Lecture Notes in Computer Science 4379

Commenced Publication in 1973
Founding and Former Series Editors:
Gerhard Goos, Juris Hartmanis, and Jan van Leeuwen

T0223240

Mario Südholt   Charles Consel (Eds.)

Object-Oriented Technology

ECOOP 2006 Workshop Reader

ECOOP 2006 Workshops
Nantes, France, July 3-7, 2006
Final Reports

 Springer

Volume Editors

Mario Südholt
École des Mines de Nantes
Département Informatique
4, rue Alfred Kastler, 44307 Nantes Cedex 3, France
E-mail: Mario.Sudholt@emn.fr

Charles Consel
INRIA/LaBRI, Domaine universitaire
351, cours de la Libération, F-33402 Talence Cedex,
E-mail: consel@labri.fr

Library of Congress Control Number: 2007925714

CR Subject Classification (1998): D.1, D.2, D.3, F.3, C.2, K.4, J.1

LNCS Sublibrary: SL 2 – Programming and Software Engineering

ISSN   0302-9743
ISBN-10   3-540-71772-2 Springer Berlin Heidelberg New York
ISBN-13   978-3-540-71772-0 Springer Berlin Heidelberg New York

Springer is a part of Springer Science+Business Media

springer.com

© Springer-Verlag Berlin Heidelberg 2007
Printed in Germany

Typesetting: Camera-ready by author, data conversion by Scientific Publishing Services, Chennai, India
Printed on acid-free paper   SPIN: 12044351   06/3180   5 4 3 2 1 0

Preface

This year, for the tenth time, the European Conference on Object-Oriented Programming (ECOOP) series, in cooperation with Springer, is glad to offer the object-oriented research community the ECOOP Workshop Reader, a compendium of workshop reports pertaining to the ECOOP 2006 conference, held in Nantes during July 3–7, 2006.

ECOOP 2006 hosted 19 high-quality research workshops covering a large spectrum of hot research topics. These workshops were chosen through a tight peer review process following a specific call for proposals. We are very grateful to the members of the Workshop Selection Committee for their careful reviews and hard work in putting together the excellent workshop program. We also want to thank all submitters, accepted or not, to whom the workshop program equally owes its quality. This selection process was then followed by a selection of workshop participants, done by each team of organizers based on an open call for papers. This participant selection process ensured that we gathered the most active researchers in each workshop research area, and therefore had fruitful working meetings.

Following the tradition of the ECOOP Workshop Reader, we strove for high-quality workshop reports that provided added-value compared with a simple summary of presentations held at the workshops. We believe that the result is a thought-provoking snapshot of the current research in object orientation, full of pointers for further exploration of the covered topics. We want to thank our workshop organizers who, despite the additional burden, did a great job in putting together these reports.

This volume consists of reports providing the reader with a starting point to understand and explore the currently debated issues in each area of concern. To do so, after summarizing the workshop goals, each report offers a critical summary of the participants' position papers and, in most cases, a transcript of the actual debates aroused by the talks. You will also typically find the full list of participants, with contact information, as well as the list of contributed position papers. Several of the reports also add a list of relevant publications and Web sites, including the workshop home page, where you will usually find the contributed position papers themselves as well as other material that goes into each covered topic more closely.

Finally, as editors, we harmonized the report titles to mention only the topics of the workshops (their abbreviations are available from the subtitles) and grouped workshops on related subjects into domains as shown in the table of contents.

February 2007

Mario Südholt
Charles Consel

Organization

Workshop Selection Committee

Uwe Aßmann   (University of Dresden, Germany)
Shigeru Chiba   (TokyoTech, Japan)
Charles Consel (Co-chair)   (ENSEIRB, LaBRI/INRIA, France)
Krystof Czarnecki   (University of Waterloo, Canada)
Eric Ernst   (Aarhus University, Danmark)
Luigi Liquori   (INRIA, France)
Wolfgang De Meuter   (VU Brussel, Belgium)
Christian Perez   (INRIA France)
Calton Puh   (Georgia Tech, USA)
Mario Südholt (Co-chair)   (INRIA-École des Mines de Nantes, France)

Sponsoring Institutions

Organization

Sponsoring Organizations

Table of Contents

Architectures and Components

Applications

Implementation, Compilation, Optimization of Object-Oriented Languages, Programs and Systems
Report on the Workshop ICOOOLPS'2006 at ECOOP'06

Roland Ducournau[1], Etienne Gagnon[2], Chandra Krintz[3], Philippe Mulet[4], Jan Vitek[5], and Olivier Zendra[6]

[1] LIRMM, France
[2] UQAM, Canada
[3] UCSB, USA
[4] IBM, France
[5] Purdue University, USA
[6] INRIA-LORIA, France

Abstract. ICOOOLPS'2006 was the first edition of ECOOP-ICOOOLPS workshop. It intended to bring researchers and practitioners both from academia and industry together, with a spirit of openness, to try and identify and begin to address the numerous and very varied issues of optimization. This succeeded, as can be seen from the papers, the attendance and the liveliness of the discussions that took place during and after the workshop, not to mention a few new cooperations or postdoctoral contracts. The 22 talented people from different groups who participated were unanimous to appreciate this first edition and recommend that ICOOOLPS be continued next year. A community is thus beginning to form, and should be reinforced by a second edition next year, with all the improvements this first edition made emerge.

1 Objectives and Call for Papers

Object-oriented languages are pervasive and play a significant role in computer science and engineering life and sometime appear as ubiquitous and completely mature. However, despite a large number of works, there is still a clear need for solutions for efficient implementation and compilation of OO languages in various application domains ranging from embedded and real-time systems to desktop systems.

The ICOOOLPS workshop thus aims to address this crucial issue of optimization in OO languages, programs and systems. It intends to do so by bringing together researchers and practitioners working in the field of object-oriented languages implementation and optimization. Its main goals are identifying fundamental bases and key current issues pertaining to the efficient implementation, compilation and optimization of OO languages, and outlining future challenges and research directions.

M. Südholt and C. Consel (Eds.): ECOOP 2006 Ws, LNCS 4379, pp. 1–14, 2007.

Topics of interest for ICOOOLPS include but are not limited to:

- implementation of fundamental OOL features:
  - inheritance (object layout, late binding, subtype test...)
  - genericity (parametric types)
  - memory management
- runtime systems:
  - compilers
  - linkers
  - virtual machines
- optimizations:
  - static and dynamic analyses
  - adaptive virtual machines
- resource constraints:
  - real-time systems
  - embedded systems (space, low power)...
- relevant choices and tradeoffs:
  - constant time vs. non-constant time mechanisms
  - separate compilation vs. global compilation
  - dynamic loading vs. global linking
  - dynamic checking vs. proof-carrying code

This workshop tries to identify fundamental bases and key current issues pertaining to the efficient implementation and compilation of OO languages, in order to spread them further amongst the various computing systems. It is also intended to extend this synthesis to encompass future challenges and research directions in the field of OO languages implementation and optimization.

Finally, this workshop is intended to become a recurrent one. Thus, the organization (most relevant format and hottest topics) of this workshop future occurrences will be adapted by the organizers and attendees according to the main outcome of this workshop discussions.

In order to have a solid basis on which the discussions could be based and to keep them focused, each prospective participant was required to submit either a short paper describing ongoing work or a position paper describing an open issue, likely solutions, drawbacks of current solutions or alternative solutions to well known problems. Papers had to be written in English and their final version could not exceed 8 pages in LNCS style.

2   Organizers

Olivier ZENDRA (chair),   INRIA-LORIA, Nancy, France.

Email:	olivier.zendra@loria.fr
Web:	http://wwW.loria.fr/~zendra
Address:	INRIA / LORIA
	615 Rue du Jardin Botanique
	BP 101
	54602 Villers-Lès-Nancy Cedex, FRANCE

Olivier Zendra is a full-time permanent computer science researcher at INRIA / LORIA, in Nancy, France. His research topics cover compilation, optimization and automatic memory management. He worked on the compilation and optimization of object-oriented languages and was one of the two people who created and implemented SmartEiffel, The GNU Eiffel Compiler (at the time SmallEiffel). His current research application domains are compilation, memory management and embedded systems, with a specific focus on low energy.

Roland DUCOURNAU (co-chair), LIRMM, Montpellier, France.
Email: ducour@lirmm.fr
Web: http://www.lirmm.fr/~ducour
Address: LIRMM,
            161, rue Ada
            34392 Montpellier Cedex 5, FRANCE

Roland Ducournau is Professor of Computer Science at the University of Montpellier. In the late 80s, while with Sema Group, he designed and developed the YAFOOL language, based on frames and prototypes and dedicated to knowledge based systems. His research topics focuses on class specialization and inheritance, especially multiple inheritance. His recent works are dedicated to implementation of OO languages.

Etienne GAGNON, UQAM, Montréal, Québec, Canada.
Email: egagnon@sablevm.org
Web: http://www.info2.uqam.ca/~egagnon
Address: Département d'informatique
            UQAM
            Case postale 8888, succursale Centre-ville
            Montréal (Québec) Canada / H3C 3P8

Etienne Gagnon is a Professor of Computer Science at Université du Québec à Montréal (UQAM) since 2001. Etienne has developed the SableVM portable research virtual machine for Java, and the SableCC compiler framework generator. His research topics include language design, memory management, synchronization, verification, portability, and efficient interpretation techniques in virtual machines.

Chandra KRINTZ, UC Santa Barbara, CA, USA.
Email: ckrintz@cs.ucsb.edu
Web: http://www.cs.ucsb.edu/~ckrintz
Address: University of California
            Engineering I, Rm. 1121
            Department of Computer Science
            Santa Barbara, CA 93106-5110, USA

Chandra Krintz is an Assistant Professor at the University of California, Santa Barbara (UCSB); she joined the UCSB faculty in 2001. Chandra's research interests include automatic and adaptive compiler and virtual runtime techniques for object-oriented languages that improve performance and increase battery life. In particular, her work focuses on exploiting repeating patterns in the time-varying behavior of underlying resources, applications, and workloads to guide dynamic optimization and specialization of program and system components.

Philippe MULET, IBM, Saint-Nazaire, France.
    Email: `philippe_mulet@fr.ibm.com`
    Address: IBM France - Paris Laboratory
                69, rue de la Vecquerie
                44600 Saint-Nazaire, France

Philippe Mulet is the lead for the Java Development Tooling (JDT) Eclipse subproject, working at IBM since 1996; he is currently located in Saint-Nazaire (France). In late 1990s, Philippe was responsible for the compiler and codeassist tools in IBM Java Integrated Development Environments (IDEs): VisualAge for Java standard and micro editions. Philippe then became in charge of the Java infrastructure for the Eclipse platform, and more recently of the entire Java tooling for Eclipse. Philippe is a member of the Eclipse Project PMC. Philippe is also a member of the expert group on compiler API (JSR199), representing IBM. His main interests are in compilation, performance, scalability and metalevel architectures.

Jan VITEK,   Purdue Univ., West Lafayette, IN, USA.
    Email: `jv@cs.purdue.edu`
    Web: `http://www.cs.purdue.edu/homes/jv`
    Address: Dept. of Computer Sciences
              Purdue University
              West Lafayette, IN 47907, USA

Jan Vitek is an Associate Professor in Computer Science at Purdue University. He leads the Secure Software Systems lab. He obtained his PhD from the University of Geneva in 1999, and a MSc from the University of Victoria in 1995. Prof. Vitek research interests include programming language, virtual machines, mobile code, software engineering and information security.

3   Participants

ICOOOLPS attendance was limited to 30 people. In addition, as mentioned in the call for paper, only people who were giving a talk were initially allowed to attend ICOOOLPS. However, since on-site there were a lot of other people interested in the workshop, the rules were relaxed to match the demand.

Finally, 22 people from 8 countries attended this first edition of ICOOOLPS, filling the allocated room, as detailed in the following table:

First name	Name	Affiliation	Country	Email
Daniel	Benquides	EMN - Nantes	France	lbenquid@emn.fr
Rhodes	Brown	Univ. of Victoria	Canada	rhodesb@cs.uvic.ca
Roland	Ducournau	Univ. of Montpellier	France	ducour@lirmm.fr
Andres	Fortier	LIFIA (UNLP)	Argentina	andres@lifia.info.unlp.edu.ar
Etienne	Gagnon	UQAM	Canada	egagnon@sablevm.org
Olivier	Gruber	IBM Research	France	ogruber@us.ibm.com
Elisa	Gonzales Bax	VUB	Belgium	egonzale@vub.ac.be
Teresa	Higuera	UCM	Spain	mthiguer@dacya.ucm.es
Yann	Hodique	USTL Lille 1	France	hodique@lifl.fr
Richard	Jones	Univ. of Kent	UK	R.E.Jones@kent.ac.uk
Susanne	Jucknath	TU Berlin	Germany	susannej@cs.tu-berlin.de
Eric	Jul	DIKU	Denmark	eric@diku.dk
Chandra	Krintz	UC Santa Barbara	USA	ckrintz@cs.ucsb.edu
Paul	McGregor	Goldman Sachs	USA	paul.regtech.mcgregor@gs.com
Philippe	Mulet	IBM Rational Software	France	philippe_mulet@fr.ibm.com
Marco	Pistoia	IBM Watson Research	USA	pistoia@us.ibm.com
Jean	Privat	Univ. of Montpellier	France	privat@lirmm.fr
Guillaume	Salagnac	Verimag lab.	France	Guillaume.Salagnac@imag.fr
Christophe	Rippert	Verimag lab.	France	Christophe.Rippert@imag.fr
Jan	Vitek	Purdue Univ.	USA	v@cs.purdue.edu
Hiroshi	Yamauchi	Purdue Univ.	USA	yamauchi@cs.purdue.edu
Olivier	Zendra	INRIA-LORIA	France	Olivier.Zendra@loria.fr

4   Contributions

All the papers and presentations are available from the ICOOOLPS web site at
http://icooolps.loria.fr.

4.1   Real-Time and Embedded Systems

This session clustered papers and questions related to real-time and/or embedded systems.

In "Java for Hard Real-Time", Jan Vitek presented the numerous challenges
caused by trying to put Java, a high-level, expressive object-oriented language,
in systems that require hard real-time guarantees (such as avionics). He detailed
OVM (Open Virtual Machine), developed at Purdue Univ.

In "Can small and open embedded systems benefit from escape analysis ?"
Gilles Grimaud, Yann Hodique and Isabelle Simplot-Rey explained how a commonly known technique, escape analysis, can be used in small constrained embedded systems to improve time through a better memory management, at low
cost.

In "Memory and compiler optimizations for low-power in embedded systems"
Olivier Zendra aimed at raising awareness about low-power and low-energy issues
in embedded systems among the object-oriented and languages communities.
He showed how mostly known time- or size-optimization techniques can be and
should observed from a different point of view, namely energy. He surveyed a
number of solutions and outlined remaining challenges.

Based on the papers, presentations and discussions in this session, several trends clearly show.

First, the ever increasing importance of embedded systems, whether they are real-time of not, in software research.

Second, it could be argued (and has in the past) that, in such highly constrained systems, the powerful features and expressiveness of object-oriented languages and their compiler are too expensive to be relied on. However, a trend can be seen in research that tries to bring these features to smaller and smaller systems, trying to bridge a gap. Hence, "object-oriented" and "embedded" are no longer opposite terms, but on the contrary form together a very active and promising research area.

Finally, new challenges (power, energy...) emerge, that require either the proper integration of known techniques, or the development of new ones. As such, being able to take into account low-level (hardware) features at high level (OO, JVM...) appear quite challenging but offer a high potential.

It is however of course always very challenging to both be able to increase the level of abstraction and at the same time get a finer, lower-level understanding of the application.

4.2   Memory Management

This session grouped papers whose main topic was memory management.

"Efficient Region-Based Memory Management for Resource-limited Real-Time Embedded Systems", by Chaker Nakhli, Christopher Rippert, Guillaume Salagnac and Sergio Yovine, presents a static algorithm to make dynamic region-based memory allocations for Java applications that have real-time constraints. M. Teresa Higuera-Toledano addresses close issues, aiming at "Improving the Scoped Memory-Region GC of Real-Time Java".

This confirms the growing importance of real-time for object-oriented languages in general, and more specifically Java, with the RTSJ (Real-Time Specification for Java). This is additional evidence for the trend we mentioned in section 4.1 towards bringing high expressiveness, easy to use languages in smaller and/or more constrained systems

Richard Jones and Chris Ryder argued, in "Garbage Collection Should be Lifetime Aware", that the efficiency of garbage collectors can be improved by making them more aware of actual objects lifetimes in the mutator. Indeed, even current generational garbage collectors generally observe the mutator with a rather coarse view, and do not provide enough flexibility when clustering objects according to their expected lifetimes. This is an area where the potential gain in performance is quite considerable.

This presentation and the following discussions where quite refreshing and confirm that even in a rather technical and well explored domain, new ideas can emerge that have both high potential and are relatively easy to grasp, especially when explained in a metaphorical way.

Finally, in "Enabling Efficient and Adaptive Specialization of Object-Oriented, Garbage Collected Programs", Chandra Krintz defended code optimizations (specialization) which are aggressively and speculatively performed and can be, if the need arises, invalidated on the fly, through OSR (On Stack Replacement).

Here again, we can spot the trend that was mentioned during the discussion for session 4.1 and tends to bridge the gap between hardware and software. Indeed, the presented technique bear some similarities with what processors do in hardware, with speculative execution and invalidation.

All the above mentioned papers and discussions make it clear that memory management is an area where a lot of progress can be made, be it in small or large strides. Memory management is furthermore an area which has an important impact over program speed. In addition to speed, memory management can also affect very significantly energy usage, as discussed during session 4.1. Memory-targeted optimizations should thus always be taken into account when trying to reach higher performance.

4.3   Optimization

This session was devoted to papers and questions related known or very specific optimizations.

In "OO specific redundancy elimination techniques", Rhodes Brown and Nigel Horspool advocated a holistic view of optimization where not only one but in fact the whole set of program properties are taken into account together, without forgetting their mutual interactions. They presented how annotations could be used, in conjunction with static and dynamic invariants, to improve program performance.

This echoes a relatively novel trend in object-oriented program optimization, that tries to analysis not only one specific optimization, but optimization composition or sequences.

"Performing loop optimizations offline", by Hiroshi Yamauchi, shows how the overhead of some loop optimizations can be removed from execution time by performing them offline. This is especially important in the context of system that require a high level of responsiveness.

This shows how even very specific and potentially common optimizations can be reconsidered in the light of new constraints, for example those of the real-time systems that were already mentioned in session 4.1.

Here again, as in session 4.1, we see that not optimization work tends to evolve. First, they more and more focus not only on one criterion which is often program speed, but also integrate other criteria, such as responsiveness, that correspond more to new current computing systems with tight real-time and/or space constraints. Second, larger sets of optimizations tend to be considered together, as optimization sequences or compositions, to better encompass the complexity inherent to real life systems and the various interactions that can take place when optimizing.

4.4   Abstraction and Frameworks

This last session aimed at regrouping papers and talks about higher level or broader points of view for optimization.

In "Efficient Separate Compilation of OO languages" Jean Privat, Floréal Morandat and Roland Ducournau present a scheme to reconcile separate and global compilation, hence global optimization. They detail their practical and implemented solution in the context of an object-oriented language.

This is truly another example of research work trying to successfully bridge a gap: the gap between separate compilation, which commonly used in industry, and global compilation, that brings the best optimization results.

"Java Framework for Runtime Modules" by Olivier Gruber and Richard Hall is a paper that takes a broad view of optimization. It proposes a framework to more easily build modules and reuse components and that could be integrated in the Java Runtime Environment.

By bringing this discussion to the workshop, the authors clearly enlarged to scope of the discussions and tried to connect the optimization and software engineering communities. This kind of openness is quite useful in a workshop so as to foster slightly unusual cooperation and work.

Finally, "The Importance of Abstraction in Efficient OO implementations" by Eric Jul, made a case for clearly and strictly separating the abstraction (language level) and the concrete (implementation) level. This indeed gives more freedom to the implementer, hence more possibilities for optimizations, while the language user does not have to worry about low-level details but only about the semantics of the program.

Here, we see that bridging the gap between what is expressed and what is implemented is important, but should not be left to the developer. That's the compiler's job, or rather the compiler implementers' job. Eric's position is thus quite important to remind us not to pollute the high level with too many low-level details. Of course, one question that remains open is how to properly abstract things, especially low-level, possible hardware, details.

This session was interesting in that it made the workshop participant not forget a high-level, software engineering oriented point of view and the related issues. Indeed, there is always a risk that, being focused on one specific optimization, the researcher forgets the larger picture. Considering issues at a high level, with abstraction, may avoids getting swamped in details. Reuse of optimizations, like reuse of modules, is a requirement to evolve from software optimizations as a craftsmanship to software optimizations as an industrial process. Of course, quite some work remains to be done before we're there, but it a goal worth aiming at.

5   Closing Debates

The presentation sessions finished later than scheduled. As a consequence, the discussion time that was planned at the end of the workshop was shorter than initially expected. This may have somehow limited the discussions.

This is one of the points that shall be improved in future occurrences of ICOOOLPS (see section 6).

The discussion session was very spontaneous, with attendees being encouraged to bring their favorite topic, main itch, etc. >From their summary emerge two main treads.

5.1 "Written Down in Code vs. Inferred"

"The user knows" what is intended and what is going on in an application. Thus, it seems to make sense to have the developer *annotate the code with meta information*, that can then be used by the compiler to optimize.

However the code — especially for libraries — can be reused in a different context. Would the annotations remain valid ? This seems to call for *context-dependent annotations*.

But what is "the context" when you write 10% and reuse 90% ?

"Annotation-guided optimization" looks quite appealing. However, the analyses done by the compiler have to be performed anyway, whether annotations are present or not. What should the compiler do if annotations appear to be *contradictory* with what it infers ?

Relying on developer annotations puts a burden on her/him. But we all know there are good developers and not-so-good ones, with a majority in the second category, so is it *realistic* ?

There are similarities between the user-software interface and the hardware-software interface: interactions are needed, as well as information passing (both ways). For example, feedback to the user is very useful, so that s/he can improve her/his coding.

The developer knows the application, but should not have to worry about the underlying OS, hardware, etc. Annotations thus should make it possible to express *what the developer wants, not how to do it.*

A lot of interest was expressed in this long debate with many attendees involved.

Annotations by the developer seem appealing but their nature is an issue. A lot depends on the developer level, so how far can annotations be trusted ?

This discussion thread certainly is worth digging deeper into during the next edition of ICOOOLPS.

5.2 "Do Threads Make Sense ?"

Isn't the threading model fundamentally flawed, that is inappropriate/problematic for object-oriented design and implementation ? Indeed, threads in Java are build on top of an existing, independent model. They thus seem poorly integrated.

See Hans-J. Boehm, "Threads Cannot Be Implemented as a Library" - PLDI 2006 and Edward A. Lee, "The Problem with Threads" - IEEE Computer, May 2006.

This topic, however, did not spark much debate, maybe because of lack of time.

6   Conclusion and Perspectives

This first edition of ICOOOLPS was able to reach one its goals: bringing together people from various horizons, in an open way, so as to foster new, original and fruitful discussions and exchanges pertaining to optimizations. The presence of people from 8 different countries, from academia and industry, researcher as well as practioners, is in itself a success. The fact that more people that expected showed up is another.

Thanks to the skills of the speakers and active participation of the attendants, the discussions were lively, open-minded and allowed good exchanges. Identifying the mains challenges for optimization is not that easy though. Indeed, as emerged more clearly during ICOOOLPS, optimizations for object-oriented languages come in variety of contexts with very different constraints (embedded, real-time, dynamic, legacy...). The optimizations criteria considered, thus the goal, also tend to differ a lot: speed, size, memory footprint, more recently energy... In addition, all these have to be tackled keeping in my higher-level, software engineering-oriented issues, such as modularity, composability, reusability, ease of use...

Some trends can however be sketched. Optimizations tend to encompass more and more target criteria (multi-criteria rather than single criterion), such as energy and speed, or memory footprint and responsiveness. Multiple optimizations tend to be evaluated in conjunction, as sequences of optimizations, rather than in an isolated way. Separating semantics and implementation is crucial, for expressiveness, ease of use and the possibility to perform optimizations at compile level. However, it appears at the same time necessary to be able to better take into account the actual execution of a program when optimizing, that is better take into account the behavior of the software and the hardware as well.

Large challenges thus remain, and should be addressed by the community. That's what ICOOOLPS intend to do in its next editions.

Indeed, the perspectives for the ECOOP-ICOOOLPS workshop appear quite bright. One of the questions was whether this workshop should be pursued in the next years, and with which periodicity. The answer was unanimously positive: attendees are in favor of continuing the workshop next year with a yearly periodicity.

Overall satisfaction is thus quite high for this very first edition of the workshop.

A few ways to improve ICOOOLPS emerged during the workshop and should be taken into account in 2007:

– Presentations should be significantly shorter, to save time for longer discussions. The later should take place during the sessions, for example one session comprising 3 talks lasting 5 to 10 minutes each, plus a 30 to 60 minutes discussion.
– More time could also be allotted for discussions at the very end of the workshop.

- Session report drafts should be written during a session (papers and talks) and maybe briefly discussed at the end of each session (not after the workshop).
- Attendees could be given the possibility to submit (written) questions to paper presenters before the workshop itself. This would give a starting base for discussions, or at the very least the question "session" at the end of each talk.
- The workshop could be open to anyone, not only authors/speakers. This year indeed, although no call for participation had been issued after the call for paper was closed, because the workshop was for presenters only, many more people asked to be admitted in. Since the aim of an ECOOP workshop is to foster discussions and exchanges, refusing interested people would have been a bad idea. Having everyone (not only authors) present themselves and their work in a few minutes would be an added value.
- A larger room is necessary. 15 attendants were expected but 22 came, so the room was very crowded, which made it difficult for some attendants to properly see the presentation slides.

7   Related Work

In order to provide a fixed point for ICOOOLPS related matters, the web site for the workshop is maintained at `http://icooolps.loria.fr`. All the papers and presentations done for ICOOLPS'2006 are freely available there.

References

1. Mohammed Javed Absar and Francky Catthoor. Compiler-based approach for exploiting scratch-pad in presence of irregular array access. In *DATE*, pages 1162–1167, 2005.
2. Wolfram Amme, Niall Dalton, Michael Franz, and Jeffery von Ronne. Safetsa: A type safe and referentially secure mobile-code representation based on static single assignment form. In *PLDI*, pages 137–147, 2001.
3. R. Athavale, Narayanan Vijaykrishnan, Mahmut T. Kandemir, and Mary Jane Irwin. Influence of array allocation mechanisms on memory system energy. In *IPDPS*, page 3, 2001.
4. Oren Avissar, Rajeev Barua, and Dave Stewart. An optimal memory allocation scheme for scratch-pad-based embedded systems. *Transaction. on Embedded Computing Systems.*, 1(1):6–26, 2002.
5. David F. Bacon, Perry Cheng, and V. T. Rajan. A real-time garbage collector with low overhead and consistent utilization. In *POPL*, pages 285–298, 2003.
6. Rajeshwari Banakar, Stefan Steinke, Bo-Sik Lee, M. Balakrishnan, and Peter Marwedel. Scratchpad memory: design alternative for cache on-chip memory in embedded systems. In *10th international symposium on Hardware/software codesign (CODES'02)*, pages 73–78, New York, NY, USA, 2002. ACM Press.
7. Matthew Q. Beers, Christian Stork, and Michael Franz. Efficiently verifiable escape analysis. In *ECOOP*, pages 75–95, 2004.

8. Stephen Blackburn, Richard Jones, Kathryn S. McKinley, and J. Eliot B. Moss. Beltway: Getting around garbage collection gridlock. In *PLDI*, pages 153–164, 2002.
9. Stephen M. Blackburn, Perry Cheng, and Kathryn S. McKinley. Oil and water? high performance garbage collection in java with mmtk. In *ICSE*, pages 137–146, 2004.
10. Bruno Blanchet. Escape analysis for object-oriented languages: Application to java. In *OOPSLA*, pages 20–34, 1999.
11. Bruno Blanchet. Escape analysis for java[tm]: Theory and practice. *ACM Trans. Program. Lang. Syst.*, 25(6):713–775, 2003.
12. Gregory Bollella and James Gosling. The real-time specification for java. *IEEE Computer*, 33(6):47–54, 2000.
13. Sigmund Cherem and Radu Rugina. Region analysis and transformation for java programs. In *ISMM*, pages 85–96, 2004.
14. Darren D. Cofer and Murali Rangarajan. Formal modeling and analysis of advanced scheduling features in an avionics rtos. In *EMSOFT*, pages 138–152, 2002.
15. Dominique Colnet, Philippe Coucaud, and Olivier Zendra. Compiler support to customize the mark and sweep algorithm. In *ISMM*, pages 154–165, 1998.
16. V. Delaluz, M. Kandemir, N. Vijaykrishnan, M. J. Irwin, A. Sivasubramaniam, and I. Kolcu. Compiler-directed array interleaving for reducing energy in multi-bank memories. In *2002 conference on Asia South Pacific design automation/VLSI Design (ASP-DAC'02)*, page 288, Washington, DC, USA, 2002. IEEE Computer Society.
17. Morgan Deters and Ron Cytron. Automated discovery of scoped memory regions for real-time java. In *MSP/ISMM*, pages 132–142, 2002.
18. David Detlefs. A hard look at hard real-time garbage collection. In *ISORC*, pages 23–32, 2004.
19. Angel Dominguez, Sumesh Udayakumaran, and Rajeev Barua. Heap data allocation to scratch-pad memory in embedded systems. *Journal of Embedded Computing (JEC)*, 1(4), 2005.
20. Matthew B. Dwyer, John Hatcliff, Robby, and Venkatesh Prasad Ranganath. Exploiting object escape and locking information in partial-order reductions for concurrent object-oriented programs. *Formal Methods in System Design*, 25(2-3): 199–240, 2004.
21. Robert P. Fitzgerald and David Tarditi. The case for profile-directed selection of garbage collectors. In *ISMM*, pages 111–120, 2000.
22. Etienne M. Gagnon and Laurie J. Hendren. Sablevm: A research framework for the efficient execution of java bytecode. In *Java Virtual Machine Research and Technology Symposium*, pages 27–40, 2001.
23. Robert Graybill and Rami Melhem. *Power aware computing*. Kluwer Academic Publishers, Norwell, MA, USA, 2002.
24. David Grove and Craig Chambers. A framework for call graph construction algorithms. *ACM Trans. Program. Lang. Syst.*, 23(6):685–746, 2001.
25. Richard S. Hall. A policy-driven class loader to support deployment in extensible frameworks. In *Component Deployment*, pages 81–96, 2004.
26. Timothy L. Harris. Dynamic adaptive pre-tenuring. In *ISMM*, pages 127–136, 2000.
27. M. Teresa Higuera-Toledano, Valérie Issarny, Michel Banâtre, Gilbert Cabillic, Jean-Philippe Lesot, and Frédéric Parain. Region-based memory management for real-time java. In *ISORC*, pages 387–394, 2001.

28. Martin Hirzel, Amer Diwan, and Matthew Hertz. Connectivity-based garbage collection. In *OOPSLA*, pages 359–373, 2003.
29. Martin Hirzel, Johannes Henkel, Amer Diwan, and Michael Hind. Understanding the connectivity of heap objects. In *MSP/ISMM*, pages 143–156, 2002.
30. J. Hom and U. Kremer. Energy management of virtual memory on diskless devices. In *Workshop on Compilers and Operating Systems for Low Power (COLP'01)*, Barcelone, Espagne, September 2001.
31. Jerry Hom and Ulrich Kremer. Inter-program optimizations for conserving disk energy. In *2005 international symposium on Low power electronics and design (ISLPED'05)*, pages 335–338, New York, NY, USA, 2005. ACM Press.
32. ITRS. International technology roadmap for semiconductors, 2005. `http:// public.itrs.net`.
33. Richard Jones and Rafael Lins. *Garbage Collection: Algorithms for Automatic Dynamic Memory Management*. Wiley, 1996.
34. M. Kandemir, N. Vijaykrishnan, M.J. Irwin, W. Ye, and I. Demirkiran. Register relabeling: A post compilation technique for energy reduction. In *Workshop on Compilers and Operating Systems for Low Power (COLP'00)*, Philadelphie, PA, USA, October 2000.
35. Chandra Krintz and Brad Calder. Using annotation to reduce dynamic optimization time. In *PLDI*, pages 156–167, 2001.
36. M. Lee, V. Tiwari, S. Malik, and M. Fujita. Power analysis and minimization techniques for embedded dsp software. *IEEE Transactions on Very Large Scale Integration*, 5, March 1997.
37. Pierre-Etienne Moreau and Olivier Zendra. Gc^2: a generational conservative garbage collector for the atterm library. *J. Log. Algebr. Program.*, 59(1-2):5–34, 2004.
38. Steven S. Muchnick. *Advanced compiler design and implementation*. Morgan Kaufmann Publishers Inc., San Francisco, CA, USA, 1997.
39. Priya Nagpurkar, Chandra Krintz, Michael Hind, Peter F. Sweeney, and V. T. Rajan. Online phase detection algorithms. In *CGO*, pages 111–123, 2006.
40. George C. Necula. Proof-carrying code. In *POPL*, pages 106–119, 1997.
41. Nathaniel Nystrom, Michael R. Clarkson, and Andrew C. Myers. Polyglot: An extensible compiler framework for java. In *CC*, pages 138–152, 2003.
42. Krzysztof Palacz and Jan Vitek. Java subtype tests in real-time. In *ECOOP*, pages 378–404, 2003.
43. Filip Pizlo, J. M. Fox, David Holmes, and Jan Vitek. Real-time java scoped memory: Design patterns and semantics. In *ISORC*, pages 101–110, 2004.
44. Francesco Poletti, Paul Marchal, David Atienza, Luca Benini, Francky Catthoor, and Jose Manuel Mendias. An integrated hardware/software approach for run-time scratchpad management. In *DAC*, pages 238–243, 2004.
45. Jean Privat and Roland Ducournau. Link-time static analysis for efficient separate compilation of object-oriented languages. In *PASTE*, pages 20–27, 2005.
46. Rajiv A. Ravindran, Robert M. Senger, Eric D. Marsman, Ganesh S. Dasika, Matthew R. Guthaus, Scott A. Mahlke, and Richard B. Brown. Partitioning variables across register windows to reduce spill code in a low-power processor. *IEEE Transaction on Computers*, 54(8):998–1012, 2005.
47. Fridtjof Siebert. Hard real-time garbage-collection in the jamaica virtual machine. In *RTCSA*, pages 96–102, 1999.
48. Sunil Soman, Chandra Krintz, and David F. Bacon. Dynamic selection of application-specific garbage collectors. In *ISMM*, pages 49–60, 2004.

49. Sriraman Tallam and Rajiv Gupta. Bitwidth aware global register allocation. In *POPL*, pages 85–96, 2003.
50. Mads Tofte and Jean-Pierre Talpin. Region-based memory management. *Inf. Comput.*, 132(2):109–176, 1997.
51. John Whaley and Martin C. Rinard. Compositional pointer and escape analysis for java programs. In *OOPSLA*, pages 187–206, 1999.
52. Seungdo Woo, Jungroin Yoon, and Jihong Kim. Low-power instruction encoding techniques. In *SOC Design Conference*, 2001.
53. Fen Xie, Margaret Martonosi, and Sharad Malik. Intraprogram dynamic voltage scaling: Bounding opportunities with analytic modeling. *ACM Transactions on Architure and Code Optimization (TACO)*, 1(3):323–367, 2004.
54. Olivier Zendra and Karel Driesen. Stress-testing control structures for dynamic dispatch in java. In *Java Virtual Machine Research and Technology Symposium*, pages 105–118, 2002.
55. Youtao Zhang and Rajiv Gupta. Data compression transformations for dynamically allocated data structures. In *11th International Conference on Compiler Construction (CC'02), Lecture Notes in Computer Science*, volume 2304, pages 14–28, London, UK, 2002. Springer-Verlag.
56. Xiaotong Zhuang, ChokSheak Lau, and Santosh Pande. Storage assignment optimizations through variable coalescence for embedded processors. In *LCTES '03: 2003 ACM SIGPLAN conference on Language, Compiler, and Tool for Embedded Systems*, pages 220–231, New York, NY, USA, 2003. ACM Press.

Lisp

Report on the "3rd European Lisp Workshop (ELW'06)" at ECOOP'06

Christophe Rhodes[1], Pascal Costanza[2], Theo D'Hondt[2], and Arthur Lemmens[3]

[1] Goldsmiths College, University of London, UK
[2] Vrije Universiteit Brussel, Belgium
[3] Amsterdam

Abstract. This report covers the activities of the 3rd European Lisp Workshop. We introduce the motivation for a workshop focussing on languages in the Lisp family, and mention relevant organisational aspects. We summarize the presentations and discussions, including Nick Levine's keynote talk, and provide pointers to related work and events.

1 Introduction

Lisp is one of the oldest computer languages still in use today. In the decades of its existence, Lisp has been a fruitful basis for language design experiments as well as the preferred implementation language for applications in diverse fields.

The structure of Lisp, and of the major dialects in use today, makes it easy to extend the language or even to implement entirely new dialects without starting from scratch. Common Lisp, including the Common Lisp Object System (CLOS), was the first object-oriented programming language to receive an ANSI standard and retains the most complete and advanced object system of any programming language, and certainly influenced many object-oriented programming languages that were to follow.

It is clear that Lisp is gaining momentum: There is a steadily growing interest in Lisp itself, with numerous user groups in existence worldwide, and in Lisp's metaprogramming notions are being transferred, as for example in Aspect-Oriented Programming, support for Domain-Specific Languages, and so on.

The theme of the workshop held at ECOOP 2006 was intentionally broad, and aimed to encourage lively discussion between researchers proposing new approaches and practitioners reporting on their experience with the strengths and limitations of current Lisp technologies; the intent was to address the near-future rôle of Lisp-based languages in research, industry and education.

2 Organisation

This section describes the organisational aspects of the workshop. The submitted papers and workshop slides can be found at the workshop's website:
`http://p-cos.net/lisp-ecoop06/`

M. Südholt and C. Consel (Eds.): ECOOP 2006, LNCS 4379, pp. 15–20, 2007.
© Springer-Verlag Berlin Heidelberg 2007

2.1   Organisers

Pascal Costanza
pascal.costanza@vub.ac.be

Theo D'Hondt
tjdhondt@vub.ac.be

Arthur Lemmens
alemmens@xs4all.nl

Christophe Rhodes
csr21@cam.ac.uk

2.2   Call for Participation

... please don't assume Lisp is only useful for Animation and Graphics, AI, Bioinformatics, B2B and E-Commerce, Data Mining, EDA/Semiconductor applications, Expert Systems, Finance, Intelligent Agents, Knowledge Management, Mechanical CAD, Modeling and Simulation, Natural Language, Optimization, Research, Risk Analysis, Scheduling, Telecom, and Web Authoring just because these are the only things they happened to list.

– Kent Pitman [7]

Potential attendees were invited to contribute a long paper (10 pages) presenting scientific or empirical results about Lisp-based uses or new approaches for software engineering purposes; a short essay (5 pages) defending a position about where research and practice based on Lisp should be heading in the near future; or a proposal for a breakout group describing the theme, an agenda for discussion and expected results. Suggested topics for presented papers included new language features or abstractions, experience reports or case studies, protocol metaprogramming and libraries, educational approaches, software evolution, development aids, persistent systems, dynamic optimization, implementation techniques, innovative applications, hardware support for lisp systems, macro-, reflective-, meta- or rule-based development approaches, and aspect-oriented, domain-oriented and generative programming.

2.3   Format

The workshop took place over one day: In the morning, the keynote talk by Nick Levine was followed by the accepted contributions (both described in Section 3.1). In the afternoon, the participants split into two groups: One group discussed concrete plans for the development of Lisp hardware. In parallel, two presenters gave tutorials on the Common Lisp Interface Manager and on the history of reflection and metaprogramming facilities in Lisp dialects. After the afternoon coffee break, the Lisp hardware breakout group join the main workshop again and gave a summary of their discussion, and then the workshop finished with an open discussion session.

This year, the Association of Lisp Users has kindly sponsored a prize fund for exceptional papers submitted to the European Lisp Workshop. The workshop organizers have selected Didier Verna's contribution as the best paper and awarded the prize after the presentation of all papers.

3   Content

3.1   Presentations

How to Stay Poor, with Macros and Closures
Nick Levine, Ravenbrook Limited

> This talk started with some of the influences that lead the author to Lisp in the first place. A number of examples were then presented that reflect major insights into the nature of Lisp, both from the perspective of a Lisp implementor and user.

Agent-Based Framework to Simulate Metabolic Processes
Marie Beurton-Aimar, LaBRI – UMR 5800 – Univ. Bordeaux 1
Nicolas Parisey, Laboratoire Physiopathologie Mitochondriale – U688 – Univ. Boreaux 2

> Since the last ten years, simulations of living systems have had new perspectives due to the availability of biological data on the one hand and the increase of computing power in terms of execution speed and memory on the other hand. Simulation of biological processes can now be considered for large sets of molecules not only with differential equations but also by modelling molecules independently as with agent-based systems. In a large project about the study of mitochondrial metabolism, the authors of this paper have designed a generic agent-based framework to test molecule behaviours where considering mean behaviour, like with differential equations, is not well adapted. The implementation of this framework is done in Common Lisp and uses the McClim interface for the graphical simulations.

Simulation of Quantum Computations in Lisp
Brecht Desmet, Ellie D'Hondt, Pascal Costanza, and Theo D'Hondt
Vrije Universiteit Brussel

> This paper introduces QLisp, a compact and expressive language extension of Common Lisp that simulates quantum computations. QLisp is an open experimental and educational platform because it translates the quantum computations into the underlying mathematical formalism and offers the flexibility to extend the postulates of quantum mechanics. Although the complexity degree of quantum mechanics is inherently exponential, QLisp includes some optimizations that prune in both space and time.

Lisp Tools for Musicology – Research aids for an Electronic Corpus of Lute Music
David Lewis and Christophe Rhodes
Goldsmiths College, University of London

This paper presents the tools that have been developed in the course of implementing a resource to assist in musicological investigation of the historically important repertoire of lute music. The majority of these tools have been developed using Common Lisp, and their development has itself spurred improvements in the libraries that they are built on.

Integrating Foreign Libraries in Common Lisp: Best Practices
Rudi Schlatte, Joanneum Research

This paper explores some of the challenges in integrating foreign libraries into Common Lisp. While generating library bindings automatically from header files and annotations can take care of some basic tasks, an API that integrates well into the language and provides the user with familiar patterns of usage must still mostly be implemented by hand. Some best practices and common pitfalls are illustrated following the example of cl-redland, a Common Lisp binding for the Redland RDF library.

Beating C in Scientific Computing Applications – On the Behavior and Performance of LISP, Part 1
Didier Verna, EPITA Research and Development Laboratory

This paper presents an ongoing research on the behavior and performance of Common Lisp with respect to C in the context of scientific numerical computing. Several simple image processing algorithms are used to evaluate the performance of pixel access and arithmetic operations in both languages. The paper demonstrates that the behavior of equivalent Common Lisp and C code is similar with respect to the choice of data structures and types, and also to external parameters such as hardware optimization. It further demonstrates that properly typed and optimized Common Lisp code runs as fast as the equivalent C code, or even faster in some cases.

3.2   Breakout Session

Lisp Hardware Revisited
Hans Hübner

Lisp is not a perfect match for today's computers. In order to make stock hardware execute Lisp code, complex compilers have to be used that make standard computers emulate Lisp's model of computation. The history of Lisp hardware is generally seen as a failure, but it seems to be common understanding that the failure was not due to the technology being inferior to the competition, but rather due to market pressure and mismanagement [6,9]. The advent of cheap reconfigurable hardware allows us to rethink the feasibility of building Lisp machines.

The following people have participated in this breakout group: Frank Buss, Hans Hübner and Robert Swindells. They have decided on some concrete actions to realize a Lisp hardware, with the goal to achieve some first results by the end of 2006, and have set up a website at `http://vaxbusters.org/workshop/` as a central starting place for their further efforts.

3.3 Tutorials

Common Lisp Interface Manager - CLIM
Christophe Rhodes

The Common Lisp Interface Manager (CLIM [5]) separates different concepts that are typically collapsed in other GUI frameworks. Input events are provided via streams, and output can also be organized by way of streams, which in this way support convenient automatic redrawing capabilities. Graphical objects on the screen are associated with presentation types that allow for convenient description of complex user interaction. The tutorial was presented using McClim, an open source implementation of the CLIM specification, and illustrated the essential concepts with some example applications.

Reflection and Metaprogramming in Lisp
Pascal Costanza

Computational reflection provides programs with the ability to inspect and change data and functions at the meta-level that represent and execute them [8]. The ability to inspect the program state is called *introspection* and the ability to change the behavior is called *intercession*. A metaobject protocol (MOP) organizes the meta-level entities such that applications can extend them in an object-oriented style [4]. A macro system distills reflective capabilities as compile-time constructs with restricted expressiveness but better performance [3].

This tutorial consisted of an overview of reflection concepts and showed how from the early days of Lisp in the 1950's up until the mid-1990's, these concepts have been realized in various Lisp dialects.

4   Discussion

Most of the contributions for this workshop describe uses of Common Lisp for particular domains. A typical claim by the presenters is that the choice of language has enabled them to achieve impressive results in a short amount of time with few people. Two papers are based on CLIM that was also presented in one of the tutorials.

A common theme is the use and reuse of "old" ideas and concepts that, in some cases, date back several decades ago. Nevertheless, they are not outdated, but sometimes seem to provide significant advantages over more recent developments. This resonates with some projects that aim to recover and resurrect "forgotten" technologies [1,2].

References

1. Bitsavers, http://bitsavers.org/ (2006)
2. Computer History Museum, http://computerhistory.org/ (2006)
3. Graham, P.: *On Lisp*. Prentice Hall, 1993.
4. Maes, P.: *Computational Reflection*. Ph.D. thesis, Vrije Universiteit Brussel, 1987.
5. McKay, S.: CLIM: The Common Lisp Interface Manager. Communicatinos of the ACM, 34, 9, September 1991.
6. Philips, E.M.: *If It Works, It's not AI: A Commercial Look at Artificial Intelligence Startup*. Master thesis, Massachusetts Institute of Technology, 1999.
7. Pitman, K.: Re: More Lisp. http://interviews.slashdot.org/comments.pl?sid=23357&cid=2543265 (2001)
8. Smith, B.: *Procedural Reflection in Programming Languages*. Ph.D. thesis, Massachusetts Institute of Technology, 1982.
9. Wikipedia: *AI winter*. http://en.wikipedia.org/wiki/AI_Winter (2006)

Models and Aspects –
Handling Crosscutting Concerns in MDSD

Report on the WS MA'06 at ECOOP'06

Iris Groher[1], Andrew Jackson[2], Christa Schwanninger[1], and Markus Völter[3]

[1] Siemens AG, Corporate Technology, Munich, Germany
{iris.groher.ext,christa.schwanninger}@siemens.com
[2] Trinity College, Distributed Systems Group, Dublin, Ireland
anjackso@cs.tcd.ie
[3] Independent Consultant, Heidenheim, Germany
voelter@acm.org

Abstract. This report summarizes the presentations and discussions of the Second Workshop on Models and Aspects – Handling Crosscutting Concerns in MDSD, held in conjunction with the 20th European Conference on Object-Oriented Programming (ECOOP) in Nantes, France on July, 3, 2006. This workshop was motivated by the fact that both Model-Driven Software Development (MDSD) and Aspect-Oriented Software Development (AOSD) are important new paradigms that both promise to change the way software is developed. While the two approaches are different in many ways – MDSD adds domain-specific abstractions, while AOSD is currently primarily seen as domain independent (de)composition mechanism – they also have many things in common – for example both approaches integrate models on different levels of abstraction and in this transformation step both have a query phase followed by a construction phase. There are many ways that these emerging paradigms may be integrated to achieve the complementary benefits of both AOSD and MDSD. This workshop aimed at exploring new approaches of using both paradigms together to investigate their differences, commonalities and possible interworking to bring new triggers to both technologies.

Keywords: Model Driven Software Development, Aspect Oriented Software Development.

1 Introduction

Both MDSD and AOSD are important new paradigms that are both expected to change the way software is developed. Both approaches attempt to separate the decision space that underlies software development. The primary goal of MDSD is to separate this decision space in to models at different levels of abstraction. AOSD separates this decision space based on concerns.

While the two approaches are different in many ways – MDSD adds domain-specific abstractions, while AOSD is currently primarily seen as domain independent (de)composition mechanism – they also have many things in common – for example

M. Südholt and C. Consel (Eds.): ECOOP 2006, LNCS 4379, pp. 21–25, 2007.

both approaches integrate models on different levels of abstraction and in this transformation step both have a query phase followed by a construction phase.

There are many ways that these emerging paradigms may be integrated to achieve the complementary benefits of both AOSD and MDSD. Two examples for combining MDSD with AOSD could be Aspect-Oriented Modeling combined with code generation, or the generation of pointcuts for AO languages from a domain model.

This workshop aimed at exploring new approaches of using both paradigms together to investigate their differences, commonalities and possible interworking to bring new triggers to both technologies.

Potential topics included, but were not limited to:

- handling crosscutting concerns in modeling
- generating aspects from models
- aspect weaving in models
- transformation of modeled aspects to non-AO languages
- separation of domain abstractions using AO
- resolving crosscutting concerns in templates

The next section summarizes the submitted position papers. Papers are categorized based on the questions they raised.

2 Workshop Questions and Positions

The aim of this workshop was to explore issues for and new approaches to using Model-Driven and Aspect-Oriented Software Development together. We invited researchers and practitioners to present their approaches and discuss the relevance for practical software development. Six papers were accepted in total. These papers raised the following questions:

1. What is the most useful way to represent a given domain? [5]
2. What kind of expressiveness is required from the chosen knowledge representation language? [5]
3. Are domain specific languages needed or is a general purpose one expressive enough? [1, 3, 4, 5]
4. What mechanism should be used for relating base code to the conceptual model? [1, 4, 5]
5. Can this mechanism be generalized? [1, 3]
6. Will the use of model-based aspects add a significant performance overhead? [5]
7. How will the conceptual model cope with structural changes in base code? [5]
8. How will models be exchanged through a tool chain? [6]
9. Can aspect models be tested? [2]

In [1] Jackson et al. take a position in relation to questions 3, 5 and 6. The position was that a generic composition operator is feasible in the Model-Driven Aspect Domain if it is extensible enough to deal with all of the issues that are related to composition.

In [2] Jackson et al. take a position in relation to question 9. The position in this case is that aspect model testing is achievable and they present an extension to Theme/UML to support aspect model testing.

In [3] Kurtev and Didonet Del Fabro take a position in relation to questions 3, 5 and 6. They argue that a domain specific language (DSL) for the definition of model composition operators is feasible. In this DSL primitive operations are defined for model composition. They show that these can build more complex operations through their DSL language.

In [4] Cleenewerck takes a position in relation to questions 3 and 4. The position is that a transformation system equipped with a meta-protocol allows the implementation of crosscutting transformations and generators as separate concerns.

In [5] Cyment et al explore questions 1-7 by describing their experiences with an AOP tool for .NET that mainly focused on making aspects rely on domain models defined in the Web Ontology Language.

In [6] Reiter et al take a position in relation to question 8. The position taken in this work is that aspect-orientation can provide a clean solution in terms of dealing with changes in models propagated through a tool chain by adding change notification infrastructure to automatically update models and avoiding the need to interfere with the tool's source code.

3 Participants

The following people participated in the workshop:

1. Iris Groher, PhD student at Siemens AG, Corporate Technology, Munich, Germany, iris.groher.ext@siemens.com
2. Andrew Jackson, PhD student at the Distributed Systems Group, Trinity College Dublin, Ireland, anjackso@cs.tcd.ie
3. Markus Völter, Independent Consultant, Heidenheim, Germany, voelter@acm.org
4. Thomas Reiter, PhD student, University of Linz, Austria, tr@ifs.uni-linz.ac.at
5. Gerti Kappel, Institute for Software Technology and Interactive Systems, Vienna University of Technology, Austria, gerti@big.tuwien.ac.at
6. Benoit Baudry, Olivier Barais and Jacques Klein, IRISA/INRIA, Rennes, France {Benoit.Baudry, Olivier.Barais, Jacques. Klein}@irisa.fr
7. Thomas Cleenewerck, Vrije Universiteit Brussel, Brussels, Belgium, tcleenew@vub.ac.be
8. Alan Cyment and Ruben Altman, University of Buenos Aires, Buenos Aires, Brazil, {acyment, raltman}@dc.uba.ar

4 Debates

As the aim of the workshop was to foster discussion rather than elaborate presentations, every participant was expected to read everyone else's paper. It was also required to complete two sentences for each paper. In the afternoon we utilized the "Open Space" format to in order to discuss topics of interest that were directly, or indirectly related to the submitted position papers.

The enduring debate that was raised in this workshop was the question on what the value is in using aspect oriented modeling in a model driven software development process. The value of MDSD was firstly discussed. In this discussion we agreed that the expected benefit of MDSD is that it raises the level of abstraction in software development. We also agreed that this abstraction is achieved through a separation of domain logic and implementation specific specification into different models. We also agreed that AOSD complements MDSD through separation of concerns at the same level of abstraction. Participants' opinions varied on the most significant benefits of the integration of these complementary approaches to software development. The list of benefits included maintainability, extensibility, reusability, testability, comprehensibility, scalability, traceability, parallel development and reduced complexity. There was a rigorous debate over which benefit was the killer application of the integration of MDSD and AOSD. There was no firm conclusion drawn in this debate and we agreed that this was due to a lack of evidence to indicate that any of these was the best. It was acknowledged that this was due to the early phase of the integration of these approaches to software development.

This debate subsumed all other debates that were related to the questions posed above. For instance, Question 1 defined in Section 2, asks what is the most useful way to define a domain? Although it was conceded by all attendees that there were many ways to do this, it was agreed that there was no perfect solution. This choice was based on how maintainable, extensible, reusable, testable, comprehensible, etc the domain model needed to be. Similarly in Questions 3-5 a debate was formed that investigated the possibility of a common AO composition mechanism at the model level. It was agreed that commonality could be achieved through a common meta-model of composition that was highly abstract. It was also noted that concrete composition mechanisms need to be tailored to achieve a balance of maintainability, extensibility, reusability, testability, comprehensibility, etc. Also question 8 asks how models will be exchanged through a tool chain. It was agreed that current tooling needs to be extended to support integrated AOSD-MDSD approaches. Advanced tooling would have many advantages as currently with respect to MDSD a lot is done manually and automation can bring many benefits.

The main discussion point was on the value of combining MDSD and AOSD. We will consider this discussion as an input for future events of this series and relate future Call for Papers to the topics that caused the most discussions.

5 Conclusion

The conclusions of the workshop were that more work needs to be done to reveal what the main benefits of an integrated AOSD-MDSD approach are. The two approaches complement each other and both have been demonstrated to improve the way software is developed. The submitted positions raised interesting questions that fostered fruitful discussions. It was agreed that more work needs to be done to fully understand the synergy between MDSD and AOSD. As a result further events for presenting solutions and discussing problems of integrated AOSD-MDSD approaches are intended.

Online Proceedings

The papers of the workshop can be found online at the URL:
http://www.kircher-schwanninger.de/workshops/MDD&AOSD/

References

1. Jackson A., Barais O., Jézéquel J.M., Clarke S., A.: Towards a Generic and Extensible Merge Operator. Models and Aspects Workshop at ECOOP, Nantes, France, July 3rd
2. Jackson A., Klein J., Baudry B., Clarke S.: Testing Executable Themes. Models and Aspects Workshop at ECOOP, Nantes, France, July 3rd
3. Kurtev I., Didonet Del Fabro M.: A DSL for Definition of Model Composition Operators. Models and Aspects Workshop at ECOOP, Nantes, France, July 3rd
4. Cleenewerck, T.: Aspects in MDSD as an Extension of a Meta-Protocol of a Transformation. Models and Aspects Workshop at ECOOP, Nantes, France, July 3rd
5. Cyment A., Kicillof N., Fernando A.: Enhancing model-based AOP with behavior representation. Models and Aspects Workshop at ECOOP, Nantes, France, July 3rd
6. Reiter T., Retschitzegger W., Schauerhuber A., Schwinger W., Kapsammer E.: Enabling API-based Tool Integration through Aspect-Orientation. Models and Aspects Workshop at ECOOP, Nantes, France, July 3rd

Aspects, Dependencies, and Interactions
Report on the WS ADI at ECOOP'06

Ruzanna Chitchyan[1], Johan Fabry[2], and Lodewijk Bergmans[3]

[1] Lancaster University, Lancaster, UK
rouza@comp.lancs.ac.uk
[2] INRIA FUTURS - LIFL, France
Johan.Fabry@lifl.fr
[3] University of Twente, Enschede, Netherlands
lbergmans@acm.org

Abstract. For Aspect-Oriented Software Development (AOSD) the topic of Aspects, Dependencies and Interactions is of high importance across the whole range of development activities – from requirements engineering through to language design. Aspect interactions must be adequately addressed all across the software lifecycle if AOSD is to succeed as a paradigm. Thus, this topic must be tackled by the AOSD community as a whole. This first workshop, initiated by AOSD-Europe project, aimed to establish a dedicated forum for discussion of this vital topic and to attract both researchers and practitioners currently engaged with related issues. The workshop has succeeded in initiating a broad community-wide discussion of this topic and has provided an initial overview of perspectives on the state of the art as well as of outstanding issues in this area.

1 Introduction

Aspects are crosscutting concerns that exist throughout software development cycle – from requirements through to implementation. While crosscutting other concerns, aspects often exert broad influences on these concerns, e.g. by modifying their semantics, structure or behaviour. Such dependencies between aspectual and non aspectual elements may lead to either desirable or (more often) unwanted and unexpected interactions.

The goal of this first workshop was to initiate a wide discussion on dependencies and interactions between aspectual and non-aspectual elements, thus investigating the lasting nature of such dependency links across all development activities:

- starting from the early development stages (i.e., requirements, architecture, and design), looking into dependencies between requirements (e.g., positive/negative contributions between aspectual goals, etc.) and interactions caused by aspects (e.g. quality attributes) in requirements, architecture, and design;
- analysing these dependencies and interactions both through modelling and formal analysis;
- considering language design issues which help to handle such dependencies and interactions (e.g. 'dominates' mechanism of AspectJ), and, last, but not least
- studying such interactions in applications, etc.

M. Südholt and C. Consel (Eds.): ECOOP 2006, LNCS 4379, pp. 26–39, 2007.
© Springer-Verlag Berlin Heidelberg 2007

In the following, we present the main topics discussed at the workshop and the questions risen, forming the broader view of the outstanding research issues in the aspects, dependencies, and interactions space.

2 Topics from Accepted Papers

Papers accepted to the workshop covered a broad spectrum of interaction-related problems. We have grouped these papers into related sets with each set briefly summarised below.

2.1 Requirements, Analysis and Design

This group of papers addresses the early stages of AOSD, talking about interaction identification and its impact assessment in requirements, architecture, and design.

In [6] an approach to estimating the impact of a change in requirements using the information about requirements interdependencies is outlined. The requirements dependencies are classified along 4 perspectives: temporal (e.g. Requirement R1 is before R2, etc.), conditional (e.g. R1 will apply only if R2 does), business rule, and task oriented (e.g., in order to complete R2 first need to complete R1). Furthermore, each of these can be related to another via forward, backward or parallel links; this is defined by the kind of impact triggered by a change in one of the concerns. The type of concern slices and their links are used to describe the dependencies triggered in case of a change. A weighting of such dependencies is also used to describe the severity of change. All these are then used to assess the change impact.

In [9] the focus is on concern interaction and resulting trade-off resolution issues when transiting from requirements to architecture. The functional requirements are modelled as concerns and refined into scenarios so that each scenario addresses only a single functional concern. The non-functional requirements are also represented as concerns and their refined sub concerns. Then the interactions between use cases and refined non-functional concerns are recorded and represented as a graph. From there the concerns for each scenario are classified as decisional if they are involved into trade-off making, or operational (i.e., not involved into tradeoffs). The decisional concerns for each scenario are then prioritised and these priorities are used in architecture derivation.

In [12] an approach to detecting aspect interactions in design models is presented. The system is modelled using UML class and state chart diagrams, produced separately for the core and aspectual concerns. These are then statically analysed and the potential interactions are pinpointed. After this the core and aspectual designs are woven together and some existing UML versification methods are used to verify the resultant design against behavioural properties. This approach combines light-weight syntactic analysis and formal versification of designs expressed in UML with a domain-specific state chart weaving language.

2.2 Techniques Related to the AOSD Domain

This set of papers looks at the traditionally non-AO software development methods and areas and draws a parallel between these and AOSD.

Paper [8] outlines the problems of interactions between aspects and proposes to use the work on feature dependency analysis to resolve some of them. A problem that may occur in incremental software development using AOP is first identified, namely invasive changes. The invasive change problem mainly comes from the lack of understanding of dependencies between features. To address this problem, a method is proposed that combines feature dependency analysis and AOP to provide support for incremental software development.

Paper [2] looks at how treating aspects as functions that transform programs reduces the potential aspect interactions. A simple algebraic approach that models aspects as functions is proposed, Using this approach, the paper shows that certain kinds of aspect dependencies caused by references and overlapping join points can be resolved by applying the notion of pseudo-commutativity. Two aspects are commutative if the order in which they are combined can be swapped, and pseudo-commutative if they are not commutative but can be transformed so that swapping them does not affect the program semantics The claim is made that each pair of aspects with referential dependencies or overlapping join points can be transformed into a corresponding pseudo-commutative pair.

In [13] there is an architecture outlined that separates clients, dispatchers and multiple service providers allowing for specific services to be found and used more flexibly. A dispatching intelligence between a message sender (a client) and the message receiver (a server) is discussed. This is said to provide malleability and flexible dispatch but requires the ability to specify protocols for the use of services, better semantic specification and interaction, and specification of dispatch strategies.

2.3 Language Design

This set of papers looks at the issues of AO language design and the sources of language-caused interactions.

Paper [4] presents a technique for semantic conflict detection between aspects applied at shared join points. The approach is based on abstracting the behaviour of advice to a resource-operation model, and detecting conflict patterns within the sequence of operations that various aspects apply to each resource.

In [10] the issues of how use of expressive pointcuts can cause unintended interactions are investigated. The source of the problem is that 'expressive pointcuts' specify join points based on the results of program analysis. Hence, if they are not carefully designed, the effects of weaving may depend on, or affect, the evaluation of expressive pointcuts.

Paper [5] outlines several categories of problematic interactions among structural aspects. It presents some ideas on how to avoid these situations, and it proposes the use of a logic engine for detecting certain types of aspect interactions.

3 Feature Interactions in Feature Based Program Synthesis and AOP [3]

The keynote speech: Feature Interactions in Feature Based Program Synthesis [3], delivered by Prof. Don Batory, presented an approach to represent and handle feature interaction with feature-based programme transformations. The speech invited the audience to compare and contrast aspects and features and learn how to utilise the work on feature interactions for AOSD.

Prof. Batory defined a feature as an increment in product functionality. Since these increments can often be dependent on the previously existing functionality, features will require/restrict the use of each other. He proposed that features are well suited for customisation of software products, and automated product generation can be based on tool-supported feature composition. Tools restrict the selection of features given previously selected features. For this features need to be represented as 1st class entities.

An example of such automated feature-based product composition tool was then demonstrated. In this tool the selection of features and their composition is stated in terms of grammar sentences. A domain specific language is developed for each given domain, defining the allowed and expected composition sequence of features (i.e., sentences) in that domain. Sentences that are specified by a user are checked against the domain knowledge for correct composition. Verified sentences are then used for generation of the software product in a selected implementation language (e.g., C++, Java, etc.).

Thus, automation of product generation with feature synthesis must start with domain knowledge accumulation, followed by development of feature model for that domain where each separate feature is identified and represented. Then rules are defined for required/restricted use of individual features due to their dependencies and their correct compositions. After this the product specification can be represented in terms of feature selection and composition, from which the product can be generated.

The speaker noted that in Feature-Oriented Programming (FOP), as in the functional world, programs are values and functions transform these values. If a programme is viewed as an object, the same function transformation corresponds to a method. He then drew parallels, comparing FOP and Aspect-Oriented Programming (AOP). He observed that:

- an introduction in AO is equal to an addition operation in FOP. However, the introduction addition operation of FOP is more general then AspectJ introductions as new classes, packages, etc. can also be introduced.
- FOP has an impoverished pointcut-advice language, as here heterogeneous advice and individual joinpoints form pointcuts.
- In AspectJ an advice is a function that maps a program and has an event-driven interpretation that is consistent with current AOP usage.
- AOP and FOP have different models of advising:
  - In FOP features extend individual methods by surrounding them, extending them with the new feature application. This model of advising is termed *bounded quantification*, as the advice is applied to the previously composed features only.
    - In AspectJ AOP the advising is global, since the advising is applied to the interpreter level. This model of advising is termed *unbounded quantification* as the advice applies not only the features composed before its application, but also those that will be added afterwards. The ideology of such advising implies that <u>all</u> the introductions are carried out before the advice is applied.

Both types of quantifications are useful in different situations.

4 Discussions on Interactions and Aspects

As this was a the first workshop on the topic of aspects, dependencies and interactions, many scientific discussions focused on identifying the important questions for the domain, some of which were also discussed in more detail during the group discussions. The list of identified questions and the essence of the group discussions are summarised below.

4.1 Questions for the Research Area

Being the first forum in the area of Aspects, Dependencies, and Interactions the ADI 2006 workshop aimed to provide some initial survey of the research space, identifying and listing the topics of interest and directions for further work. Below follows the list of identified topics:

- How do we define or detect semantic interaction? How do we specify semantics of a concern?
- What taxonomy, categories, granularity and kind of interactions are there?
- What scope, binding time and binding mode do we have for composition rules? How do we do interaction detection in this context?
- How are interactions detected, propagated and resolved through different stages in the development process? What information do we need to perform this?
- Are there any interaction problems specific to the design of the pointcut language or joinpoint model.
- How can we deal with ad-hoc constraints, e.g. expert intuition?
- How does unbounded quantification combine with top-down design?
- What abstraction granularity do we need to define precedence or ordering constrains?
- How do we deal with interference, e.g. use total order or partial order?
- What language mechanisms or new operators beyond aspect precedence do we need to specify resolution?
- How do we detect interactions when an aspect suppresses a join-point needed by another aspect?
- How do we analyze aspect interactions without having the base code?
- How can refactoring techniques be used to simplify dependencies and interactions?

4.2 Group Discussions

Several of the above listed topics had repeatedly recurred at the ADI 2006 workshop. Thus, five of these recurrent topics were discussed at the group-work sessions.

4.2.1 Group 1: How Do We Define/Detect Semantic Interaction? How Do We Specify the Semantics of a Concern?

The topic of this group is an active research area; in the discussion it became clear that no profound answers to these questions could be given. Instead, several observations were made about the nature of semantic interactions and the possible forms or contexts in which semantic interactions may appear. These observations have been structured according to the following topics:

- Where do the semantic interactions occur
- What kind of properties need to be modelled for detecting interactions
- How to obtain these properties
- How do we specify the semantics of an aspect?

For semantic interactions, the focus of active research, and the group discussion, is mostly on the semantic interactions among advices. Such interactions are most common and easy to reason about at *shared join points:* join points in the program where multiple advices need to be executed. Interactions can be related to control or – shared– state, and may be influenced by the order in which advice is executed at shared join points. Detecting such interactions can be organized by iterating over all (potential) shared join points in the program. However, aspects may also interact through advices that are *not* sharing the same join point. This may be the case either because the advices have some shared state, or because one advice affects the control flow, thereby affecting the other (e.g. because some expected join point may no longer occur).

To model interactions, or design algorithms for detecting interactions, certain properties about the elements in the program must be modelled. What properties these exactly are depends on the type of interactions. Such properties need to be defined for one or more of the following elements: aspects, base code, or the woven system.

In the worst case, the software engineer must specify all properties for each program element. This yields a load for the software engineer that prohibits most practical applications. Ideally, these properties are derived automatically from the program source code. This is considered infeasible in general: because not all relevant properties can always be derived statically from a program source code, and because very quickly the size and complexity of the interaction detection grow out of hand. To this extent it is necessary to reason about a subset of all properties, for a subset of all program elements in the source code. Two approaches were discussed: firstly abstraction/focusing about the analyzed program, thereby ignoring many details, hopefully without compromising the conclusions from the detection analysis. Secondly, slicing as an alternative means to observe only a part of the complete program by leaving out many details.

Finally, the ways to represent the semantics of an aspect were discussed: here we distinguish between representing the behaviour of the aspect (i.e. of the advice), and representing the pointcuts. For representing the behaviour of advice, formal semantics such as small step semantics, state machine representations or control flow models can be used. For representing pointcuts in a precise way, possible formalisms are predicate logic or the approach followed by Event-based AOP.

4.2.2 Group 2: What Taxonomy, Categories, Granularity and Kind of Interactions Do We Have?

The first question faced by the group was whether there are any good techniques for analyzing pointcuts, but without having access to the base-level code. The goal is to be able to reason about aspects individually, in a modular fashion. However, if we would have access to the source code, then the question is if computing intersections of pointcuts would be useful enough.

The second question treated by the group was if, and how, refactoring techniques can be used to simplify dependencies among aspects, and check them separately. The analyst should not have to look at the final woven program to verify it. Instead, she/he should be able to verify the program by looking at its different aspects. It has been shown that in some cases it is possible to change the dependency order. This can be used to simplify dependencies between particularly hard to check aspects.

4.2.3   Group 3: What Scope and Binding Time/Binding Mode Do We Have for Composition Rules? How Do We Do Interaction Detection in This Context?

To get a better feeling for the concepts of scope and binding time, the group members started with defining a grid showing the possible combinations between binding time and scope. This grid was then filled in with example aspect languages or features of aspect languages with the corresponding combination. The grid is shown in Fig. 1.

	Compile Time	Run-Time
Static	AspectJ/Josh	CesarJ Deploy/ Association Aspects
Dynamic	Reflex/ JAC	AspectS/ Gepetto/ SteamLoom

Fig. 1. Binding Time versus Binding Mode

The discussion then focused on the need for both static and dynamic composition rules, and if these rules should be applied at the level of the aspect or each of the affected element. Participants wanted to find convincing examples of both static and dynamic cases.

For static composition rules the example found is an on-line auction site, where buyers can participate in a number of auctions. The aspects applied here are logging and access control. These need to be applied on all operations of an auction: joining the auction, placing a bid, and getting an overview of all placed bids. All attempts to join the auction need to be logged, regardless if authentication is successful or not, but to be able to place a bid, or get an overview of bids placed the buyer needs to be logged in successfully. In the former case, therefore, the logging aspect has a higher precedence than the access control aspect, and in the latter two cases, the reverse is the case.

Dynamic composition of aspects can also be encountered in this setting, albeit on the lower level of network management. All incoming network messages need to be validated for correctness, as a protection against hacking attacks. Also, incoming messages need to be logged, for traceability purposes. Two aspects are used: a validator and a logger aspect. In normal operations, the validator aspect has precedence over the logger, as only correct messages need to be logged. In case of an intensive attack by hackers, the malicious messages should however also be logged, for analysis and counter-measures. Therefore, in this case, the aspects need to be switched dynamically, whenever the validator aspect detects that an intensive attack is in progress.

4.2.4 Group 4: How Are Interactions Detected, Propagated and Resolved Through Different Stages of Development Process

The group members started by setting a basis for further discussion by agreeing that there are multiple views or models of aspects at different levels of the development lifecycle. Thus, the aspects are defined for each level of development as concerns that have a broad influence on the elements of the model at the level where the aspect is defined. They also agreed that an aspect at one level does not always need to be represented as aspect at another level. This is because a solution to a problem at one level becomes a problem to be solved at the following level. This is illustrated in Fig. 2, where a problem "Reduce operational costs for car dealers" stated at requirements will be represented as, for instance, a requirements template (solution), this template will then need to be represented as a part of architecture design (problem), leading to creation of multiple alternatives architectures and finally a choice of one of them (solution). The chosen architecture solution (problem for Design) will have to be elaborated into a detailed design solution, etc.

With the above view, we can define the requirements -> architecture -> etc. as a chain of problems and solutions. In this case, if a model is created for each level, we can use the model transformation techniques to move from one level to another. With the correct transformations we would be able to preserve the semantics of aspects. Moreover, if decisions on interaction resolution for the higher level are made, and a 1-to-1 transformation is appropriate, these interaction resolutions can be used at the lower level as well. Otherwise in case of 1-n mapping, we need to optimize the transformations from multiple perspectives.

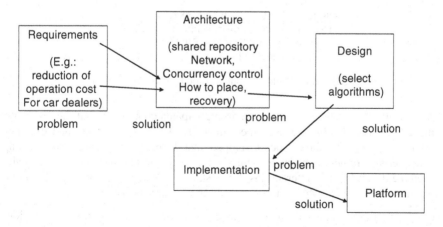

Fig. 2. The Problem-Solution Chain for Aspect Modelling

The information about interactions should be obtained from domain knowledge, past experience (similar to design patterns), e.g. selection of a decisions (e.g. topology is related to response time). But more research needs to be done to clarify and define as to what details do we need to know in order to realize these transformations.

The group participants carried out an initial brainstorming to answer the above questions, and suggested that some information that could be used is:

- The call graph with call probability can be used to estimate the performance of some communication at different levels (e.g., collect the statistics of car dealers, simulate the algorithms with the given statistics, put the priorities from the statistical information into the architectural trade-offs)
- If we know the values for the relative importance of concerns in requirements, these can be passed to components and connectors to preserve the same constraints in the architecture.
- Prepare and reuse trade-off catalogues for various concerns and their mapping

4.2.5 Group 5: Are There Specific Problems to Pointcut Languages in Terms of Aspect Interactions?

The group participants thought that most problems of interactions in pointcut languages are particularly related to system evolution. Such problems are, for instance, that:

- non-local edits to the code results in changes of the set of matching join points. This in turn can result in aspect interactions, making two aspects inadvertently picked up due to code modification being applied to the same join points.
- pointcuts can be based on runtime types. This for instance, may result in *proceed* changing the runtime types, and *arguments* can check runtime types. An example of this is presented in Fig. 3.
- aspects can modify the type hierarchy (e.g., declare parents), etc.

```
after(Float f) returning: args(f) && ... {}
around(Number n) : execution(foo) && args(n)
     { proceed(new Double(0.5)); }
void foo(Number n) { ... }
```

Fig. 3. An Example of Pointcut-Based Aspect Interaction

- As a result of this discussion, the group participants concluded, that the pointcuts, indeed are most likely to cause aspect interactions. Thus, they reasoned that new kinds of joinpoints should be developed that leverage this interaction-causing characteristic rather than try to neutralize it. Such joinpoints may intentionally promote desired aspect interactions. For instance, advice execution at such a point may enable an aspect which in turn may disable other aspects, or alike.

The group participants also discussed weather static joinpoints have lesser interaction-related problems than the dynamic ones. They agreed that both static and dynamic joinpoints are equally likely to cause interactions, though in the case of static joinpoints such interactions could be resolved in the implementation of the compilers.

5 Do Aspectual Dependencies and Interactions Prevent Modular Reasoning?

A panel of experts from the AOSD-Europe project discussed the question *Do aspectual dependencies and interactions prevent modular reasoning?* Each of the four panellists presented a specific view on the issue, which are briefly outlined below.

5.1 Panel Positions

Adrian Colyer questioned how could an approach that gives better modularity not improve modular reasoning? This is a contradiction. He pointed out that any new modularity mechanism, by virtue of allowing new ways of modularity, will have to provide new ways of composition. So if the aspectual modules and compositions "break modular reasoning", then what kind of reasoning is broken? He argued that it is the "old" modularity that will be broken, but a new form of modular reasoning will arise from new modular representation and composition. Adrian drew a parallel of the AOSD acceptance with that of past paradigm shifts by recounting that before procedures the developers had needed to do global reasoning. With procedures they could do local reasoning, but still had global data. With objects they could also locally define data. Aspects are the next step in this ladder of evolution, allowing to locally define functionality and data used in multiple locations by objects or procedures.

Adrian summarised the argument of AO opponents as "if we need to know about all aspects to reason about a module, how can we have modular reasoning"? He then explained that, in his view, such argument means that modular reasoning implies complete locality. However, modular reasoning is not "all or nothing", but a mechanism to support partial reasoning about partially localised code or modules in the same way as, for instance, procedures allow useful analysis about the procedure content, but they do need to refer to the instance variables. Thus, AOP supports better partial modular reasoning.

Awais Rashid stated that aspects are about abstraction (abstracting away from the details of how that aspect might be scattered and tangled with other functionality), modularity (allowing to modularise the details of interest, hence facilitating modular reasoning), and composability [11]. He noted that in his view composability is of a paramount importance as modules need to relate to each other in a systematic and coherent fashion. Aspects provide advancement in composition mechanisms, thus complementing the traditional modular reasoning with compositional reasoning, i.e., the ability to reason about global and emergent properties of the system using the modularised information. Awais underlined that in his view, the important contribution of AOP is the support for this compositional reasoning, which helps developers to more effectively reason about dependencies and interactions compared to traditional software engineering techniques. Hence, aspects do not prevent modular reasoning as this is supported via the abstraction and modularity support. Furthermore, the composability properties of aspect-oriented techniques enhance the compositional reasoning support available to developers.

Theo D'Hondt suggested that maybe such questions as the topic of this panel were rising because the AO community has approached the notion of aspects from the wrong perspective. Theo pointed out that historically Computer Science has developed by increasing the level of abstraction of the main elements used in development. However, this progression trend was broken in case of aspects. The break was in that historically each new theory had worked to show that the newly proposed abstraction (e.g., procedure, object) is the "rule" for the development in that suggested paradigm. However, in case of AO, aspects are treated as "an exception" to the existing abstractions. Thus, Theo asked if the AO community should try and view objects and hierarchical decomposition as a "specialisation" of aspects? He proposed that, aspects should be <u>more general abstractions</u> than those of the previous theory. In conclusion, Theo suggested that aspects should be studies "on their own" as modules, along with their reasoning support. However, this will only be possible if aspects are viewed as more general, subsuming previous abstraction types, so the view on aspects should be revisited.

Mario Sudholt was sceptical that modularity and full obliviousness were possible with aspects. Mario explained that traditionally, when writing a system, one would start with modules and interfaces and when writing them he or she would have a good knowledge of the program structure and behaviour. However, with AOP, as it is today, the development is moving from this modular development, into the style of <u>evolutionary</u> development. He concluded that he does not believe that the current state of art provides any proof that AO supports an adequate modularity. Current approaches to modular properties in the presence of aspects (e.g.,[1, 7]) are either too restrictive or not powerful/systematic enough to render a solution. He suggested that this point will remain to be seen in the future.

5.2 Discussion

The discussion turned to the question of what is the simplest mental image of aspect. It was suggested that in most cases aspect is understood as "interrupt routine plus interrupt processing". However, this is a very primitive view and the community should work to move away from this primitive image of aspect to more appropriate image for a fully fledged module. Indeed, an aspect has state and behaviour, as a class has state and methods. A class has called methods running over variables, and aspect has pointcuts, advice and state, with advice running when the pointcut is matched. So aspect is as much a module as a class.

The workshop participants also agreed that one should not think that "an aspect belongs to a class". Aspects are for modular reasoning about the aspects themselves, not the class. The claim that aspects change the classes in an unintended way can be equally well stated about the classes changing each other as well. The claim that the class does not know which aspects will apply on it, is also valid about the call to procedures: one does not know which procedure will be called, particularly in cases of late binding.

Adrian Colyer also argued that successive levels of modular reasoning are possible with AspectJ, looking at the aspect only; then at aspects with the type of applying advice, i.e., before, after or around; after this the details about the body of the advice can be included into the reasoning. Thus, different levels of detail for reasoning can be available at the different element consideration views.

The discussants talked about global versus local design with aspects versus OO. It was argued that in OO the global design is hard but the local effects are very clear. On the other hand, with AO global design is clear and relatively easy, though its effects on local reasoning are more difficult to account for. Tool support can help in assisting local reasoning by completing the local details recovered from global compositions. However, no tool support can adequately recover the global details from local ones, supporting global reasoning. Thus, AO seems to progress along the right path.

Additionally, the participants agreed that aspects bring into programming languages the notions of quantification over temporal and conditional references which are broadly used in natural language (e.g., notions about history of the programme execution, etc.). Thus aspects enrich the current programming languages.

After a lively discussion, in summary, most workshop participants agreed that aspect interactions need to be addressed, but they do not, in principle, prevent modular reasoning.

6   Conclusion

This AOSD-Europe workshop on Aspects, Dependencies and Interactions provided an opportunity for presentations and lively discussion between researchers working on AOSD and dependencies and interactions in general from all over the world. As a first workshop on the topic, it has established a list of important questions which will stimulate and guide the further research in this area. We intend to continue the work stared at this event in the future years by organising a series of follow up workshops.

7   Workshop Organisers and Participants

7.1   List of Organizers

- Ruzanna Chitchyan: Lancaster University, UK (Co-chair).
  Email: rouza@comp.lancs.ac.uk
- Johan Fabry: Vrije Universiteit Brussel, Belgium (Co-chair).
  Email: johan.fabry@vub.ac.be
- Lodewijk Bergmans: Universiteit Twente, The Netherlands.
  Email: L.M.J.Bergmans@ewi.utwente.nl
- Andronikos Nedos: Trinity College Dublin, Ireland. Email: nedosa@gmail.com
- Arend Rensink: Universiteit Twente, The Netherlands.
  Email: rensink@cs.utwente.nl

7.2   List of Attendees

The list of attendees officially registered for the workshop is presented below (a number of unregistered attendees also participated, but are not listed):

1. Mehmet Akşit (University of Twente, The Netherlands)
2. Tomoyuki Aotani (University of Tokyo, Japan)
3. Don Batory (University of Taxes at Austin, USA)

4. Lodewijk Bergmans (University of Twente, The Netherlands)
5. Walter Cazzola (DICo Università di Milano, Italy)
6. Ruzanna Chitchyan (Lancaster University, UK)
7. Adrian Colyer (Interface21, UK)
8. Theo D'Hondt (Vrije Universiteit Brussel, Belgium)
9. Remi Douence (INRIA, France)
10. Pascal Dürr (University of Twente, The Netherlands)
11. Johan Fabry (Vrije Universiteit Brussel, Belgium)
12. Safoora Khan (Lancaster University, UK)
13. Kwanwoo Lee (Hansung University, Korea)
14. Jose Mango (Instituto Politecnico de Leiria, Portugal)
15. Hidehiko Masuhara (University of Tokyo, Japan)
16. Sonia Pini (DISI, Università di Genova, Italy)
17. Awais Rashid (Lancaster University, UK)
18. Pouria Shaker (Memorial University of Newfoundland, Canada)
19. Pablo Sánchez (University of Malaga, Spain)
20. Frans Sanen (Katholieke Universiteit Leuven, Belgium)
21. Daniel Speicher (University of Bonn, Germany)
22. Maximilian Störzer (Universitat Passau, Germany)
23. Mario Südholt (INRIA, France)
24. Éric Tanter (University of Chile, Chile)
25. Tim Walsh (Trinity College Dublin, Ireland)

References

[1] J. Aldrich and C. Chambers, "Ownership Domains: Separating Aliasing Policy from Mechanism", ECOOP'04, 2004, LNCS, 3086, pp. 1-25.
[2] S. Apel and J. Liu, "On the Notion of Functional Aspects in Aspect-Oriented Refactoring", in Aspects, Dependencies, and Interactions Workshop (held at ECOOP), Lancaster University Computing Department Technical Report Series, ISSN 1477447X. Lancaster, 2006, pp. 1-9.
[3] D. Batory, "Feature Interactions in Feature-Based Program Synthesis", University of Texas at Austin, Dept. Computer Sciences, Austin, Technical Report TR-06-52, September 2006.
[4] P. Durr, L. Bergmans, and M. Aksit, "Reasoning about Semantic Conflicts between Aspects", in Aspects, Dependencies, and Interactions Workshop (held at ECOOP), Lancaster University Computing Department Technical Report Series, ISSN 1477447X. Lancaster, 2006, pp. 10-18.
[5] B. Kessler and É. Tanter, "Analyzing Interactions of Structural Aspects", in Aspects, Dependencies, and Interactions Workshop (held at ECOOP), Lancaster University Computing Department Technical Report Series, ISSN 1477447X. Lancaster, 2006, pp. 70-76.
[6] S. Khan and A. Rashid, "Analysing Requirements Dependencies and Change Impact Using Concern Slicing", in Aspects, Dependencies, and Interactions Workshop (held at ECOOP), Lancaster University Computing Department Technical Report Series, ISSN 1477447X. Lancaster, 2006, pp. 33- 42.

[7] G. Kiczales and M. Mezini, "Aspect-oriented programming and modular reasoning", 27th International Conference on Software Engineering (ICSE 2005), 2005, ACM, pp. 49-58.

[8] K. Lee, "Using Feature Dependency Analysis and AOP for Incremental Software Development", in Aspects, Dependencies, and Interactions Workshop (held at ECOOP), Lancaster University Computing Department Technical Report Series, ISSN 1477447X. Lancaster, 2006, pp. 62-69.

[9] J. Magno and A. Moreira, "Concern Interactions and Tradeoffs: Preparing Requirements to Architecture", in Aspects, Dependencies, and Interactions Workshop (held at ECOOP), Lancaster University Computing Department Technical Report Series, ISSN 1477447X. Lancaster, 2006, pp. 43-52.

[10] H. Masuhara and T. Aotani, "Issues on Observing Aspect Effects from Expressive Pointcuts", in Aspects, Dependencies, and Interactions Workshop (held at ECOOP), Lancaster University Computing Department Technical Report Series, ISSN 1477447X. Lancaster, 2006, pp. 53-61.

[11] A. Rashid and A. Moreira, "Domain Models are NOT Aspect Free", MoDELS/UML, 2006, Springer LNCS, 4199, pp. 155-169.

[12] P. Shaker and D. K. Peters, "Design-level Detection of Interactions in Aspect-Oriented Systems", in Aspects, Dependencies, and Interactions Workshop (held at ECOOP), Lancaster University Computing Department Technical Report Series, ISSN 1477447X. Lancaster, 2006, pp. 23-32.

[13] T. Walsh, D. Lievens, and W. Harrison, "Dispatch and Interaction in a Service-Oriented Programming Language", in Aspects, Dependencies, and Interactions Workshop (held at ECOOP), Lancaster University Computing Department Technical Report Series, ISSN 1477447X. Lancaster, 2006, pp. 19-22.

AOSD and Reflection:
Benefits and Drawbacks to Software Evolution
Report on the WS RAM-SE at ECOOP'06

Walter Cazzola[1], Shigeru Chiba[2], Yvonne Coady[3], and Gunter Saake[4]

[1] DICo - Department of Informatics and Communication,
Università degli Studi di Milano, Milano, Italy
cazzola@dico.unimi.it
[2] Department of Mathematical and Computing Sciences,
Tokyo Institute of Technology, Tokyo, Japan
chiba@is.titech.ac.jp
[3] Department of Computer Science,
University of Victoria, Victoria, Canada
ycoady@cs.uvic.ca
[4] Institute für Technische und Betriebliche Informationssysteme,
Otto-von-Guericke-Universität Magdeburg, Magdeburg, Germany
saake@iti.cs.uni-magdeburg.de

Abstract. Following last two years' RAM-SE (Reflection, AOP and Meta-Data for Software Evolution) workshop at the ECOOP conference, the RAM-SE 2006 workshop was a successful and popular event. As its name implies, the workshop's focus was on the application of reflective, aspect-oriented and data-mining techniques to the broad field of software evolution. Topics and discussions at the workshop included mechanisms for supporting software evolution, technological limits for software evolution and tools and middleware for software evolution.

The workshop's main goal was to bring together researchers working in the field of software evolution with a particular interest in reflection, aspect-oriented programming and meta-data. The workshop was organized as a full day meeting, partly devoted to presentation of submitted position papers and partly devoted to panel discussions about the presented topics and other interesting issues in the field. In this way, the workshop allowed participants to get acquainted with each other's work, and stimulated collaboration. We hope this helped participants in improving their ideas and the quality of their future publications.

The workshop's proceedings, including all accepted position papers can be downloaded from the workshop's web site and a post workshop proceeding, including an extension of the accepted paper is published byt the University of Magdeburg.

In this report, we first provide a session-by-session overview of the presentations, and then present our opinions about future trends in software evolution.

Workshop Description and Objectives

Software evolution and adaptation is a research area, as also the name states, in continuous evolution, that offers stimulating challenges for both academic and industrial

M. Südholt and C. Consel (Eds.): ECOOP 2006, LNCS 4379, pp. 40–52, 2007.

researchers. The evolution of software systems, to face unexpected situations or just for improving their features, relies on software engineering techniques and methodologies. Nowadays a similar approach is not applicable in all situations e.g., for evolving nonstopping systems or systems whose code is not available.

Features of reflection such as transparency, separation of concerns, and extensibility seem to be perfect tools to aid the dynamic evolution of running systems. Aspect-oriented programming (AOP in the next) can simplify code instrumentation whereas techniques that rely on meta-data can be used to inspect the system and to extract the necessary data for designing the heuristic that the reflective and aspect-oriented mechanism use for managing the evolution.

We feel the necessity to investigate the benefits brought by the use of these techniques on the evolution of object-oriented software systems. In particular we would determine how these techniques can be integrated with more traditional approaches to evolve a system and the benefits we get from their use.

The overall goal of this workshop was that of supporting circulation of ideas between these disciplines. Several interactions were expected to take place between reflection, aspect-oriented programming and meta-data for the software evolution, some of which we cannot even foresee. Both the application of reflective or aspect-oriented techniques and concepts to software evolution are likely to support improvement and deeper understanding of these areas. This workshop has represented a good meeting-point for people working in the software evolution area, and an occasion to present reflective, aspect-oriented, and meta-data based solutions to evolutionary problems, and new ideas straddling these areas, to provide a discussion forum, and to allow new collaboration projects to be established. The workshop was a full day meeting. One part of the workshop was devoted to presentation of papers, and another to panels and to the exchange of ideas among participants.

Workshop Topics and Structure

Every contribution that exploits reflective techniques, aspect-oriented programming and/or meta-data to evolve software systems were welcome. Specific topics of interest for the workshop have included, but were not limited to:

- aspect-oriented middleware and environments for software evolution;
- adaptive software components and evolution as component composition;
- evolution planning and deployment through aspect-oriented techniques and reflective approaches;
- aspect interference and composition for software evolution;
- feature- and subject-oriented adaptation;
- unanticipated software evolution supported by AOSD or reflective techniques;
- MOF, code annotations and other meta-data facilities for software evolution;
- software evolution tangling concerns;
- techniques for refactoring into AOSD and to get the separation of concerns.

To ensure lively discussion at the workshop, the organizing committee has chosen the contributions on the basis of topic similarity that will permit the beginning of new collaborations. To grant an easy dissemination of the proposed ideas and to favorite an ideas interchange among the participants, accepted contributions are freely download-able from the workshop web page:

http://homes.dico.unimi.it/RAM-SE06.html.

The workshop was a full day meeting organized in four sessions. The first session was devoted to the Awais Rashid's keynote speech on *"Aspects and Evolution: The Case for Versioned Types and Meta-Aspect Protocols"*. Each of the remaining sessions has been characterized by a dominant topic that perfectly describes the presented papers and the related discussions. The three dominant topics were: *aspect-oriented modeling for software evolution, tools and middleware for software evolution,* and *technological limits to software evolution.* During each session, half time has been devoted to papers presentation, and the rest of the time has been devoted to debate about the on-going works in the area, about relevance of the approaches in the software evolution area and the achieved benefits. The discussion related to each session has been brilliantly lead respectively by Theo D'Hondt, Mario Südholt and Hidehiko Masuhara.

The workshop has been very lively, the debates very stimulating, and the high number of participants (see appendix A) testifies the growing interest in the application of reflective, aspect- and meta-data oriented techniques to software evolution.

Important References

The following publications are important references for people interested in learning more about the topics of this workshop:

- Pattie Maes. Computational Reflection. PhD thesis, Vrije Universiteit Brussel, Brussels, Belgium, 1987.
- Gregor Kiczales, John Lamping, Anurag Mendhekar, Chris Maeda, Cristina Videira Lopes, Jean-Marc Loingtier, and John Irwin. Aspect-Oriented Programming. In *11th European Conference on Object Oriented Programming (ECOOP'97)*, LNCS 1241, pages 220–242, Helsinki, Finland, June 1997. Springer-Verlag.
- The proceedings of the International Conference on Aspect-Oriented Software Development (AOSD) from 2002 to 2006. See also http://aosd.net/archive/index.php.
- Several tracks related to aspect-oriented software development and evolution at the International Conference on Software Maintenance (ICSM) and the Working Conference on Reverse Engineering (WCRE), from 2002 onward.
- The software evolution website at the Program Transformation wiki:

http://www.program-transformation.org/twiki/bin/view/Transform/SoftwareEvolution.

1   Workshop Overview: Session by Session

In this section of the report we summarize the workshop. In particular, Shigeru Chiba, in the role of chairman of the invited talk session, will comment the Nierstrasz's talk and the discussions raised from the talk, then a short summary of the the remaining sessions will follow.

Session on Aspects and Evolution
Keynote Speech by Awais Rashid (*Lancaster University, UK*)
Summary by Shigeru Chiba (Session Chair, *Tokyo Institute of Technology*)

In the first morning session, we had a keynote talk by Dr. Awais Rashid:

– Aspects and Evolution: The Case for Versioned Types and Meta-Aspect Protocol.

Abstract. One of the often cited advantages of aspect-oriented programming (AOP) is improved evolvability. No doubt the modularisation support provided by aspects helps to localise changes thus supporting evolution. However, evolution often requires keeping track of changes in order to make them reversible. Furthermore, often such changes (and their reversal) needs to be done online, e.g., in case of business and mission critical systems that can't be taken offline. In this talk, I will discuss whether current AOP mechanisms are suited to such evolution needs. I will highlight the need for first class support for versioned types as well as fully-fledged meta-aspect protocols and present some practical experiences of implementing these in the Vejal aspect language and its associated dynamic evolution framework. The talk will conclude with a roadmap of key research issues that need to be tackled to ensure that the full potential of aspects can be realised with regards to improving the evolvability of software systems.

Dr. Rashid's keynote was very interesting and led active discussion among participants. In particular, the first half of his talk was about a classic problem in AOP, which is the problem of obliviousness and quantification. Although it was first proposed by Filman and Friedman [10] that the primary properties of AOP are obliviousness and quantification, this issue has been actively discussed by many researchers. Dr. Rashid's claim was that obliviousness and quantification are not mandatory properties of AOP but they are only desirable properties. According to his talk, the obliviousness property often makes modular reasoning difficult. Hence, open modules and XPIs have been proposed as technique for limiting the obliviousness property and enabling easier modular reasoning. This fact shows that this property is not necessary (therefore, it can be limited). The quantification property is also useful but most of aspects, for example, in the database transaction domain, are not heterogeneous aspects but homogeneous aspects. Homogeneous aspects do not need the complex functionality of the quantification property. His claim was appealing and led a number of comments, objections, and supports from the floor.

Session on Aspect-Oriented Modeling for Software Evolution

The second session was related to the use of the aspect-oriented modeling to support the software evolution, Theo D'Hondt (Vrije Universiteit Brussel, Belgium) was the chairman. Three papers have been presented:

[7] Improving AOP Systems' Evolvability by Decoupling Advices from Base Code. *Alan Cyment, Nicolas Kicillof, Rubén Altman,* and *Fernando Asteasuain* (University of Buenos Aires, Argentina).

Alan Cyment gave the talk.

[16] Making Aspect Oriented System Evolution Safer. *Miguel Ángel Pérez Toledano, Amparo Navasa Martinez, Juan M. Murillo Rodriguez,* (University of Extremadura, Spain) and *Carlos Canal* (University of Málaga).

Miguel Ángel Pérez Toledano gave the talk.

[6] Design-Based Pointcuts Robustness Against Software Evolution. *Walter Cazzola* (DICo Università degli Studi di Milano, Italy), *Sonia Pini,* and *Massimo Ancona* (DISI Università degli Studi di Genova, Italy).

Sonia Pini gave the talk.

Session on Tools and Middleware for Software Evolution

The papers in this session covered the topic of adaptive middleware to support software evolution. Mario Südholt (École de Mines de Nantes) has chaired the session. Three papers have been presented:

[1] Evolution of an Adaptive Middleware Exploiting Architectural Reflection. *Francesca Arcelli,* and *Claudia Raibulet* (Università degli Studi di Milano-Bicocca, Italy).

Claudia Raibulet gave the talk.

[3] An Aspect-Oriented Adaptation Framework for Dynamic Component Evolution. *Javier Cámara Moreno, Carlos Canal, Javier Cubo* (University of Málaga, Spain), and *Juan M. Murillo Rodriguez* (University of Extremadura, Spain).

Javier Cámara Moreno gave the talk.

[12] An Aspect-Aware Outline Viewer. *Michihiro Horie,* and *Shigeru Chiba* (Tokyo Institute of Technology, Japan).

Michihiro Horie has given the talk.

Session on Technological Limits for Software Evolution

The papers in this session explore the technological limits of the AOP and reflective techniques to support software evolution. Hidehiko Masuhara (University of Tokyo, Japan) has lead the session. Four papers have been presented:

[18] Solving Aspectual Semantic Conflicts in Resource Aware Systems. *Arturo Zambrano, Tomás Vera,* and *Silvia Gordillo* (University of La Plata, Argentina).

Arturo Zambrano has given the talk.

[8] Statement Annotations for Fine-Grained Advising. *Mark Eaddy,* and *Alfred Aho* (Columbia University, USA).

Mark Eaddy gave the talk.

[9] Dynamic Refactorings: Improving the Program Structure at Run-time. *Peter Ebraert* and *Theo D'Hondt* (Vrije Universiteit Brussel, Belgium).

Peter Ebraert gave the talk.

[13] Implementing Bounded Aspect Quantification in AspectJ. *Christian Kästner, Sven Apel,* and *Gunter Saake* (Otto-von-Guericke-Universität Magdeburg, Germany).

Christian Kästner gave the talk.

2   Software Evolution Trends: The Organizers' Opinion

The authors, with this report, would like to go beyond the mere presentation of statistical and generic information related to the workshop and to its course. They try to speculate about the current state of art of the research in the field and to evaluate the role of reflection, AOSD and meta-data in the software evolution.

Can or Cannot the AOP Support the Software Evolution?
Comment by Walter Cazzola (*Università di Milano, Italy*)

In [2], software evolution is defined as a kind of software maintenance that takes place only when the initial development was successful. The goal consists of adapting the application to the ever changing user requirements and operating environment.

Software systems are often asked for promptly evolving to face critical situations such as to repair security bugs, to avoid the failure of critical devices and to patch the logic of a critical system. It is fairly evident the necessity of improving the software adaptability and its promptness without impacting on the activity of the system itself. This statement brings forth to the need for a system to manage itself to some extent, to dynamically inspect component interfaces, to augment its application-specific functionality with additional properties, and so on.

Independently of the mechanism adopted for planning the evolution, it requires a mechanism that permits of concreting the evolution on the running system. In particular this mechanism should be able of i) extruding the code interested by the evolution from the whole system code, ii) carrying out the patches required by the planned evolution on the located code. Often, both these steps must occur without compromising the system stability and the services availability (that is, without stopping the system providing them).

AOP [14] provides some mechanisms (join points, pointcut and aspect weaving) that allow of modifying the behavior and the structure of an application. The AOP technology better addresses functionality that crosscut the whole implementation of the application. Evolution is a typical functionality that crosscut the code of many objects in the system. Moreover, the AOP technology seems suitable to deal with the detection of the code to evolve and with the instrumentation of such a code.

From AOP characteristics, it is fairly evident that AOP has the potential for providing the necessary tools for instrumenting the code of a software system, especially when aspects can be plugged and unplugged at run-time. Pointcuts should be used to pick out a region of the code involved by the evolution, whereas the advices should be used to define how the selected region of code should evolve. Weaving such an aspect on the running system should either inject new code or manipulate the existing code, allowing the dynamic evolution of the system.

Unfortunately, to define pointcuts that point out the code interested by the evolution is a hard task because such modifications can be scattered and spread all around the code and not confined to a well-defined area that can be taken back to a method call. Moreover the changes could entail only part of a statement, e.g., the exit condition of a loop or an expression, and not the entire statement.

The AOP technology could be the right approach to deal with the evolution concern but some scenarios are difficult to administrate with the current aspect-oriented frameworks. The main issues that obstacle the use of the AOP approaches are: the *granularity* of the requested manipulation and the *locality* of the code to manipulate. The necessary granularity for the pointcut is too fine, traditional join point models refer to method invocation in several way whereas we want to be able to manipulate a single statements or a group of statements in somehow related. This means that we can manipulate the method execution at its beginning and at its ending but we cannot alter its computational flow requiring the execution of another statement between two statements of its body.

These problems are due to the poor expressiveness of the pointcut definition languages and of the related join point models provided by most of the actual AOP frameworks. Nowadays AOP languages provide very basic pointcut definition languages that heavily rely on the structure and syntax of the software application neglecting its semantics. The developer has to identify and to specify in the correct way the pointcut by using, what we call the linguistic pattern matching mechanism; it permits of locating where an advice should be applied by describing the join points as a mix of references to linguistic constructs (e.g., method calls) and of generic references to their position, e.g., before or after it occurs. Therefore, it is difficult to define generic, reusable and comprehensible pointcuts that are not tailored on a specific application. Moreover, current join point model is too abstract. Join points are associated to a method call whereas a finer model should be adopted to permit of altering each single statement.

Therefore, to benefit from the AOP technology, this one and the underlying join point models, have to support a finer granularity of the join point model with a pointcut declaration language that abstracts from the syntax and deals with the semantics/behavior of the application. A few attempts in this direction are under development [5, 11, 15].

Unanticipated Software Evolution: Does It Exist?
Comment by Shigeru Chiba (*Tokyo Institute of Technology, Japan*)

An interesting issue on software evolution is what kind of evolution we must support. For example, if we use AOP or reflection, we can extend our applications so that they can fit new requirements. However, if we anticipate future changes of requirements when we design the applications, we can prepare against those future changes. We will define extra interfaces for better modularity. We may apply some design patterns such as the visitor pattern. If we can perfectly anticipate future changes, we will not need

AOP or reflection. We will be able to prepare within confines of existing technologies such as object-oriented programming.

Some readers might say the value of AOP and reflection is that they provide better syntax. Although preparation by existing technologies is often complicated, preparation by AOP or reflection is much simpler or unnecessary. However, I think that the real value of AOP and reflection is that they can be used for implementing unanticipated evolution. If we use AOP or reflection, we do not have to prepare against future changes at all when we design and implement a first version of our applications. On the other hand, existing technologies such as object oriented programming do not address unanticipated evolution. To adapt applications to new requirements, those technologies force developers to edit and modify source code of the applications. I think that the study in this research field should consider differences between anticipated evolution and unanticipated one.

AOP vs. Reflection for Evolution
Comment by Gunter Saake (*University of Magdeburg, Germany*)

Evolution of software artifacts means continuous adaptation to a changing environment and changing requirements. However, this process can be performed on different abstraction levels and in different kinds of environments. Important dimensions for adaptation are the following:

- Anticipated evolution can be foreseen at software production time. Typical techniques can be built-in parametrization and reconfiguration methods, e.g., based on components or design patterns. Unanticipated adaptation means the reaction on unforeseen changes, which is of course much harder.
- The adaption process can be performed manually as part of the maintenance process. Automatic adaptation is possible in some situations but requires the detection of environmental changes and planning and validation of adaption steps by the software system itself.
- Adaptation can take place on different abstraction levels, from the model level (for example UML) down to the code level.

These dimensions are not independent and usually they overlap. For example, planning of an adaptation requires in most case a semantic-rich representation of the system and it is hard to plan on the syntactic code-level.

How do AOSD and reflection fit to this general picture? Figure 1 shows the current situation for AOP and reflection techniques.

AOP techniques can directly manipulate (syntactic) code. However, since common AOP techniques are based on the syntactic structure of the program it is hard to use them for semantic based tasks which are used for a fully automatic adaption. AOP is general enough to allow manual adaptation to unforeseen changes.

Reflection and meta-programming on the other hand is based on an internal model of the software. Current technology can use reflection for automatic reconfiguration at runtime, which can be used for reaction on anticipated changes. Unanticipated changes are hard to cope with basic reflection techniques, because that would require besides the

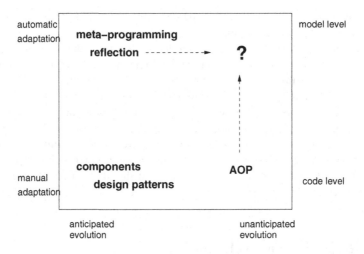

Fig. 1. AOP versus Reflection

internal model of the software also a complete model of the environment which has to be general enough to capture all unforeseen changes. Also it is hard to use these techniques for the code level.

So, AOP and reflection are currently playing in different corners of the adaptation techniques landscape. What is their interplay?

First of all, AOP techniques can be used to prepare software for reflection. Pointcuts can identify points of interaction between meta-level and base-level in the code. This can be used to built in the necessary communication between the base-level objects and the meta-level objects.

Second, a combination of techniques from both approaches may shift one of them a little bit toward the "hard" corner (automatic reaction to unanticipated changes [4]). Pointcuts related to semantic properties as described for example in [15] in combination with dynamic weaving may become a (semi) automatic technique for performing semantic adaptation resulting of a plan generated by a reflective analysis of the changed environment.

Natural Selection and System Microevolution:
A New Modularity for RAM-SE'07?
Comment by Yvonne Coady (*University of Victoria, Canada*)

Microevolution can be thought of on a small scale, within a single population, while *macroevolution* transcends the boundaries of a single species. Despite their differences, evolution on both of these scales relies on the same mechanisms of evolutionary change, such as *natural selection*. Natural selection is the differential survival of a subset of a population over other subsets. In terms of software, we can apply theories of microevolution within single, open source systems, and can see how natural selection drives evolution. For example, if we consider a single population such as Linux, natural selection determines which kernel extensions survive as the system evolves. But what factors determine survival of the fittest? Why do some extensions survive while others do not?

Companies and governments alike are relying upon evolution of Linux to reduce the cost and time-to-market of developing WiFi routers, cell phones, and telecommunications equipment and of running services on specialized servers, clusters, and high-performance supercomputers. One important benefit of starting from the same Linux source for all of these systems is that developers have access to this open source project and can easily create variants that are directly tailored for their application domain. Major evolutionary variants of a mainline Linux kernel are typically created by incrementally adding kernel extensions by fine grained instrumentation of source.

Current best practice is to implementing such extensions is by directly instrumenting the code-base of a mainline Linux kernel. Upon completing the development of an extension, developers extract the instrumentation as a whole with tools such as diff to create a "patch". They can then share the resulting patch with others, who in turn integrate the extension into their version of the kernel using tools such as patch.

It is interesting to note that patch sets must be approved before they can be incorporated into a mainline version of the kernel. As a result, all instrumentation must be reasoned about and tested comprehensively. The problem is that, though well localized, patch sets themselves are almost impossible to reason about at a high-level, as their granularity of interaction is expressed in terms of line numbers with very little surrounding context.

Given that there are a number of highly invasive patch sets that have yet to be mainlined, it is indeed reasonable to assume that it is ultimately their lack of explicit representation of interaction with the rest of the system that may be an ultimate determining factor in survival. That is, highly invasive patches are exterminated due to natural selection, meaning that *modularity is indeed an evolutionary factor in system microevolution*.

For most of these extensions however, the answer does not come in the form of aspects as we know them today. This is due to the aggressive nature of the required refactoring necessary to reveal suitable join points given current join point models. Aggressive refactoring is not an option in this context, within this domain, as it would make the entire patch set less likely to be adopted into a mainline kernel.

Others have suggested a need for a finer-grained join point model, and this challenge problem of microevolution seems to echo that same call. At the same time however, it is necessary that these new mechanisms provide substantially more semantic leverage than that which is currently available in tools such as diff and patch. The question as to how a new modularity can be developed to simultaneously provide (1) fine-grained points of interaction, along with (2) a high enough level of abstraction upon which semantic conflicts can be reasoned about, is an interesting challenge problem for participants at RAM-SE'07!

3   Final Remarks

The workshop's main goal was to bring together researchers interested in the field and to allow them to get to know each other and each other's work. The workshop lived up to its expectations, with high-quality submissions and presentations, and lively and stimulating discussions. We hope participants found the workshop interesting and useful, and encourage them to finalize their position papers and submit them as full papers to international conferences interested in the topics of this workshop.

Acknowledgements. We wish to thank Awais Rashid, Theo D'Hondt, Mario Südholt and Hidehiko Masuhara both for their interest in the workshop, and for their help during the workshop as chairmen and speakers. We wish also to thank all the researchers that have participated to the workshop.

We have also to thank the Department of Informatics and Communication of the University of Milan, the Department of Mathematical and Computing Sciences of the Tokyo institute of Technology and the Institute für Technische und Betriebliche Informationssysteme, Otto-von-Guericke-Universität Magdeburg for their various supports.

References

1. Francesca Arcelli and Claudia Raibulet. Evolution of an Adaptive Middleware Exploiting Architectural Reflection. In Walter Cazzola, Shigeru Chiba, Yvonne Coady, and Gunter Saake, editors, *Proceedings of ECOOP'2006 Workshop on Reflection, AOP and Meta-Data for Software Evolution (RAM-SE'06)*, pages 49–58, Nantes, France, July 2006.
2. Keith H. Bennett and Václav T. Rajlich. Software Maintenance and Evolution: a Roadmap. In Anthony Finkelstein, editor, *The Future of Software Engineering*, pages 75–87. ACM Press, 2000.
3. Javier Cámara Moreno, Carlos Canal, Javier Cubo, and Juan M. Murillo Rodriguez. An Aspect-Oriented Adaptation Framework for Dynamic Component Evolution. In Walter Cazzola, Shigeru Chiba, Yvonne Coady, and Gunter Saake, editors, *Proceedings of ECOOP'2006 Workshop on Reflection, AOP and Meta-Data for Software Evolution (RAM-SE'06)*, pages 59–70, Nantes, France, July 2006.
4. Walter Cazzola, Ahmed Ghoneim, and Gunter Saake. Software Evolution through Dynamic Adaptation of Its OO Design. In Hans-Dieter Ehrich, John-Jules Meyer, and Mark D. Ryan, editors, *Objects, Agents and Features: Structuring Mechanisms for Contemporary Software*, Lecture Notes in Computer Science 2975, pages 69–84. Springer-Verlag, Heidelberg, Germany, July 2004.
5. Walter Cazzola, Sonia Pini, and Massimo Ancona. AOP for Software Evolution: A Design Oriented Approach. In *Proceedings of the 10th Annual ACM Symposium on Applied Computing (SAC'05)*, pages 1356–1360, Santa Fe, New Mexico, USA, on 13th-17th of March 2005. ACM Press.
6. Walter Cazzola, Sonia Pini, and Massimo Ancona. Design-Based Pointcuts Robustness Against Software Evolution. In Walter Cazzola, Shigeru Chiba, Yvonne Coady, and Gunter Saake, editors, *Proceedings of ECOOP'2006 Workshop on Reflection, AOP and Meta-Data for Software Evolution (RAM-SE'06)*, pages 35–45, Nantes, France, July 2006.
7. Alan Cyment, Nicolas Kicillof, Rubén Altman, and Fernando Asteasuain. Improving AOP Systems' Evolvability by Decoupling Advices from Base Code. In Walter Cazzola, Shigeru Chiba, Yvonne Coady, and Gunter Saake, editors, *Proceedings of ECOOP'2006 Workshop on Reflection, AOP and Meta-Data for Software Evolution (RAM-SE'06)*, pages 9–21, Nantes, France, July 2006.

8. Mark Eaddy and Alfred Aho. Statement Annotations for Fine-Grained Advising. In Walter Cazzola, Shigeru Chiba, Yvonne Coady, and Gunter Saake, editors, *Proceedings of ECOOP'2006 Workshop on Reflection, AOP and Meta-Data for Software Evolution (RAM-SE'06)*, pages 89–99, Nantes, France, July 2006.
9. Peter Ebraert and Theo D'Hondt. Dynamic Refactorings: Improving the Program Structure at Run-time. In Walter Cazzola, Shigeru Chiba, Yvonne Coady, and Gunter Saake, editors, *Proceedings of ECOOP'2006 Workshop on Reflection, AOP and Meta-Data for Software Evolution (RAM-SE'06)*, pages 101–110, Nantes, France, July 2006.
10. Robert E. Filman and Daniel P. Friedman. Aspect-Oriented Programming is Quantification and Obliviousness. In *Proceedings of OOPSLA 2000 Workshop on Advanced Separation of Concerns*, Minneapolis, USA, October 2000.
11. Jeff Gray, Janos Sztipanovits, Douglas C. Schmidt, Ted Bapty, Sandeep Neema, and Aniruddha Gokhale. Two-Level Aspect Weaving to Support Evolution in Model-Driven Synthesis. In Robert E. Filman, Tzilla Elrad, Siobhàn Clarke, and Mehmet Akşit, editors, *Aspect-Oriented Software Development*, chapter 30, pages 681–709. Addison-Wesley, October 2004.
12. Michihiro Horie and Shigeru Chiba. An Aspect-Aware Outline Viewer. In Walter Cazzola, Shigeru Chiba, Yvonne Coady, and Gunter Saake, editors, *Proceedings of ECOOP'2006 Workshop on Reflection, AOP and Meta-Data for Software Evolution (RAM-SE'06)*, pages 71–75, Nantes, France, July 2006.
13. Christian Kästner, Sven Apel, and Gunter Saake. Implementing Bounded Aspect Quantification in AspectJ. In Walter Cazzola, Shigeru Chiba, Yvonne Coady, and Gunter Saake, editors, *Proceedings of ECOOP'2006 Workshop on Reflection, AOP and Meta-Data for Software Evolution (RAM-SE'06)*, pages 111–122, Nantes, France, July 2006.
14. Gregor Kiczales, John Lamping, Anurag Mendhekar, Chris Maeda, Cristina Videira Lopes, Jean-Marc Loingtier, and John Irwin. Aspect-Oriented Programming. In *11th European Conference on Object Oriented Programming (ECOOP'97)*, Lecture Notes in Computer Science 1241, pages 220–242, Helsinki, Finland, June 1997. Springer-Verlag.
15. Klaus Ostermann, Mira Mezini, and Christoph Bockisch. Expressive Pointcuts for Increased Modularity. In Andrew P. Black, editor, *Proceedings of the 19th European Conference on Object-Oriented Programming (ECOOP'05)*, LNCS 3586, pages 214–240, Glasgow, Scotland, July 2005. Springer.
16. Miguel Ángel Pérez Toledano, Amparo Navasa Martinez, Juan M. Murillo Rodriguez, and Carlos Canal. Making Aspect Oriented System Evolution Safer. In Walter Cazzola, Shigeru Chiba, Yvonne Coady, and Gunter Saake, editors, *Proceedings of ECOOP'2006 Workshop on Reflection, AOP and Meta-Data for Software Evolution (RAM-SE'06)*, pages 23–34, Nantes, France, July 2006.
17. Awais Rashid. Aspects and Evolution: The Case for Versioned Types and Meta-Aspect Protocols. In Walter Cazzola, Shigeru Chiba, Yvonne Coady, and Gunter Saake, editors, *Proceedings of ECOOP'2006 Workshop on Reflection, AOP and Meta-Data for Software Evolution (RAM-SE'06)*, pages 3–5, Nantes, France, July 2006.
18. Arturo Zambrano, Tomás Vera, and Silvia Gordillo. Solving Aspectual Semantic Conflicts in Resource Aware Systems. In Walter Cazzola, Shigeru Chiba, Yvonne Coady, and Gunter Saake, editors, *Proceedings of ECOOP'2006 Workshop on Reflection, AOP and Meta-Data for Software Evolution (RAM-SE'06)*, pages 79–88, Nantes, France, July 2006.

A   Workshop Attendee

The success of the workshop is mainly due to the people that have attended it and to their effort to participate to the discussions. The following is the list of the attendees in alphabetical order.

Name	Affiliation	Country	e-mail
Altman, Rubén	Universidad de Buenos Aires	Argentina	ruben.altman@miva.com
Bernard, Emmanuel	jBoss Europe	France	
Beurton-aimar Marie	LaBRI, Université de Bordeaux 1	France	aimar@labri.u-bordeaux.fr
Cámara Moreno, Javier	Universidad de Málaga	Spain	jcamara@lcc.uma.es
Cazzola, Walter	Università degli Studi di Milano	Italy	cazzola@dico.unimi.it
Chiba, Shigeru	Tokyo Institute of Technology	Japan	chiba@is.titech.ac.jp
Cyment, Alan	Universidad de Buenos Aires	Argentina	acyment@yahoo.com
David, Pierre-Charles	France Télécom R&D	France	pierrecharles.david@francetelecom.com
D'Hondt, Theo	Vrij Universiteit Brussel	Belgium	tjdhondt@vub.ac.be
Dubochet, Gilles	École Polytechnique Fédérale de Lausanne	Switzerland	gilles.dubochet@epfl.ch
Eaddy, Mark	Columbia University	USA	eaddy@cs.columbia.edu
Ebraert, Peter	Vrij Universiteit Brussel	Belgium	pebraert@vub.ac.be
Horie, Michihiro	Tokyo Institute of Technology	Japan	horie@csg.is.titech.ac.jp
Kästner, Christian	University of Magdeburg	Germany	christian.k@stner.de
Masuhara, Hidehiko	University of Tokyo	Japan	masuhara@graco.c.u-tokyo.ac.jp
Meister, Lior	Rafael	Israel	meister@rafael.co.il
Nguyen, Ha	École des Mines de Nantes	France	ha.nguyen@emn.fr
Pérez Toledano, Miguel Ángel	University of Extremadura	Spain	toledano@unex.es
Pini, Sonia	Università degli Studi di Genova	Italy	pini@disi.unige.it
Raibulet, Claudia	Università di Milano Bicocca	Italy	raibulet@disco.unimib.it
Rashid, Awais	Lancaster University	United Kingdom	marash@comp.lancs.ac.uk
Saake, Gunter	University of Magdeburg	Germany	saake@iti.cs.uni-magdeburg.de
Shakil Khan, Safoora	Lancaster University	United Kingdom	safoorashakil@hotmail.com
Stein, Krogdahl	University of Oslo	Norway	stein.krogdahl@ifi.uio.no
Südholt, Mario	École des Mines de Nantes	France	sudholt@emn.fr
Tsadock, Carmit	Rafael	Israel	
Zambrano, Arturo	Universidad de La Plata	Argentina	arturo@sol.info.unlp.edu.ar

Formal Techniques for Java-Like Programs
Report on the WS FTfJP at ECOOP'06

Davide Ancona, Sophia Drossopoulou, Atsushi Igarashi, Gary T. Leavens,
Arnd Poetzsch-Heffter, and Elena Zucca

davide@disi.unige.it, scd@doc.ic.ac.uk, igarashi@kuis.kyoto-u.ac.jp,
leavens@cs.iastate.edu, poetzsch@informatik.uni-kl.de,
zucca@disi.unige.it

Abstract. This report gives an overview of the eighth ECOOP Workshop on Formal Techniques for Java-like Programs. It summarizes the workshop preparation, contributions, debates and conclusions.

1 Objectives

This workshop was the eighth in the series of workshops on "Formal Techniques for Java-like Programs (FTfJP)" held at ECOOP. It was a follow-up to FTfJP workshops held at the previous ECOOP conferences in 2005, 2004 [1], 2003 [2], 2002 [3], 2001 [4], 2000 [5], and 1999 [6], and the "Formal Underpinnings of the Java Paradigm" workshop held at OOPSLA'98 [7].

FTfJP workshops have the objective to bring together people working on formal techniques and tool support for Java, or closely related languages such as C#, either with the aim to describe, analyse, and verify aspects and properties of these programming languages themselves (type system, semantics, bytecode verification, etc.), or of programs written in these languages. Java-like languages provide a good platform to bridge the gap between formal techniques and practical program development, because of their reasonably clear semantics and standardised libraries. Starting from 2002 the name of the workshop has been slightly changed — from "Formal Techniques for Java Programs" to "Formal Techniques for Java-like Programs" — to include not just work on Java, but also work on related languages such as C#.

2 Organizers

The workshop was organized by

- Davide Ancona (University of Genova, Italy), davide@disi.unige.it, co-chair,
- Sophia Drossopoulou (Imperial College, Great Britain), scd@doc.ic.ac.uk,
- Susan Eisenbach (Imperial College, Great Britain), sue@doc.ic.ac.uk,
- Gary T. Leavens (Iowa State University, USA), leavens@cs.iastate.edu
- Peter Müller (ETH Zurich, Switzerland), peter.mueller@inf.ethz.ch

M. Südholt and C. Consel (Eds.): ECOOP 2006, LNCS 4379, pp. 53–58, 2007.

- Arnd Poetzsch-Heffter (University of Kaiserlautern, Germany),
  `poetzsch@informatik.uni-kl.de`,
- Erik Poll (University of Nijmegen, the Netherlands), `erikpoll@cs.ru.nl`,
  and
- Elena Zucca (University of Genova, Italy), `zucca@disi.unige.it`, chair.

3   Call for Papers

The call for papers sought contributions (of up to 10 pages) on open questions, new developments, or interesting new applications of formal techniques in the context of Java or similar languages. We encouraged contributions that not merely presented completely finished work, but also raised challenging open problems or proposed speculative new approaches; in particular, contributions that simply suggested good topics for discussion at the workshop, or raised issues deserving the attention of the research community.

We recalled that contributions would have been formally reviewed for originality, relevance, and the potential to generate interesting discussions, and that a special journal issue was planned to collect selected contributions as done for the previous FTfJP workshops.

The deadline for submission was April 8, 2006.

The Program Committee of the workshop included

- Davide Ancona (University of Genova, Italy), co-chair,
- Bernhard Beckert (University Koblenz-Landau, Germany),
- Yoonsik Cheon (University of Texas at El Paso, USA),
- Dave Clarke (CWI, Netherlands),
- Sophia Drossopoulou (Imperial College, UK),
- Erik Ernst (University of Aarhus, Denmark),
- Paola Giannini (University of Piemonte Orientale, Italy),
- Michael Hicks (University of Maryland, College Park, USA),
- Atsushi Igarashi (Kyoto University, Japan),
- Rustan Leino (Microsoft Research, USA),
- Elena Zucca (University of Genova, Italy), chair.

4   Structure

There was lively interest in the workshop. We were very pleased with the high quality of the submissions. Out of 15 submissions, 9 position papers were selected by the Program Committee for presentations. Moreover, for the first time in the workshop series, the Program Committee decided to have an invited talk, by Erik Meijer (Microsoft Research). 23 people from 10 countries attended the workshop.

The one-day workshop consisted of a technical part during the day and a workshop dinner in the evening. The program of the workshop and the presented position papers are available on the web at `http://www.disi.unige.it/person/AnconaD/FTfJP06/`.

The presentations at the workshop were structured as follows:

- 9:00-10:30 Session 1 (Chair: Sophia Drossopoulou)
  - *Invited Talk: The Long Road From Theory To Practice*
    Erik Meijer
  - *When Separation Logic Met Java*
    Matthew Parkinson
- 11:00-12:30 Session 2 (Chair: Arnd Poetzsch-Heffter)
  - *Specifying and Verifying Heap Space Allocation with JML and ESC/Java2*
    Robert Atkey
  - *Towards Support for Non-null Types and Non-null-by-default in Java*
    Patrice Chalin
- 14-15.30 Session 3 (Chair: Atsushi Igarashi)
  - *A State Abstraction for Coordination in Java-like Languages*
    Elena Giachino
  - *Dynamic Linking of Polymorphic Bytecode*
    Giovanni Lagorio
  - *Simple Loose Ownership Domains*
    Jan Schäfer
- 16-17:00 Session 4 (Chair: Gary Leavens)
  - *Temporal Verification Theories for Java-like Classes*
    Suad Alagić
  - *Verification of Programs with Inspector Methods*
    Bart Jacobs

5   List of Participants

Name	Affiliation	Email
Davide Ancona	University of Genova, Italy	davide@disi.unige.it
Suad Alagić	University of Southern Maine, USA	alagic@cs.usm.maine.edu
Robert Atkey	University of Edinburgh, UK	bob.atkey@ed.ac.uk
Patrice Chalin	Concordia University, Canada	chalin@cs.concordia.ca
Julien Charles	INRIA, France	julien.charles@inria.fr
Ferruccio Damiani	University of Torino, Italy	damiani@di.unito.it
Sophia Drossopoulou	Imperial College, UK	scd@doc.ic.ac.uk
Erik Ernst	University of Aarhus, Denmark	eernst@daimi.au.dk
Manuel Fahndrich	Microsoft Research, USA	maf@microsoft.com
Elena Giachino	University of Torino, Italy	giachino@di.unito.it
Paola Giannini	University of Piemonte Orientale, Italy	giannini@di.unito.it
Atsushi Igarashi	Kyoto University, Japan	igarashi@kuis.kyoto-u.ac.jp
Bart Jacobs	Katholieke Universiteit Leuven, Belgium	bart.jacobs @cs.kuleuven.be
Giovanni Lagorio	University of Genova, Italy	lagorio@disi.unige.it
Gary T. Leavens	Iowa State University, USA	leavens@cs.iastate.edu
Eric Madelaine	INRIA, France	eric.madelaine@sophia.inria.fr
Matthew Parkinson	University of Cambridge, UK	matthew.parkinson@cl.cam.ac.uk
Arnd Poetzsch-Heffter	University of Kaiserlautern, Germany	poetzsch@informatik.uni-kl.de
Jan Schäfer	University of Kaiserlautern, Germany	jschaefer@informatik.uni-kl.de
Elena Zucca	University of Genova, Italy	zucca@disi.unige.it

6 Summary of Contributions and Debates

The workshop started with Erik Meijer's invited talk where he discussed the usefulness and feasibility of adding advanced theoretical concepts such as monads and monad comprehensions to mainstream practical programming languages.

His experience working with industry was that often advanced concepts are needed, and the practitioners adopt them enthusiastically, but the requirement is for these concepts to be simplified and tailored to the particular task. There is ongoing work in the design and implementation of C# 3.0 and Visual Basic 9, where many such advanced features are being adapted and adopted.

Matthew Parkison presented his work in modular reasoning, adapting separation logic to the object oriented paradigm, and in particular, dealing with the fact that behavioural subtyping is too strong a requirement. In his approach, abstract predicate families alleviate the restriction, and mirror dynamic dispatch in the logic. The debate concentrated on the comparison of approaches such as those in Boogie and Spec#, and the one suggested by Matthew.

Session 2 was about new aspects and constructs of specification languages for program properties. Such specification languages allow to express the properties in a concise way and provide support for checking and verification. To keep the syntactical and semantic gap between the specification and programming language small, specification languages have been developed that are taylored to their host language. In particular, the Java Modeling Langue JML is widely used for the specification of Java programs and Spec# for C#. In this session three contributions were presented and discussed that focussed on specification constructs for different kinds of program properties.

In his presentation, Robert Atkey investigated JML's support for specifying properties of heap space allocation in Java. Essentially, JML allows to specify an upper bound for the total number of bytes that are allocated during executions of a method. The talk and paper presented solutions to overcome some shortcomings of the current specification constructs and discussed aspects of the extended specification expressions. The positive remarks after the talk conveyed that there is still work to be done in the area of specifying space properties.

In the second talk, Patrice Chalin addressed the support for non-null properties in programming and specification languages. The main part of his contribution was concerned with the question: What would be the effects if one interpreted ordinary types as non-null types in JML and Java? He considered both the effects to the languages and their semantics as well as to the migration of existing code. The following discussion revealed further aspects concerning for example particular features of the Spec# type system and the virtual machine infrastructure.

As mentioned above, specification languages like JML and Spec# aim to keep the gap between specification and programming concepts small, in particular to simplify their application for the programmer. This comes at a price: The support for purely declarative data types and functions is not satisfactory and has negative implication for formal verification. Julien Charles presented an extension to JML to overcome this problem. The extension supports the declaration and use of so-called native functions, predicates, and types in JML specifications. A short discussion after the presentation was concerned with relating the work to similar approaches.

In Session 3, three papers on language constructs and types were presented. In Elena Giachino's presentation, the language construct of state classes for controlling concurrent threads and its type and effect system were proposed. A state class is equipped with a finite number of states, each of which provides different fields and methods. The type and effect system estimates possible method-wise state changes in order to prevent a thread from accessing unavailable fields. After her presentation, there was some discussion about accuracy of the type system.

In JVML, each instruction is annotated with type information: for example, a field access instruction comes with its receiver type and field type. However, since those types have to be fixed class names, even very small changes cause recompilation. Polymorphic bytecode had been proposed to solve this problem by allowing (constrained) type variables in bytecode. Giovanni Lagorio, in his presentation, showed a formal operation semantics for such polymorphic bytecode with the mechanism of dynamic loading/liking as in JVM; such semantics will be a basis of the implementation of polymorphic code on top of JVM.

Finally, Jan Schäfer presented a paper about a new ownership type system by introducing the notion of boundary domains and relaxing the principle of "onwer-as-dominator" to "border-as-dominator". It improves over previous ownership type/domain systems in that the new system can now express iterators, which has been known to be hard. Similarity (and differences) of the idea to (from) Lu and Potter's paper "On Ownership and Accessibility", presented at the main conference, was pointed out and discussed.

Session 4 was about specification and verification techniques. Suad Alagić presented an approach for translating JML class specifications into PVS theories, including specifications that use generic parameters. In the translation, the theory of a subclass is presented as a subtheory of the theory of its superclass. Conditions for behavioral subtyping are given in terms of the PVS theories, which formalize and extend to temporal logic the definitions of Liskov and Wing. The speaker stated that in comparison to the Alagić's earlier work "the main contribution of this paper is in matching this theory of behavioral compatibility with the tools and techniques based on the PVS system."

Bart Jacobs addressed the problem of how do specification and verification with inspector methods in the presence of both aliasing and information hiding. The paper deals with the frame problem of how to specify the effects of modifications on the results of inspector methods. That is, when an object's state is mutated, one would like to know what inspectors may have their results changed, and which are constant with respect to that mutation. The paper presents a series of solutions, each of which uses increasingly relaxed (and hence more flexible) restrictions on what storage the value of an inspector methods may depend on. Dealing with object invariants is a key concern, and the solutions adapt the Boogie methodology's ownership system.

7 Conclusions

Looking back on the workshop, the Program Committe is very pleased with the quality of the submitted papers and with the attendance at the workshop. There were both familiar and new faces at the workshop, and both familiar and new topics were being addressed.

After the workshop, the Program Committee has selected the best presentations for invitation to a special issue of the "Journal of Object Technology" (JOT) dedicated to FTfJP'2006.

References

1. A. Coglio, M. Huisman, J. R. Kiniry, P. Müller, and E. Poll. Formal techniques for Java-like programs. In J. Malenfant and B. M. Østvold, editors, *Object-Oriented Technology. ECOOP 2004 Workshop Reader*, volume 3344 of *Lecture Notes in Computer Science*, pages 76–83. Springer, 2005.
2. S. Eisenbach, G. T. Leavens, P. Müller, A. Poetzsch-Heffter, and E. Poll. Formal techniques for Java-like programs. In F. Buschmann, A. P. Buchmann, and M. Cilia, editors, *Object-Oriented Technology. ECOOP 2003 Workshop Reader*, volume 3013 of *Lecture Notes in Computer Science*, pages 62–71. Springer, 2003.
3. G. T. Leavens, S. Drossopoulou, S. Eisenbach, A. Poetzsch-Heffter, and E. Poll. Formal techniques for Java-like programs. In J. Hernandez and A. Moreira, editors, *Object-Oriented Technology. ECOOP 2002 Workshop Reader*, volume 2548 of *Lecture Notes in Computer Science*, pages 203–210. Springer, 2002.
4. G. T. Leavens, S. Drossopoulou, S. Eisenbach, A. Poetzsch-Heffter, and E. Poll. Formal techniques for Java programs. In A. Frohner, editor, *Object-Oriented Technology. ECOOP 2001 Workshop Reader*, volume 2323 of *Lecture Notes in Computer Science*, pages 30–40. Springer, 2001.
5. S. Drossopoulou, S. Eisenbach, B. Jacobs, G. T. Leavens, P. Müller, and A. Poetzsch-Heffter. Formal techniques for Java programs. In J. Malenfant, S. Moisan, and A. Moreira, editors, *Object-Oriented Technology. ECOOP 2000 Workshop Reader*, volume 1964 of *Lecture Notes in Computer Science*, pages 41–54. Springer, 2000.
6. B. Jacobs, G. T. Leavens, P. Müller, and A. Poetzsch-Heffter. Formal techniques for Java programs. In A. Moreira and D. Demeyer, editors, *Object-Oriented Technology. ECOOP 1999 Workshop Reader*, volume 1743 of *Lecture Notes in Computer Science*, pages 97 – 115. Springer, 1999.
7. S. Eisenbach. Formal underpinnings of Java. Workshop report, 1998. Available from `www-dse.doc.ic.ac.uk/~sue/oopsla/cfp.html`.

Program Analysis for Security and Privacy
Report on the WS PASSWORD at ECOOP'06

Marco Pistoia[1] and Francesco Logozzo[2]

[1] IBM T. J. Watson Research Center, Hawthorne, New York, USA
pistoia@us.ibm.com
[2] École Normale Supérieure, Paris, France
Francesco.Logozzo@polytechnique.edu

Abstract. Software security has become more important than ever. Unfortunately, still now, the security of a software system is almost always retrofitted to an afterthought. When security problems arise, understanding and correcting them can be very challenging. On the one hand, the program analysis research community has created numerous static and dynamic analysis tools for performance optimization and bug detection in object-oriented programs. On the other hand, the security and privacy research community has been looking for solutions to automatically detect security problems, privacy violations, and access-control requirements of object-oriented programs. The purpose of the First Program Analysis for Security and Safety Workshop Discussion (PASSWORD 2006), co-located with the Twentieth European Conference on Object-Oriented Programming (ECOOP 2006), was to bring together members of the academic and industrial communities interested in applying analysis, testing, and verification to security and privacy problems, and to encourage program analysis researchers to see the applicability of their work to security and privacy—an area of research that still needs a lot of exploration. This paper summarizes the discussions and contributions of the PASSWORD workshop.

1   Introduction

Security has progressively become more interesting to the program analysis community. Both static and dynamic program analysis have been extensively applied to security issues, such as access control [6] and information flow [5,16]. However, there is still high potential for more research on how to apply analysis, testing, and verification to security and privacy problems, including:

1. Evaluation of security and privacy policies
2. Identification of vulnerabilities that could lead to denial of service attacks
3. Verification of access control
4. Computation of access control requirements
5. Identification of mutability, accessibility, and isolation policy violations
6. Verification of complete authorization
7. Intrusion detection
8. Secure programming

M. Südholt and C. Consel (Eds.): ECOOP 2006, LNCS 4379, pp. 59–68, 2007.
© Springer-Verlag Berlin Heidelberg 2007

This paper summarizes the contributions of the First Program Analysis for Security and Safety Workshop Discussion (PASSWORD 2006), co-located with the Twentieth European Conference on Object-Oriented Programming (ECOOP 2006), which was held in Nantes, France in July 2006.

2 Objective and Call for Papers

With the advent of the Internet, software security has become more important than ever. Unfortunately, still now, the security of a software system is almost always an afterthought. When security problems arise, understanding and correcting them can be very challenging. On the one hand, the program analysis research community has created numerous static and dynamic analysis tools for performance optimization and bug detection in object-oriented programs. On the other hand, the security and privacy research community has been looking for solutions to automatically detect security problems, privacy violations, and access-control requirements of object-oriented programs. The purpose of PASSWORD 2006 was to bring together members of both these communities and to encourage program analysis researchers to see the applicability of their work to security and privacy—an area of research that still needs exploration.

Two types of papers were welcomed at PASSWORD 2006: *technical papers*, which present mature technical and research material, and *position, exploratory, or preliminary-work papers*, which may describe work in progress or new research ideas.

Topics of interest for PASSWORD included, but were not limited to:

- Analysis of cryptographic systems and implementations
- Analysis of network and security protocols
- Automatic detection of attacks against networks and machines
- Automated tools for source- and compiled-code analysis
- Authentication and authorization of users, systems, and applications
- Bug finding
- Detection of mutability, accessibility, and isolation policy violations
- Identification of denial-of-service attacks
- Input validation
- Intrusion and anomaly detection
- Language-based security
- Operating system security
- Privacy analysis
- Security in heterogeneous and large-scale environments
- Security in the presence of agents and mobile code
- Security policy analysis
- Static analysis for program verification
- Static analysis techniques for soundness, precision, and scalability

3 Program Organization and Participants

3.1 Organizers

PASSWORD 2006 was organized by Marco Pistoia and Francesco Logozzo.

- **Marco Pistoia, Ph. D.** is a Research Staff Member in the Programming Languages and Software Engineering Department at the IBM T. J. Watson Research Center in Hawthorne, New York, USA. He has written ten books, filed thirteen patents, and published numerous papers and journal articles on all areas of Java and program analysis for security. Most recently, he has published his Ph.D. thesis, and has been the lead author of the books *Enterprise Java Security*, published by Addison-Wesley in 2004 (and now available in Chinese), and *Java 2 Network Security*, published by Prentice Hall PTR in 1999. He has published and presented at several conferences worldwide and has been invited to give lectures and teach at several universities and research centers. He received his Ph. D. in Mathematics from Polytechnic University, Brooklyn, New York in May 2005 with a thesis entitled *A Unified Mathematical Model for Stack- and Role-Based Authorization Systems*, and his Master of Science and Bachelor of Science degrees in Mathematics *summa cum laude* from the University of Rome, Italy in 1995, with a research thesis entitled *Theory of Reductive Algebraic Groups and Their Representations*.
- **Francesco Logozzo, Ph. D.** is a Postdoctoral Researcher at the École Normale Supérieure, Paris, France. He graduated from École Polytechnique, Paris, France in June 2004 with a thesis entitled *Modular Static Analysis of Object-oriented Languages*. His Ph. D. advisor was Dr. Radhia Cousot. He was a former student of the Scuola Normale Superiore of Pisa, Italy. He is the author of more than ten papers on static analysis of object-oriented languages. He co-chaired the First Workshop on Abstract Intepretation of Object-Oriented Languages (AIOOL 2005) and the Seventh Workshop of Formal Techniques for Java-like Programs (FTfJP 2005).

3.2 Program Committee Members

The committee members were program analysis and security experts from academia and industry:

- **Sabrina De Capitani Di Vimercati**, University of Milan, Milan, Italy
- **Stephen J. Fink**, IBM T. J. Watson Research Center, Hawthorne, New York, USA
- **Robert J. Flynn**, Polytechnic University, Brooklyn, New York, USA
- **Charles Hymans**, European Aeronautic Defence and Space Company, Paris, France
- **Trent Jaeger**, Pennsylvania State University, University Park, Pennsylvania, USA
- **Francesco Logozzo**, École Normale Supérieure, Paris, France
- **Nasir Memon**, Polytechnic University, Brooklyn, New York, USA

- **Greg Morrisett**, Harvard University, Cambridge, Massachusetts, USA
- **David A. Naumann**, Stevens Institute of Technology, Hoboken, New Jersey, USA
- **Marco Pistoia**, IBM T. J. Watson Research Center, Hawthorne, New York, USA
- **Jan Vitek**, Purdue University, West Lafayette, Indiana, USA
- **Eran Yahav**, IBM T. J. Watson Research Center, Hawthorne, New York, USA
- **Steve Zdancewic**, University of Pennsylvania, Philadelphia, Pennsylvania, USA
- **Xiaolan Zhang**, IBM T. J. Watson Research Center, Hawthorne, New York, USA
- **Roberto Zunino**, University of Pisa, Pisa, Italy

3.3   Participants

Participation to the PASSWORD 2006 workshop was allowed also through remote connection for people unable to attend in person. The list of participants included:

- **Paolina Centonze**, IBM T. J. Watson Research Center, Hawthorne, New York, USA
- **Tzi-cker Chiueh**, Computer Science Department, Stony Brook University, Stony Brook, New York, USA
- **Holger Grandy**, University of Augsburg, Augsburg, Germany
- **Francesco Logozzo**, École Normale Supérieure, Paris, France
- **Yi Lu**, School of Computer Science and Engineering, The University of New South Wales, Sydney, Australia
- **Eric Madelaine**, INRIA, Centre Sophia Antipolis, Sophia Antipolis, France
- **Michael McIntosh**, IBM T. J. Watson Research Center, Hawthorne, New York, USA
- **Nicholas Nguyen**, Department of Informatics, University of Sussex, Brighton, UK
- **Marco Pistoia**, IBM T. J. Watson Research Center, Hawthorne, New York, USA
- **Jan Vitek**, Purdue University, West Lafayette, Indiana, USA
- **Jian Yin**, IBM T. J. Watson Research Center, Hawthorne, New York, USA
- **Xiaolan Zhang**, IBM T. J. Watson Research Center, Hawthorne, New York, USA

4   Summary of Contributions

An important area of application for program analysis is intrusion detection. Host-based intrusion detection systems attempt to identify attacks by discovering program behaviors that deviate from expected patterns. While the idea of performing behavior validation on-the-fly and terminating errant tasks as soon as a violation is detected is appealing, this presents numerous practical and theoretical challenges. Vitek [20] focuses on automated intrusion detection techniques—techniques that do not require human intervention. Of particular interest are techniques that rely on, or leverage, programming language semantics to find novel ways of detecting attacks [3]. Vitek reviews the main attack models, describes the state of the art in host-based intrusion detection techniques, and concludes with a list of challenges for the research community.

Another interesting area of research is program analysis applied to access control and information flow. Pistoia [13] presents a static analysis framework for statically representing the execution of software programs and the flow of security information in those programs. The results of the analysis can be used to automatically identify security properties of software and evaluate security policies. The analysis can be applied to define or evaluate security policies in both Stack-Based Access Control (SBAC) systems [6], such as Java, Standard Edition (SE) [18] and .NET Common Language Runtime (CLR) [2], and Role-Based Access Control (RBAC) systems [14], such as Java, Enterprise Edition (EE) [17] and CLR. In an SBAC system, when access to a security-sensitive resource is attempted, all the callers on the current stack of execution must prove possession of the right to access that resource. In an RBAC system, access rights typically represent responsibilities inside an organization; rights are aggregated into sets called *roles*, which are then assigned to users and groups. For both SBAC and RBAC system, Pistoia's security-policy inference algorithm assumes that the program execution is represented as a call graph. Security requirements are determined at the authorization points and then propagated backwards in the call graph, performing set unions at the merge points. Another application of this technique is the automatic identification of portions of trusted code that should be made "privilege-asserting" to exempt client code in an SBAC system from unnecessary access-right requirements. A typical example is a library that accesses a configuration or log file. While the library is required to exhibit the necessary file-access right, its clients are not. To achieve this result, the portion of library code that wraps the code responsible for the file-system access can be made privilege-asserting. The problem is how to determine which code should be made privilege-asserting without allowing tainted variables to transfer untrusted data from unauthorzed code into the trusted privilege-asserting code—an integrity problem. Pistoia presents a static-analysis technique based on static program slicing to automatically detect optimum placement of privilege-asserting code without allowing unsanitized tainted data to contaminate trusted code [16].

Resource access control has its origins in the field of operating systems research, but more recently has gained attention for use in programming language research. With the growth of the global computing paradigms, this is particularly true of programming languages to support distributed applications. The essence of resource access control is to enable untrusted programs to execute in a system in a manner prescribed by the system policy. Systems policies represents allowable behaviors by third party code and can range in their sophistication from simple access matrices to sophisticated RBAC schemes. Policies may not only protect access to privileged resources but also ensure that code respects dynamic behaviors in the form of specified protocols. Nguyen and Rathke [12] do not focus on the policy specification but rather on the policy enforcement mechanism. They make use of type and effect systems to extract effects as models, and to statically check that each thread separately satisfies a global policy before using a reduced state space exploration of the interleaved behavior models. The particular language used is a simply-typed λ-calculus augmented with constructs for thread creation and Java style monitor primitives with synchronized expressions. They make use of these by noticing that within a monitor the thread has mutually exclusive access to system resources and, by virtue of this, it is sufficient to verify the policy state only at strategic points within transactions, such as monitor entry points. This observation helps to reduce the size of the state space when it comes to checking interleavings of threads. Behavior models during model extraction are decorated with summaries which instruct the model checker on how to track the policy state. A summary takes the form of a mapping, which relates the policy state at the current point of execution, backwards, to the state at the beginning of either the current transaction, or, the most recent function call. Their type and effect system performs an interprocedural analysis, which tracks the state of the policy across the boundaries of transactions and function calls. The resource accesses are abstracted from the behavior models and replaced with summaries of policy state changes.

Grandy, Stenzel, and Reif [4] illustrate the mapping of abstract data types to a real programming language during a refinement of security protocol specifications. They show that new security and correctness problems arise on the concrete level and describe a possible solution. Their initial observation is that it is hard to get communication protocols secure on the design level. Research has brought a variety of methods to ensure security, for example model-checking-based approaches or specialized protocol analyzers. Their approach for the analysis of security protocols uses Abstract State Machines and interactive verification with an interactive theorem prover called KIV. However, ensuring security of a protocol on the design level is not sufficient. It is an equally important step to get a correct and secure implementation. The verification of sequential Java programs is supported in KIV with a calculus and semantics. Together with the established refinement approach of Downward Simulation, which has been adapted to Abstract State Machines, the correctness of a protocol implementation can be proven. An implementation is *correct* if it makes the same state changes and has the same input/output behavior as an abstract specification.

With the rapid adoption of the Service Oriented Architecture (SOA), sophisticated software systems are increasingly built by composing coarse-grained service components offered by different organizations through standard Web Services interfaces. The ability to quantify end-to-end security risks of composite software services is extremely valuable to businesses that increasingly rely on Web applications to interact with their customers and partners. Yin, Tang, Zhang, and

McIntosh [21] propose a framework that predicts the probability of end-to-end security breaches of a software service by using a combination of three models:

1. A software security model that describes the probability distribution of security bugs in individual components,
2. A service composition model that describes the interactions of components and the contribution of security bugs in individual components to the overall security of the service, and
3. A hacking exposure model that estimates hackers' knowledge of individual components and hence the probability that a security hole, if exists, may be exploited.

Comparing the system call sequence of a network application against a sandboxing policy is a popular approach to detecting control-hijacking attack, in which the attacker exploits such software vulnerabilities as buffer overflow to take over the control of a victim application and possibly the underlying machine. The long-standing technical barrier to the acceptance of this system call monitoring approach is how to derive accurate sandboxing policies for Windows applications whose source code is unavailable. In fact, many commercial computer security companies take advantage of this fact and fashion a business model in which their users have to pay a subscription fee to receive periodic updates on the application sandboxing policies, much like anti-virus signatures. Li, Lam, and Chiueh [7] describe the design, implementation and evaluation of a sandboxing system called BASS that can automatically extract a highly accurate application-specific sandboxing policy from a Win32/X86 binary, and enforce the extracted policy at run time with low performance overhead. BASS is built on a binary interpretation and analysis infrastructure called BIRD, which can handle application binaries with dynamically linked libraries, exception handlers and multi-threading, and has been shown to work correctly for a large number of commercially distributed Windows-based network applications, including IIS and Apache.

Centonze [1,11] observes that, although RBAC allows restricting access to privileged operations, a deployer may actually intend to restrict access to privileged data. Centonze describes a theoretical foundation for correlating an operation-based RBAC policy with a data-based RBAC policy. Relying on a location-consistency property, Centonze shows how to infer whether an operation-based RBAC policy is equivalent to any data-based RBAC policy.

Centonze and Pistoia discuss the pros and cons of static and dynamic analysis for security. Dynamic analysis is typically unsound. Its precision depends on the completeness of the test case suite used during testing. In absence of a complete suite of test cases, the results of dynamic analysis are going to be incomplete. For an analysis that is aimed at detecting certain security requirements of an application, for example authorization requirements [6,16,14,15,1,10], missing certain requirements can cause run-time failures. On the other hand, static analysis is potentially conservative, and may detect unfeasible security requirements. For example, an authorization-requirement analysis may report unnecessary access-right requirements—a violation of the Principle of Least Privilege [19]. Therefore,

Centonze and Pistoia observe that combining static and dynamic analysis is often crucial when it comes to security analyses, and these two approaches should be combined.

Logozzo describes how automatic inference of class invariants may be relevant to security issues [8,9].

Static program analysis of incomplete programs is still an open issue. Yet, most of the programs that need to be analyzed for security are libraries. Another point of discussion that deserves further research is a better quantification of the tradeoffs between precision and scalability of static program analysis for security.

5   Workshop Material

All the papers and presentations of the PASSWORD 2006 workshop are available at the workshop Web site at `http://research.ihost.com/password/`.

6   IBM Research Best Paper Student Award

The *Security and Privacy* and *Programming Languages and Software Engineering* departments at the IBM T. J. Watson Research Center in Hawthorne, New York, USA jointly sponsored the *IBM Research Best Paper Student Award*. The purpose of this recognition was to encourage talented students to submit papers with high research contents. To qualify for this award, at least one of the lead authors of the paper had to be a full-time undergraduate or graduate university student at the time the paper was submitted. Based on the research quality and originality of the paper *Automatic Application-Specific Sandboxing for Win32/X86 Binaries* [7], the Program Committee unanimously decided to confer the IBM Research Best Paper Student Award on Wei Li, lead author of the paper and Ph. D. student at Stony Brook University, Stony Brook, New York, USA.

References

1. Paolina Centonze, Gleb Naumovich, Stephen J. Fink, and Marco Pistoia. Role-Based Access Control Consistency Validation. In *Proceedings of the International Symposium on Software Testing and Analysis (ISSTA '06)*, Portland, Maine, USA, July 2006.
2. Adam Freeman and Allen Jones. *Programming .NET Security*. O'Reilly & Associates, Inc., Sebastopol, CA, USA, June 2003.
3. Rajeev Gopalakrishna, Eugene H. Spafford, and Jan Vitek. Efficient Intrusion Detection Using Automaton Inlining. In *Proceedings of the 2005 IEEE Symposium on Security and Privacy*, pages 18–31, Oakland, CA, USA, May 2005. IEEE Computer Society.
4. Holger Grandy, Kurt Stenzel, and Wolfgang Reif. Refinement of Security Protocol Data Types to Java. In *First Program Analysis for Security and Safety Workshop Discussion (PASSWORD 2006), co-located with the Twentieth European Conference on Object-Oriented Programming (ECOOP 2006)*, Nantes, France, July 2006.

5. Christian Hammer, Jens Krinke, and Gregor Snelting. Information Flow Control for Java Based on Path Conditions in Dependence Graphs. In *Proceedings of IEEE International Symposium on Secure Software Engineering*, Arlington, Virginia, USA, 2006.
6. Larry Koved, Marco Pistoia, and Aaron Kershenbaum. Access Rights Analysis for Java. In *Proceedings of the 17th ACM SIGPLAN Conference on Object-Oriented Programming, Systems, Languages, and Applications*, pages 359–372, Seattle, WA, USA, November 2002. ACM Press.
7. Wei Li, Lap chung Lam, and Tzi cker Chiueh. Application Specific Sandboxing for Win32/Intel Binaries. In *First Program Analysis for Security and Safety Workshop Discussion (PASSWORD 2006), co-located with the Twentieth European Conference on Object-Oriented Programming (ECOOP 2006)*, Nantes, France, July 2006.
8. Francesco Logozzo. Class-level modular analysis for object oriented languages. In *Proceedings of the 10th Static Analysis Symposium (SAS '03)*, volume 2694 of *Lectures Notes in Computer Science*. Springer-Verlag, June 2003.
9. Francesco Logozzo. Automatic inference of class invariants. In *Proceedings of the 5th International Conference on Verification, Model Checking and Abstract Interpretation (VMCAI '04)*, volume 2937 of *Lectures Notes in Computer Science*. Springer-Verlag, January 2004.
10. Gleb Naumovich. A Conservative Algorithm for Computing the Flow of Permissions in Java Programs. In *Proceedings of the International Symposium on Software Testing and Analysis (ISSTA '02)*, pages 33–43, Rome, Italy, July 2002.
11. Gleb Naumovich and Paolina Centonze. Static Analysis of Role-Based Access Control in J2EE Applications. *SIGSOFT Software Engineering Notes*, 29(5):1–10, September 2004.
12. Nicholas Nguyen and Julian Rathke. Typed Static Analysis for Concurrent, Policy-Based, Resource Access Control. In *First Program Analysis for Security and Safety Workshop Discussion (PASSWORD 2006), co-located with the Twentieth European Conference on Object-Oriented Programming (ECOOP 2006)*, Nantes, France, July 2006.
13. Marco Pistoia. Keynote: Static Analysis for Stack-Inspection and Role-Based Access Control Systems. In *First Program Analysis for Security and Safety Workshop Discussion (PASSWORD 2006), co-located with the Twentieth European Conference on Object-Oriented Programming (ECOOP 2006)*, Nantes, France, July 2006.
14. Marco Pistoia, Stephen J. Fink, Robert J. Flynn, and Eran Yahav. When Role Models Have Flaws: Static Validation of Enterprise Security Policies. Technical Report RC24056 (W0609-065), IBM Corporation, Thomas J. Watson Research Center, Yorktown Heights, NY, USA, September 2006.
15. Marco Pistoia and Robert J. Flynn. Interprocedural Analysis for Automatic Evaluation of Role-Based Access Control Policies. Technical Report RC23846 (W0511-020), IBM Corporation, Thomas J. Watson Research Center, Yorktown Heights, NY, USA, November 2005.
16. Marco Pistoia, Robert J. Flynn, Larry Koved, and Vugranam C. Sreedhar. Interprocedural Analysis for Privileged Code Placement and Tainted Variable Detection. In *Proceedings of the 9th European Conference on Object-Oriented Programming*, Glasgow, Scotland, UK, July 2005. Springer-Verlag.
17. Marco Pistoia, Nataraj Nagaratnam, Larry Koved, and Anthony Nadalin. *Enterprise Java Security*. Addison-Wesley, Reading, MA, USA, February 2004.
18. Marco Pistoia, Duane Reller, Deepak Gupta, Milind Nagnur, and Ashok K. Ramani. *Java 2 Network Security*. Prentice Hall PTR, Upper Saddle River, NJ, USA, second edition, August 1999.

19. Jerome H. Saltzer and Michael D. Schroeder. The Protection of Information in Computer Systems. In *Proceedings of the IEEE*, volume 63, pages 1278–1308, September 1975.

20. Jan Vitek. Keynote: Advance in Intrusion Detection. In *First Program Analysis for Security and Safety Workshop Discussion (PASSWORD 2006), co-located with the Twentieth European Conference on Object-Oriented Programming (ECOOP 2006)*, Nantes, France, July 2006.

21. Jian Yin, Chunqiang Tang, Xiaolan Zhang, and Michael McIntosh. On Estimating the Security Risks of Composite Software Services. In *First Program Analysis for Security and Safety Workshop Discussion (PASSWORD 2006), co-located with the Twentieth European Conference on Object-Oriented Programming (ECOOP 2006)*, Nantes, France, July 2006.

Object-Oriented Reengineering

Roel Wuyts[2], Serge Demeyer[1], Yann-Gaël Guéhéneuc[3], Kim Mens[4], and Stéphane Ducasse[5]

[1] Department of Mathematics and Computer Science, University of Antwerp — Belgium
[2] Département d'Informatique, Université Libre de Bruxelles — Belgium
[3] Group of Open and Distributed Systems, Université de Montréal — Canada
[4] Département d'Ingénierie Informatique, Université catholique de Louvain — Belgium
[5] LISTIC Laboratory, University of Savoie — France

1 Introduction

The ability to reengineer object-oriented legacy systems has become a vital matter in today's software industry. Early adopters of the object-oriented programming paradigm are now facing the problems of transforming their object-oriented "legacy" systems into full-fledged frameworks.

To address this problem, a series of workshops have been organised to set up a forum for exchanging experiences, discussing solutions, and exploring new ideas. Typically, these workshops are organised as satellite events of major software engineering conferences, such as ECOOP'97 [1], ESEC/FSE'97 [3], ECOOP'98 [6], ECOOP'99 [5], ESEC/FSE'99 [4], ECOOP'03 [2], ECOOP'04 [7], ECOOP'05 [8]. The last of this series so far has been organised in conjunction with ECOOP'06 and this report summarises the key discussions and outcome of that workshop.

As preparation to the workshop, participants were asked to submit a position paper which would help in steering the workshop discussions. As a result, we received @@@TOFIX— ?? @@ position papers, of which @@@TOFIX— ?? @@ authors were present during the workshop. Together with @@@TOFIX— ?? @@ organisers and @@@TOFIX— ?? @@ participants without position paper, the workshop numbered @@@TOFIX— ?? @@ participants. The position papers, the list of participants, and other information about the workshop are available on the web-site of the workshop at http://smallwiki.unibe.ch/WOOR.

For the workshop itself, we chose a format that balanced presentation of position papers and time for discussions, using the morning for presentations of position papers and the afternoon for discussions in working groups. @@@TOFIX— Following has been used a number of years. Any suggestions for improvement ? @@ Due to time restrictions, we could not allow every author to present. Instead, we invited two authors to summarise the position papers. This format resulted in quite vivid discussions during the presentations, because authors felt more involved. Various participants reported that it was illuminating to hear other researchers present their own work.

Before the workshop, the workshop organisers (Serge Demeyer, Kim Mens, Roel Wuyts, and Stéphane Ducasse) classified the position papers in @@@TOFIX— ?? @@ groups, one group on *??* and one group on *??*. Consequently, in the afternoon, the workshop participants separated in @@@TOFIX— ?? @@ working sessions, during

M. Südholt and C. Consel (Eds.): ECOOP 2006, LNCS 4379, pp. 69–71, 2007.

which they could discuss and advance their ideas. The workshop was concluded with a plenary session where the results of the working groups were exposed and discussed in the larger group. Finally, we discussed practical issues, the most important one being the idea to organise a similar workshop next year which would be the 10th anniversary edition.

2   Summary of Position Papers

In preparation to the workshop, we received **@@@TOFIX—** ?? **@@** position papers (none of them was rejected), which naturally fitted into **@@@TOFIX—** ?? **@@** categories: (a) Category1 and (b) Category2.

– CategoryX
  1. authors, "title".

For each of these categories, we asked one reporter to summarise the position papers; their summaries are presented in the next two sections.

2.1   Position Papers on Category1

@@@TOFIX— Can someone summarize the position papers here ? **@@**

3   Working Groups

Given the above position papers, we decided to split up in **@@@TOFIX—** ?? **@@** working groups. The working groups would focus on ...

3.1   Working Group 1

4   Conclusion

In this report, we have listed the main ideas that were generated during the workshop on object-oriented reengineering. Based on a full day of fruitful work, we can make the following recommendations.

– *Viable Research Area.* Object-Oriented Reengineering remains an interesting research field with lots of problems to be solved and with plenty of possibilities to interact with other research communities. Therefore its vital that we organise such workshops outside of the traditional reengineering community (with conferences like ICSM, WCRE, CSMR, ...).
– *Research Community.* All participants agreed that it would be wise to organise a similar workshop at next year's ECOOP. There is an open invitation for everyone who wants to join in organising it: just contact the current organisers. **@@@TOFIX—** Something abouth 10th anniversary edition **@@**
– *Workshop Format.* The workshop format, where some authors were invited to summarise position papers of others worked particularly well.
– more items more conclusions

References

1. E. Casais, A. Jaasksi, and T. Lindner. FAMOOS workshop on object-oriented software evolution and re-engineering. In J. Bosch and S. Mitchell, editors, *Object-Oriented Technology (ECOOP'97 Workshop Reader)*, volume 1357 of *Lecture Notes in Computer Science*, pages 256–288. Springer-Verlag, Dec. 1997.
2. S. Demeyer, S. Ducasse, and K. Mens. Workshop on object-oriented re-engineering (WOOR'03). In F. Buschmann, A. P. Buchmann, and M. Cilia, editors, *Object-Oriented Technology (ECOOP'03 Workshop Reader)*, volume 3013 of *Lecture Notes in Computer Science*, pages 72–85. Springer-Verlag, July 2003.
3. S. Demeyer and H. Gall. Report: Workshop on object-oriented re-engineering (WOOR'97). *ACM SIGSOFT Software Engineering Notes*, 23(1):28–29, Jan. 1998.
4. S. Demeyer and H. Gall, editors. *Proceedings of the ESEC/FSE'99 Workshop on Object-Oriented Re-engineering (WOOR'99)*, TUV-1841-99-13. Technical University of Vienna - Information Systems Institute - Distributed Systems Group, Sept. 1999.
5. S. Ducasse and O. Ciupke. Experiences in object-oriented re-engineering. In A. Moreira and S. Demeyer, editors, *Object-Oriented Technology (ECOOP'99 Workshop Reader)*, volume 1743 of *Lecture Notes in Computer Science*, pages 164–183. Springer-Verlag, Dec. 1999.
6. S. Ducasse and J. Weisbrod. Experiences in object-oriented reengineering. In S. Demeyer and J. Bosch, editors, *Object-Oriented Technology (ECOOP'98 Workshop Reader)*, volume 1543 of *Lecture Notes in Computer Science*, pages 72–98. Springer-Verlag, Dec. 1998.
7. R. Wuyts, S. Ducasse, S. Demeyer, and K. Mens. Workshop on object-oriented re-engineering (WOOR'04). In J. Malenfant and B. M. Østvold, editors, *Object-Oriented Technology (ECOOP'04 Workshop Reader)*, volume 3344 of *Lecture Notes in Computer Science*, pages 177–186. Springer-Verlag, June 2004.
8. R. Wuyts, S. Ducasse, S. Demeyer, and K. Mens. Workshop on object-oriented re-engineering (WOOR'05). In *Object-Oriented Technology (ECOOP'05 Workshop Reader)*, Lecture Notes in Computer Science. Springer-Verlag, 2005.

Coordination and Adaptation Techniques: Bridging the Gap Between Design and Implementation

Report on the WS WCAT at ECOOP'06

Steffen Becker[1], Carlos Canal[2], Nikolay Diakov[3], Juan Manuel Murillo[4], Pascal Poizat[5], and Massimo Tivoli[6]

[1] Universität Karlsruhe (TH), Institute for Program Structures and Data Organization
sbecker@ipd.uka.de
[2] Universidad de Málaga, GISUM Software Engineering Group
canal@lcc.uma.es
[3] Centrum voor Wiskunde en Informatica (CWI)
nikolay.diakow@cwi.nl
[4] Universidad de Extremadura, Quercus Software Engineering Group
juanmamu@unex.es
[5] IBISC FRE 2873 CNRS - Université d'Evry Val d'Essonne
ARLES Project, INRIA Rocquencourt, France
Pascal.Poizat@inria.fr
[6] Università degli Studi dell'Aquila, Software Engineering and Architecture Group
tivoli@di.univaq.it

Abstract. Coordination and Adaptation are two key issues when developing complex distributed systems. Coordination focuses on the interaction among software entities. Adaptation focuses on solving the problems that arise when the interacting entities do not match properly. This is the report of the third edition of the WCAT workshop, that took place in Nantes jointly with ECOOP 2006. In this third edition, the topics of interest of the participants covered a large number of fields where coordination and adaptation have an impact: models, requirements identification, interface specification, extra-functional properties, automatic generation, frameworks, middleware, and tools.

1 Introduction

The new challenges raised by complex distributed systems have promoted the development of specific fields of Software Engineering such as Coordination [1]. This discipline addresses the interaction issues among software entities (either considered as subsystems, modules, objects, components, or web services) that collaborate to provide some functionality.

A serious limitation of currently available interface descriptions of software entities is that they do not provide suitable means to specify and reason on the

M. Südholt and C. Consel (Eds.): ECOOP 2006, LNCS 4379, pp. 72–86, 2007.

interacting behaviour of complex systems. Indeed, while the notations commonly used provide convenient ways to describe the typed signatures of software entities, they offer a quite limited support to describe their interaction protocol or concurrent behaviour.

To deal with such problems, a new discipline, Software Adaptation, is emerging [2]. Software Adaptation promotes the use of adaptors - specific computational entities with a main goal of guaranteeing that software components will interact in the right way not only at the signature level, but also at the protocol, Quality of Service, and semantic levels. In particular, Adaptation focuses on the dynamic/automatic generation of adaptors. In this sense, models for software adaptation can be considered as a new generation of coordination models. An introduction to Software Adaptation, its state-of-the-art, the description of the main research lines in the field, and some of its open issues can be found in [3].

This report summarizes the third edition of the WCAT workshop, that took place in Nantes jointly with ECOOP 2006. WCAT'06 tried to provide a venue where researchers and practitioners on these topics could meet, exchange ideas and problems, identify some of the key issues related to coordination and adaptation, and explore together and disseminate possible solutions. The topics of interest of the workshop were:

- Coordination Models separating the interaction concern.
- Identification and specification of interaction requirements and problems.
- Automatic generation of adaptors.
- Dynamic versus static adaptation.
- Enhanced specification of components to enable software composition and adaptation.
- Behavioral interfaces, types, and contracts for components, coordinators and adaptors.
- Formal and rigorous approaches to software adaptation.
- The role of adaptation in the software life-cycle.
- Patterns and frameworks for component look-up and adaptation.
- Metrics and prediction models for software adaptation.
- Prediction of the impact of software adaptation on Quality of Service.
- Extra-functional properties and their relation to coordination and adaptation.
- Aspect-oriented approaches to software adaptation and coordination.
- Coordination and adaptation middleware.
- Tools and environments.
- Coordination and adaptation in concurrent and distributed object-oriented systems.
- Interface and choreography description of Web-Services.
- Using adaptors for legacy system integration.
- Industrial and experience reports.
- Surveys and case studies.

The rest of this report is organized as follows: In Section 2 we enumerate the contributions received, and also the participants of the workshop. Then, Section 3, presents a comparative outline of these contributions. Section 4 summarizes the results of the three discussion groups that worked during the workshop, and Section 5 presents the conclusions of the workshop. Finally, we provide some references to relevant works on coordination and adaptation.

2   Contributions and Workshop Participants

To enable lively and productive discussions, prospective participants were required to submit in advance a short position paper, describing their work in the field, open issues, and their expectations on the workshop. From the contributions received, we decided to invite ten position papers. Both the Call for Papers, and the full text of these papers can be found at the Website of the workshop:

`http://wcat06.unex.es`

The list of accepted papers, together with the names and affiliations of their authors is as follows:

- Software Adaptation in Integrated Tool Frameworks for Composite Services
  Nikolay Diakov (*), and Farhad Arbab
  {nikolay.diakow, farhad.arbab}@cwi.nl
  CWI, The Netherlands
- Coordination and Adaptation for Hierarchical Components and Services
  Pascal André, Gilles Ardourel (*), and Christian Attiogbé
  {Pascal.Andre, Gilles.Ardourel,
  Christian.Attiogbe}@univ-nantes.fr
  University of Nantes, France
- Towards Unanticipated Dynamic Service Adaptation
  Marcel Cremene (*) (cremene.marcel@com.utcluj.ro)
  Technical University of Cluj-Napoca, Romania
  Michel Riveill (riveill@unice.fr)
  University of Nice, France
  Christian Martel (christian.martel@univ-savoie.fr)
  University of Savoie, France
- Dynamic Adaptation Using Contextual Environments
  Javier Cámara, Carlos Canal (*), Javier Cubo, and Ernesto Pimentel
  {jcamara, canal, cubo, ernesto}@lcc.uma.es
  University of Málaga, Spain
- Aspect-Oriented Approaches for Component Coordination
  Lidia Fuentes, and Pablo Sánchez (*)
  {lff,pablo}@lcc.uma.es
  University of Málaga, Spain

- Towards Unification of Software Component Procurement Approaches
  Hans-Gerhard Gross (*) (h.g.gross@tudelft.nl)
  Delft University of Technology, The Netherlands
- On Dynamic Reconfiguration of Behavioral Adaptations
  Pascal Poizat (*) (poizat@lami.univ-evry.fr), University of Evry, France
  Gwen Salaün (Gwen.Salaun@inrialpes.fr), INRIA Rhône-Alpes, France
  Massimo Tivoli (*) (tivoli@di.univaq.it), University of L'Aquila, Italy
- Capitalizing Adaptation Safety: a Service-oriented Approach
  Audrey Occello (*), and Anne-Marie Dery-Pinna
  {occello, pinna}@essi.fr
  University of Nice, France
- Safe Dynamic Adaptation of Interaction Protocols
  Christophe Sibertin-Blanc (*) (sibertin@univ-tlse1.fr)
  University of Toulouse 1, France
  Philippe Mauran, and Gérard Padiou
  {mauran, padiou}@frenseeiht.fr
  Institut de Recherche en Informatique de Toulouse
  Pham Thi Xuan Loc (phamtxloc@yahoo.com)
  Can Tho University, Vietnam
- An Aspect-Oriented Adaptation Framework for Dynamic Component Evolution
  Javier Cámara, Carlos Canal (*), and Javier Cubo
  {jcamara, canal, cubo}@lcc.uma.es
  University of Málaga, Spain
  Juan Manuel Murillo (*) (juanmamu@unex.es)
  University of Extremadura (Spain)

Authors that were in fact present at the workshop are marked with and asterisk in the relation above. Apart from those, also attended the workshop, without presenting a paper:

- *Steffen Becker* (sbecker@ipd.uka.de)
  Technical University of Karlsruhe, Germany
- *Jérémy Buisson* (jbuisson@irisa.fr)
  IRISA, France
- *Fabien Dagnat* (Fabien.dagnat@enst-bretagne.fr)
  Ecole Nationale Supérieure des Télécommunications de Bretagne, France
- *Leonel Gayard* (leonel.gayard@ic.unicamp.br)
  State University of Campinas, Brasil
- *Arnaud Lanoix* (lanoix@loria.fr)
  LORIA, France
- *Inès Mouakher* (mouakher@loria.fr)
  LORIA, France

In total, seventeen participants coming from seven different countries attended the workshop.

3   Comparative Summary of the Contributions

The position papers presented in the workshop covered a wide number of issues related to coordination and adaptation, both from the theoretical and the practical point of view.

3.1   Coordination Models

Some of the papers focused on coordination techniques for software composition and interaction. Coordination Models and Languages provide mechanisms to specify the coordination constraints of a software system. Such constraints involve all the dependencies between the computational entities of the system, that is, their interactions. Thus, Coordination Languages could be good tools to support adaptation when the subject of the adaptation is the way in which software entities interact.

Coordination Models can be classified in two categories [1] named *Endogenous* and *Exogenous*. Such categories are motivated by the different mechanisms used by coordination models to deal with the coordination constraints of the system.

Endogenous coordination languages provide primitives that are incorporated within the computational entities for their coordination. The most representative language in this category is Linda [4]. If the interaction protocol is to be adapted, it could be done adapting the behaviour of the primitives to access the tuple space and the pattern matching mechanism.

In contrast, exogenous coordination languages place the coordination primitives in entities external to those to be coordinated. Such clear separation between processes functionality and interaction protocols provides a better support for adaptation. Hence, adapting the interaction protocols can be managed manipulating the coordinators. Design time adaptation can be easily managed recoding the interaction protocols implemented by coordination processes. Moreover, runtime adaptation is also supported.

Following this approach, Diakov [5] presented an adaptation framework for the construction of composite Web Services (WS) for distributed computing environments, developed in collaboration with F. Arbab. Their position was that current Web Service description languages, such as WSDL or WSBPEL do not sufficiently address compositionality at the level of their formal semantics and dynamic execution model. Thus, they applied their previous theoretical results in formal techniques for exogenous coordination of software components, namely using the coordination model Reo [6]. The major issues addressed are: *(i)* the implication of synchrony in the way in which software is designed, *(ii)* the bridging of protocols with fundamentally different coordination models, and *(iii)* the enriching of theoretical models so that they become usable in practical applications. They also presented a tool framework for WS composition that includes visual editing and a graphical user interface.

Combining both Coordination and Aspect-Oriented Software Development (AOSD) techniques, Sánchez [7] presented an Aspect-Oriented approach for component coordination that complements their work on adaptation developed for the preceding edition of the workshop [8]. His position was that the coordination protocol that governs the interchange of messages among interacting software components is usually entangled with the base functionality of those components, especially in the field of endogenous coordination. In this work, the authors advocate for the use of Aspect-Oriented techniques for the separation of coordination patterns and components' functionality, in order both to reuse them and to make composition easier. Their paper includes a survey on some recent publications that combine CBSD and AOSD with success, including component and aspect models such as MALACA, programming languages such as JAsCo (Java Aspect Components), and aspectized component platforms such as CAM/DAOP [9], which gives a broad view of the technologies required and the current state of the art in aspect-oriented coordination.

3.2 Software Adaptation

The rest of the works presented addressed specifically different adaptation issues. In his paper, Gross [10] presented his proposal towards the unification of software component procurement and integration. Component procurement deals with how to map customer component requirements to provider's component specifications. His position was that the mechanisms currently available only deal with lower levels of abstraction, close to the implementation level. The goal of his research work is to elevate typical component featuring mapping mechanisms from the implementation level up onto the design and requirements engineering levels. He outlined a research agenda that includes (i) the formalization of component specifications equipped with provided and required behaviour models, in order to automate the currently manually performed component mapping and integration effort; (ii) the definition of an integrated requirements specification method based on natural language; (iii) the derivation of model artifacts from the these requirements specifications documents; and (iv) the development of mapping mechanisms to other commonly used component specification notations such as UML.

3.3 Adaptation of Behaviour

Also dealing with how to express component specifications, Ardourel [11] presented a Behavioural IDL (BIDL) for the coordination and adaptation of hierarchical components and services. The paper presented an approach in which a service is like a formal operation with a signature (name and parameters), a contract (pre/post-conditions), a signature interface (with provided and required services, from which the service's hierarchical structure can be inferred), and a BIDL that describes the dynamic evolution of the service. The proposal is exemplified by means of a classical Automatic Teller Machine example. In this setting the kind of adaptation that can be performed includes both message and parameter names, message ordering, and one-to-many relations between clients and servers.

One of the big issues of the workshop was how to address dynamic adaptation. Several papers presented the proposals of their authors to this problem. For instance, Canal [12] presented an approach for dynamic adaptation based on the use of contextual environments. In this work it is shown how to perform adaptation following flexible polices. The goal is to describe a context-dependent mapping between the interfaces of the components being adapted, as opposed to static mappings presented in the authors' previous work [13]. Mappings are described using a map calculus that defines a small set of operations over environments and mappings, designed to express various encapsulation policies, composition rules, and extensibility mechanisms. On the other hand, component's interface description is achieved by means of a BIDL based on process algebraic notation (namely the π-calculus). From that, an algorithm would automatically develop an adaptor for the components involved, following the flexible adaptation policies specified in the mapping. The proposal is exemplified by means of a Video-On-Demand system.

A similar approach, also dealing with dynamic behavioural adaptation was that of Poizat [14], who presented a proposal for the dynamic reconfiguration of behavioural adaptations. His position was that, since the development of software adaptors is costly, it is crucial to make adaptor reconfiguration possible when one wants to modify or update some parts of a running system involving adaptors. In an initial approach, the problem of dynamically reconfigurable adaptors was presented, and some ideas for a solution to this problem were sketched. The proposal is built on previous work [15] in which component behavioral interfaces are specified by labelled transition systems (LTS), and in order to find out if a system made up of several components presents behavioural mismatch, the synchronous product of these LTS is computed, and then the absence of deadlock is checked on it. Then, an abstract description of an adaptor is specified again by an LTS which, put into a non-deadlock-free system, keeps it deadlock-free. From this starting point, the possible changes that can be applied dynamically to a system and may result in incompatible behavior (namely, component addition, upgrading, or suppression) are identified, and some hints on how to deal with the automatic handling of the reconfiguration process in order to maintain the system deadlock-free are given.

An aspect-orientated approach was also advocated by Murillo [16]. AOSD provides techniques to deal with the separation of crosscutting concerns along the software life cycle. Within that, Aspect Oriented Programming (AOP) is focused on the implementation step proposing programming languages supporting the separated codification of system features that crosscut several software entities (classes, subprograms, processes,...). The code specifying the separated properties is located in a new kind of module commonly called an *aspect*. In addition, one should also specify how aspects affect software entities. In order to obtain the original system behaviour, this information is used to weave the code inside aspects with the software entities. Such weaving can be done both statically, before the application starts, or dynamically, when the application is already running.

Murillo presented an adaptation framework for dynamic component evolution. The approach combined both aspect-oriented programming with reflection and with adaptation techniques in order to support and speed up the process of dynamic component evolution by tackling issues related to signature and proto-col interoperability. The goal was to provide the first stage of a semi-automatic approach for syntactical and behavioural adaptation. Murillo pointed out that when performing component adaptation it is necessary to have information that is only available at runtime. Moreover, if one wants to take advantage of this information, he or she has to find a way to apply it at runtime as well. His position was that aspect-oriented techniques serve for the purpose, and two dif-ferent strategies may be considered: (i) Dynamic aspect generation, allowing runtime generation, application and removal of aspects implementing adapta-tion concerns. However, this is not a realistic scenario yet, considering the state-of-the-art on aspect-oriented languages and runtime platforms. Moreover, the computational overhead caused by these additional tasks may be too heavy for the system. (ii) Dynamic adaptor management, a more reasonable approach with respect to to overhead, in which the aspects that manage adaptation are precompiled, and an adaptation manager is able to retrieve, interpret and use the dynamic information required for runtime adaptation.

3.4 Unanticipated Adaptation

The important issue of unanticipated orientation was raised by the work of Cremene et al. [17]. Indeed, the adaptation proposals described above deal with dynamism either by assuming predefined adaptation policies or by passing through a phase of system re-design. In contrast, Cremene's presentation dealt with unanticipated service adaptation at runtime. Their position is that auto-matically solving unanticipated adaptation is a must, since the context (user profile, physical resources, and other elements) may change while the service is running. However, the current service adaptation approaches require the predic-tion of all the possible variations in the context, and need to specify beforehand rules for each possible situation. The authors presented a solution based on a context-service common representation that enables them to discover the adap-tation rules and strategies rather than to fix them a priori. For that, they use a service-context description that explains how the service and the context in-teract. This description is based on a three-layered model, including a context layer, a component layer and a profile layer. They are currently developing a prototype of service adaptation based on their proposals.

3.5 Safe Adaptation

The remaining two papers addressed safety issues. Sibertin-Blanc [18] presented an approach to safe dynamic adaptation of interaction protocols between the actors of a computer-aided learning system based on the notion of a moderator. In this proposal, moderators are components managing interactions described and formalized by means for Petri nets. Then, dynamic adaptation is performed by specific transformations of the net representing the moderator. These trans-formations permit to satisfy adaptation demands, insofar as these changes do not alter the integrity of the base system. The flexibility of the approach is illustrated by a real case study for the adaptation of a protocol for controlling accesses to documents during an examination.

Finally, Occello et al. [19] presented a service-oriented approach for capitalizing adaptation safety. They assume that the different adaptation mechanisms for modifying system's structure and components' behaviour dynamically may lead the application to an unsafe state. Current approaches facing this problem can be divided into *(i)* formal approaches, that provide deep theoretical results but are generally not linked with an implementation; and *(ii)* practical solutions, that lack of formal foundations and cannot be reused in other platforms. From this description of the problem, their proposal consists of computing the required adaptation at model level in order to make adaptation generic, and thus reusable. The authors presented the *Satin* safety service that can be queried by technological platforms to determine whether the adaptations to be done at the platform level are safe or not. This work makes benefits of a model driven engineering (MDE) approach for validation purposes. Among the open issues of this work was the development of a methodology for model validation.

4   Discussion Groups

Invited participants made five-minute presentations of their positions, followed by discussions that served to identify a list of open issues in the field. We divided these issues into three categories or groups: *Fundamental Issues*, *Incremental Composition and Testing of Dynamic Architectures*, and *Industrial Knowledge Transfer*. Participants were then assigned to one of them, attending to their interests. The task of each group was be to discuss about a subset of the previously identified issues.

4.1   Fundamental Issues

This group was formed by Jeremy Buisson, Carlos Canal, Marcel Cremene, Fabien Dagnat, Inès Mouakher, Audrey Occello, and Pablo Sánchez. The topics assigned to the group covered a number of general and fundamental issues on adaptation and coordination, including component models, in particular semantic models, exogenous (external) coordination vs. endogenous (intracomponent) coordination, context compliance, and context dependent reasoning. These topics lead the discussion to other even more general issues on components, aspects, interfaces, coordination, etc.

At the end of the session, each participant was asked to write down a conclusion or *motto*, which afterwards was discussed and voted for acceptance/rejection by the rest of the group.

- *"Coordination is more than just message coordination"*. This issue was raised by the common perception that most of the works presented in the workshop (and also in the literature) on Coordination deal with message interaction. Moreover, adaptation techniques also address mainly message passing issues, both at the signature and behaviour levels. However, Coordination should also address other issues such as, for instance, memory consumption. Such issues can profoundly affect the interaction of components and the performance and global behaviour of the whole system.

- *"Existing component models do not contain enough elements in order to define components interaction with the environment"*. Indeed one of the classical issues in Software Adaptation and also in CBSD is how to effectively model and represent the dependencies and interrelations both among the components of the system, and between the system and its environment. This problem was also raised by the next *motto*.

- *"The four levels of contracts (syntactical, behavioural, quality of service, semantics) are enough to represent adaptation requirements, but we do not have language tools to express them"*. As we have already mentioned, current component models and IDLs only focus on the signature of the messages exchanged. Many research proposals in the field address also behavioural specification using BIDLs, but many other important properties of components (for instance, QoS and functionality) lack a sufficient description.

- *"Component should declare all their dependencies in their interfaces and this declaration should be as abstract as possible"*. Only by means of abstract, platform-independent interface descriptions would it be possible to perform third-party and interplatform composition and adaptation.

- *"Context dependency is complementary to contract specification"*. That is, the more explicitly the context dependencies of a component are described in its interface, the less context-dependent would the component become, since all these dependencies could be then addressed with composition and adaptation techniques.

- *"Context is a component that should be contracted"*. We can take this *motto* as the conclusion/summary of the group discussions, since it tries to drive attention and incitate discussion by being controversial, paving the path for future discussions on these and other related issues.

4.2 Incremental Composition and Testing of Dynamic Architectures

The group was formed by Gilles Ardourel, Leonel Gayard, Juan Manuel Murillo, Pascal Poizat, and Christophe Sibertin-Blanc. The main issue assigned to the group was how (and when) to address dynamic adaptation, an underlying topic in most of the papers presented in the workshop.

First, the group started by agreeing and setting the context of the problem. It falls obviously in the grounds of CBSD and, in general, in any other context where the integration of different components or software units is required (for instance, in team development). One less obvious but yet significant field of application is *"the jungle of"* Pervasive Computing, as it was named by some of the participants, and in general, any system which has a high degree of dynamism in its architecture, and changing environment conditions. In this context, adaptation is not only required to make components match, but it must also collaborate with service discovery and software composition to build new emerging services from a jungle of components.

Then, if we assume that the architecture of the system can be dynamic (with components continuously entering and leaving the system, possibly evolving themselves, and with dynamic reconfiguration of component relations), the adaptation process needs to be also inherently dynamic. This establish a series of links with implementation issues, such as adaptative middleware [20], and runtime overload.

As a consequence, it was agreed that there was a need for *incremental* adaptation: when something changed in the system, not everything had to be re-computed. Incremental adaptation would require to adapt the adaptors themselves, or alternatively, to make them evolve attending to the changing conditions of the system. Techniques for this kind of adaptation have to be developed.

The group also discussed how the incremental development of the system relates to the need for compositionality. It is a fact that some properties of software can be lifted from the local (components) to the global (system), but this seems to require some kind of compositionality of properties. If that could be expressed, incremental adaptation would be solved by using hierarchical adaptors (i.e. adaptors of adaptors). However, some properties (for instance, deadlock freedom) are not compositional in that sense, and this means that an additional specific step of system-wide adaptation has to be computed.

4.3   Industrial Knowledge Transfer

The group —formed by Steffen Becker, Nikolay Diakow, Hans-Gerhard Gross, Arnaud Lanoix, and Massimo Tivoli— has been assigned to discuss on several issues. The overall question has been why there is no widespread use of adaptation techniques in industrial practice although there exist quite several working and useful algorithms. As a consequence, the main issue dealt with was what can be done to transfer this scientific knowledge into industry. The group came up with a discussion on the stakeholders involved in to transfer process, the reasons for them to actually do knowledge transfer, the problems faced, why this transfer is performed insufficiently and what means can help to change the situation.

Initially, the group identified three stakeholders mostly involved in a knowledge transfer process: academic institutions, research units in companies, and production units in companies. In the first category there are usually universities and technology transfer institutes which are usually associated to one or more university institutes. They develop research ideas and report on them in academic publications. Research units in companies also develop new ideas but are mainly concerned with customizing research results of academic institutions in order to make them applicable in their companies operational goals. Finally, the production units are involved with their daily work. They have the possibility to report on their problems either to their research units or to universities. One of the most often used way of transferring knowledge goes from academic institutions over research units into production. But there is also a direct link between universities and production which is used implicitly by people coming from universities into production practice. This is often the case with interns, but also when students finish their studies and go into industry.

The next question was to investigate why companies and universities are motivated to do knowledge transfer. This motivation can be used to increase the transfer amount. For companies there are short term and long term goals driving them to participate in technology transfer. Two major factors have been identified: business advantages and prestige/vanity. Business advantages directly result gaining a higher efficiency often by the possibility to decrease costs using the new knowledge. Other factors can result from the ability to produce the same products but with increased quality attributes or by getting the same products faster into a market (decreased time-to-market). Prestige and vanity which can be used in marketing and project acquisition come from the fact that companies can show that they have experience in new fields of technology. This is often supported by the use of current buzz-words to communicate their expertise.

Scientific people are motivated to do technology transfers for scientific and social reasons. The scientific value of doing knowledge transfer comes from the possibility to do validations, verification or proof-of-concept studies of the developed ideas. Additionally, after doing such studies there is usually a lot of gained new experiences. This kind of feedback can afterwards lead to the development of enhancements of the existing methods or even to the initiation of new research. The social factor comes from the fact that scientists get to know people and develop long term cooperations.

Given the above highlighted motivations for the participants in knowledge transfers, there is the question why there are problems in doing technology transfers. The main issue here is how to convince the companies that a newly developed idea is worth trying. The ideas developed against this issue contained the two suggestions. Either the transfer should be done in small steps or in pilot projects for new buzz-word related technologies. In performing small introductory steps those steps should be selected which are easy to introduce but show their usefulness in large parts of the companies. After a successful initial step of this kind larger projects can be initiated as follow up projects. Buzz-word related projects may be larger because they usually target at the prestige motivation of companies.

To get started into the discussion what can be done to alter the current situation the question was how can scientific people convince companies of the usefulness of their ideas. The group came up with several organizational issues which can help. In order to reduce the costs and hence the risk for companies, student projects are well suited. Additionally, also well defined reference projects with little financial risk can be suited to get a knowledge transfer started. An other means to reduce the financial risk of larger projects can be to participate in governmental projects which cover most of the costs. A different means is to found a spin-off company in which research ideas are evolved into a mature state. Additionally, given a spin-off company the spin-off has to deal with the economic risks alone and not a third-party.

A different issue is that many of the developed ideas in science take a while to communicate and comprehend. During a scientific presentation, company representatives do not get the impression that a research idea is useful. This can often be altered when a tool is available. Tools are able to hide the complexity of algorithms and hence, are better suited to communicate the benefits and the possible automation of the methods. A remaining problem is that even if a tool exists, for productive use often tool customizations are still needed.

Finally, the group discussed the idea that presenting research ideas with more suited, problem-oriented models can also help. For example, in adaptation methods often difficult to understand models like process algebras are applied. This kind of complexity should be hidden by using different models in the interaction with the end users of the methods. In our example, graphical languages to model protocols are better suited for communication than the same model written as process algebra. In order to realize tools which offer easy to understand problem or domain oriented models, model transformations (like in MDA) can help to automatically come from the user representation to the internal algorithm oriented representation. Additionally, model transformations can also be applied in the opposite direction. In this direction, they transform the results of the algorithms into a user understandable way. In tool prototypes it would be therefore a task of the researches to implement in their tools also such a user understandable model and presentation. Moreover, having such a transformation approach in place it is also easier to integrate several different analysis methods in a single tool which also increases the acceptance probability when doing industry presentations.

5   Conclusion of the Workshop

Finally, a plenary session was held, in which each group presented their conclusions to the rest of the participants, followed by a general discussion. During this session attendants were asked for their general impression about the third edition of WCAT. While the first two editions of WCAT [21,22] tried to define adaptation and its limits with reference to other domains such as evolution or maintenance, during this third edition, people agreed that they had been able to discuss on more precise and technical issues. These issues were namely the differences between techniques for adaptation at runtime and design time, and mechanisms to implement or generate adaptors. Implementation, the third part of the detect-correct-implement adaptation triplet, is often eluded in adaptation proposals.

Some future work for next editions of WCAT can be seen in the following issues for which several complementary domains should be investigated:

- the relation with ontologies and automatic service composition approaches [23] for the automatic specification of adaptation mappings;
- the relation with distributed and real-time domains for the detection of adaptation needs, and the online application of adaptation (either using design time or runtime techniques);

– the relation with AOSD and MDA techniques, languages and component models for the implementation of adaptors: should we use weaving (AOSD) or refinement (MDA)?

Finally, the community interested in adaptation and coordination identified the task of developing a common suite of example problems found in adaptation and coordination. It is envisioned to use this suite in the future to estimate strengths and weaknesses of proposed adaptation methods, to compare methods with each other, and finally, to validate the usefulness of the proposed approaches.

References

1. Arbab, F.: What Do You Mean Coordination? Bulletin of the Dutch Association for Theoretical Computer Science (NVTI) (1998)
2. Canal, C., Murillo, J.M., Poizat, P.: Report on the First International Workshop on Coordination and Adaptation Techniques for Software Entities. In: Object-Oriented Technology. ECOOP 2004 Workshop Reader. Volume 3344 of Lecture Notes in Computer Science., Springer (2004) 133–147
3. Canal, C., Murillo, J.M., Poizat, P.: Software adaptation. L'Objet **12-1** (2006) 9–31
4. N. Carreiro, D.G.: Linda in Context. Communications of the ACM **32** (1989) 133–147
5. Diakov, N., Arbab, F.: Software adaptation in integrated tool frameworks for composite services. [24] 9–14
6. Arbab, F.: Reo: A channel-based coordination model for component-composition. Mathematical Structures in Computer Science **14-1** (2004) 329–366
7. Fuentes, L., Sánchez, P.: Aspect-oriented approaches for component coordination. [24] 43–51
8. Fuentes, L., Sánchez, P.: AO approaches for Component Adaptation. [22] 79–86
9. Pinto, M., Fuentes, L., Troya, J.M.: A dynamic component and aspect-oriented platform. The Computer Journal **48-4** (2005) 401–420
10. Gross, H.G.: Towards unification of software component procurement approaches. [24] 53–59
11. André, P., Ardourel, G., Attiogbé, C.: Coordination and adaptation for hierarchical components and services. [24] 15–23
12. Cámara, J., Canal, C., Cubo, J., Pimentel, E.: Dynamic adaptation using contextual environments. [24] 35–42
13. Bracciali, A., Brogi, A., Canal, C.: A Formal Approach to Component Adaptation. Journal of Systems and Software **74-1** (2005) 45–54
14. Poizat, P., Salaün, G., Tivoli, M.: On dynamic reconfiguration of behavioral adaptations. [24] 60–69
15. Canal, C., Poizat, P., Salaün, G.: Synchronizing behavioural mismatch in software composition. In: Formal Methods for Open Object-Based Distributed Systems (FMOODS'06). Volume 4037 of Lecture Notes in Computer Science., Springer (2006) 63–77
16. Cámara, J., Canal, C., Cubo, J., Murillo, J.M.: An aspect-oriented adaptation framework for dynamic component evolution. [24] 91–99

17. Cremene, M., Riveill, M., Martel, C.: Towards unanticipated dynamic service adaptation. [24] 25–34
18. Sibertin-Blanc, C., Xuan-Loc, P.T., Mauran, P., Padiou, G.: Safe dynamic adaptation of interaction protocols. [24] 81–90
19. Occello, A., Dery-Pinna, A.M.: Capitalizing adaptation safety: a service-oriented approach. [24] 71–79
20. Agha, G.A., ed.: Special Issue on Adaptative Middleware. Volume 45(6) of Communications of the ACM. ACM Press (2002)
21. Canal, C., Murillo, J.M., Poizat, P., eds.: First International Workshop on Coordination and Adaptation Techniques for Software Entities (WCAT'04). Held in conjunction with the 18th European Conference on Object-Oriented Programming (ECOOP'2004). Available at http://wcat04.unex.es/. (2004)
22. Becker, S., Canal, C., Murillo, J.M., Poizat, P., Tivoli, M., eds.: Second International Workshop on Coordination and Adaptation Techniques for Software Entities (WCAT'05). Held in conjunction with the 19th European Conference on Object-Oriented Programming (ECOOP'2005). Available at http://wcat05.unex.es/. (2005)
23. Mokhtar, S.B., Georgantas, N., Issarny, V.: Ad hoc composition of user tasks in pervasive computing environments. In: Software Composition. (2005) 31–46
24. Becker, S., Canal, C., Diakov, N., Murillo, J.M., Poizat, P., Tivoli, M., eds.: Third International Workshop on Coordination and Adaptation Techniques for Software Entities (WCAT'06). Held in conjunction with the 20th European Conference on Object-Oriented Programming (ECOOP'2006). Available at http://wcat06.unex.es/. (2006)
25. Ciancarini, P., Hankin, C., eds.: First International Conference on Coordination Languages and Models, (COORDINATION '96). Volume 1061 of Lecture Notes in Computer Science., Springer (1996)
26. Arbab, F.: The IWIM model for coordination of concurrent activities. [25]

Quantitative Approaches in Object-Oriented Software Engineering
Report on the WS QAOOSE at ECOOP'06

Fernando Brito e Abreu[1], Coral Calero[2], Yann-Gaël Guéhéneuc[3],
Michele Lanza[4], and Houari Sahraoui[5]

[1] Univ. of Lisbon, Portugal
[2] Univ. of Castilla, Spain
[3] Univ. of Montreal, Canada
[4] Univ. of Lugano, Switzerland
[5] Univ. of Montreal, Canada

Abstract. The QAOOSE 2006 workshop brought together, for a full day, researchers working on several aspects related to quantitative evaluation of software artifacts developed with the object-oriented paradigm and related technologies. Ideas and experiences were shared and discussed. This report includes a summary of the technical presentations and subsequent discussions raised by them. 12 out of 14 submitted position papers were presented, covering different aspects such as metrics, components, aspects and visualization, evolution, quality models and refactorings. In the closing session the participants were able to discuss open issues and challenges arising from researching in this area, and they also tried to forecast which will be the hot topics for research in the short to medium term.

1 Historical Background and Motivation

QAOOSE 2006 is a direct continuation of nine successful workshops, held at previous editions of ECOOP in Glasgow (2005), Oslo (2004), Darmstadt (2003), Malaga (2002), Budapest (2001), Cannes (2000), Lisbon (1999), Brussels (1998) and Aarhus (1995).

The QAOOSE series of workshops has attracted participants from both academia and industry that are involved / interested in the application of quantitative methods in object-oriented software engineering research and practice. Quantitative approaches in the OO field is a broad but active research area that aims at the development and/or evaluation of methods, techniques, tools and practical guidelines to improve the quality of software products and the efficiency and effectiveness of software processes. The workshop is open to other technologies related to OO such as aspects (AOP), component-based systems (CBS), web-based systems (WBS) and agent-based systems (ABS). The relevant research topics are diverse, but include a strong focus on applying empirical software engineering techniques.

M. Südholt and C. Consel (Eds.): ECOOP 2006, LNCS 4379, pp. 87–96, 2007.

2   Workshop Overview

23 people attended the workshop. They were representing 18 different organizations from 10 different countries.

Among the attendants, 6 people were not authors, as it is normally the case in these kind of workshops. They have asked the organizers to attend the workshop, which is an additional evidence of the interest raised by this area.

This workshop encompassed 4 sessions, the first 3 bring presentation sessions, while the last one was a pure discussion session. The topics of each presentation session were, respectively: (1) Metrics, Components, Aspects (chaired by H. A. Sahraoui), (2) Visualization, Evolution (chaired by F. Brito e Abreu), and (3) Quality Models, Metrics, Detection, Refactoring (chaired by C. Calero.

Each presentation, plus corresponding discussion, took around 25 minutes. Those presentations were based on submitted position papers that went through an evaluation process conducted by the organizers.

In the final session, a collective effort was performed to discuss open issues that rose from the three previous sessions and to identify future trends for this workshop.

In the next three sections (one per session), we will present for each discussed paper an abstract and a summary of the consequent discussion.

2.1   Session 1: Metrics, Components, Aspects

"Measuring the Complexity of Aspect-Oriented Programs with Multiparadigm Metric" - N. Pataki, A. Sipos, Z. Porkoláb

The position of the authors, presented by Norbert, is that nowadays multiparadigm metrics are necessary to compare programs written using different paradigms or to measure programs that use multiple paradigms. They defined a complexity metric, called AV, that can be extracted from programs written in AOP, OOP or procedural programs. They use this metric to compare the complexity of design patterns when implemented in Java or in AspectJ. The conclusion was that thanks to this multiparadigm metric, we can claim that AOP is well suited for some patterns, but not for others, i.e., increases the complexity in comparison with the OO version. The discussion that took place after the presentation concerned two points. First, a participant asked whether it is interesting to adapt a paradigm specific metric to other paradigms or to define new ones. The position of Norbert is that existing metrics are paradigm dependent. The adaptation can be biased by this dependence. for the second point, a participant asked if the metric is defined using a model that contains the important concepts (from the concerned paradigms) involved in the measurement. Norbert explained that this was the basis of the work. The paper presents the part that concerns AOP.

"On the Influence of Practitioners' Expertise in Component Based Software Reviews" - M. Goulão, F. Brito e Abreu

Fernando presented his (and his colleague) position on the importance of expertise in component code inspection. This position is supported by an empirical study performed using student subjects. Expertise was determined based on their independently assessed academic record. Inspection outcome was evaluated by the diversity of defects found at two levels of abstraction. As a result, a significant correlation was found between the two variables. Some participants questioned the fact that the expertise was determined based on the student academic results in general and not on components specifically. Although Fernando recognized that this is an issue, he explained that they consider only software engineering results which attenuates the impact. Another possible threat that was discussed is the influence of the domain knowledge of the inspected program on the results. This threat is in fact circumvented by the training on the control domain (application domain) that was given to the subjects. Finally one participant wondered if the age of the expertise is important. As all the students have recent expertise, it is difficult to evaluate the importance of this factor.

"A Substitution Model for Software Components" - B. George, R. Fleurquin, and S. Sadou

The position of the authors, as reported by Bart, concerned the problem of searching components in libraries. Indeed, in the context of CBSD, a software component is described by its functional and non-functional properties. Then, the problem is to know which component satisfies a specific need in a specific composition context, during software design or maintenance. The position is that this is a substitution problem in any of the two cases. From this statement, they propose a need-aware substitution model that takes into account functional and non-functional properties. Following this presentation, a participant asked for a clarification on if the matching concerns at the same time the functional and non-functional properties of the components. Bart explained that the non-functional matching is evaluated only if there is a functional matching. The search strategy was also discussed to see if it is better to compare concrete component between them than to compare each component with an ideal one. The conclusion was that as the search is done in a specific context, direct comparison is not suitable. Many questions concerned the definition and the measurement of component quality. More specifically, a participant questioned the use of ISO9126 to define a single metric for each property. Some properties can be better measured using more than one metric. Another participant highlighted the fact that the quality of a component is different from the quality of the system after the composition, i.e., finding the best component using local properties doesnt mean that this will lead to the best option from the system point of view. Bart however, minimized the impact of the locality by the argument that the composition is performed sequentially. Finally, some participant warned the presenter on the risks of using expertise-base weighting and on the need of evaluating the approach on real component libraries.

2.2 Session 2: Visualization, Evolution

Four position papers were presented and discussed in this session. All of them dealt with software visualization and/or software evolution aspects.

"Towards Task-Oriented Modeling Using UML" - C.F.J. Lange, M.A.M. Wijns, M.R.V. Chaudron

The authors claim that since software engineering is becoming increasingly model-centric, tasks such as the analysis or prediction of system properties require additional information, namely of quantitative nature, that must be easily visualized along with the diagrams. For this purpose they have developed a prototype tool, named MetricView Evolution tool, that allows 2D views of UML diagrams superimposed with a 3rd dimension for representing metrics values. Industrial case studies and a light-weight user experiment to validate the usefulness of the proposed views were reported. The presentation ended with a tool demo.

Several issues were raised in the discussion that followed the presentation. Questioned on the forecasted improvements on the demonstrated tool, Christian referred that there is an undergoing work with an industrial partner regarding tool usability and integration with other UML tools. Another issue pointed out was that of the ability to scale up to large systems. Christian recognized that they are indeed having problems of this sort for systems above a few hundred classes. However, he claimed that this problem can be somehow mitigated with the appropriate usage of model partitioning (packaging) and zooming. Another participant questioned which was the model input format used for the tool, since it has no editing capabilities. Since the answer was XMI, a question was then raised on the positioning information of model elements, which is only available on the new XMI 2 version. Regarding this issue, Christian argued that they are using Rose and Together tools, which generate extended (non-standard) XMI files with positioning information. Finally, someone questioned if the new views causes, or not, an increased navigation difficulty. While recognizing that UML 2 has already 13 diagram types and that adding more information may actually reduce the navigability, Christian argued that integrating / tracing information in the diagrams is a way of mitigating this problem.

"Animation Coherence in Representing Software Evolution" - G. Langelier, H.A. Sahraoui, and P. Poulin

The authors start by recognizing that the study of software evolution requires the analysis of large amounts of data, which is not easily tractable in a manual fashion. To mitigate this problem they propose a semi-automatic approach based on diachronic visualization to represent software versions. Animation is used to represent the transitions (code modifications) between versions. This representation allows the user to perceive visually the coherence between two successive versions. The presentation included a demo of a 3D city-like class visualization tool, where evolution situations provoked (re)placements plus characteristics modifications (e.g. building twist or height modification).

After the presentation, the participants were able to raise several questions. Both the presenter and another co-author also present (Houari Sahraoui) answered them. The first question related to the representation (in the tool) of a typical basic refactoring operation class renaming. The authors replied that they did not consider it, because they want to reduce automatic processing by just allowing the user to detect the movement. Nevertheless this could be performed by matching new classes (appearing) with discarded ones, by simply comparing their contents (renamed classes keep the same features). Another participant asked if some kind of patterns of modification were identified. Guillaume answered that indeed several patterns such as the already mentioned appear/disappear pattern, have been identified, but are still being systematized. A final question tackled the suitability of visual attributes for evolution analysis. The presenter mentioned that if we take the psychological perspective, some attributes such as texture or colour can in fact be much less appropriate than, for instance, twist. However, further investigation on this issue must still be performed.

"Computing Ripple Effect for Object Oriented Software" - H. Bilal and S. Black

The work presented aims at proposing a quantification of the ripple effect, that is, the impact that a local change causes on the remaining parts of a software system. Keeping this effect low is typically a maintenance desideratum. The authors propose to calculate the ripple effect based upon the effect that a change to a single variable has on the rest of a program and consider its applicability as a software complexity measure for object oriented software. Extensions to the PhD work of Sue Black (2001) are proposed to the computation of ripple effect to accommodate different aspects of the object oriented paradigm.

As in previous presentations, we had a period for questions after the oral presentation. The presenter was first asked to prognosticate the deployment of this ripple effect detection in industry. He was not able to produce such a prognosis because, at the current stage of their research and tool support, they cannot yet scale-up to real-world examples. Another participant asked what kind of ripple detection model the authors are using. Haider replied that they have not yet developed a ripple estimation model for object-oriented software. They are planning to do so while extending a locally developed tool for calculating ripple effect for C++ code (currently it only supports C programs).

"Using Coupling Metrics for Change Impact Analysis in Object-Oriented Systems" - M.K. Abdi, H. Lounis, and H.A. Sahraoui

The authors start by recalling that maintenance costs are usually much larger than development ones, and as such, systems modifications and their effects should be assessed rigorously. They propose an analytical and experimental approach to evaluate and predict change impacts in object-oriented systems. This approach uses a meta-model based impact calculation technique. They presented the conclusions of an empirical study, upon a real system, in which a correlation hypothesis between coupling and change impact was evaluated, using three machine-learning algorithms. This session ended with a final period for questions. A participant remarked that the authors apparently have only considered one granularity level the class one which was corroborated by Houari. Then, the question was raised on the justification for the absence of other granularity levels. Houari replied that considering other levels like package, subsystem or system will, in the end, imply, in this case, computing coupling values at class level.

2.3   Session 3: Quality Models, Metrics, Detection, Refactoring

"A Maintainability Analysis of the Code Produced by an EJBs Automatic Generator" - I. García, M. Polo, M. Piattini

The paper presents the tool the authors have built for the automatic generation of multilayer web components- based applications to manage databases. The goal is to deal with the problem of the decrease of its quality and maintainability of web applications due to the successive changes on the code and databases. The source code of these applications is automatically generated by the tool, being optimized, corrected and already pre-tested and standardized according to a set of code templates. The paper makes an overview of the code generation process and, then, shows some quantitative analysis related to the obtained code, that are useful to evaluate its maintainability. Someone on the audience asked about the ability of the tool for the detection of the errors of the database. This issue is not considered yet but will be. The authors were also asked about the prediction of the complexity of the program based on the complexity of the database and they answered that this was considered. Also from a question the authors explained that the business logic is considered in the solution.

"Validation of a Standard- and Metric-Based Software Quality Model" - R. Lincke and W. Löwe

This paper describes the layout of a project of the authors. The objective was to validate the automated assessment of the internal quality of software according to the ISO 9126 quality model. In selected real world projects, automatically derived quality metric values shall be compared with expert opinions and information from bug and test databases. As a side effect, the authors create a knowledge base containing precise and reusable definitions of automatically assessable metrics and their mapping to factors and criteria of the ISO quality model. After the exposition, and after a question, the authors explained that the approach was proven on different languages. Also was remarked the fact that the separation of models automated and manual is strange because ones need the others. About the state of the quality model, the authors explained that they were improving it. The authors also clarified that the metrics on their proposal are calculated on the source code. Finally, somen one suggested to the authors that to consider the semantics of the languages when translating programs in different languages the values of the metrics are calculated but perhaps they are capturing wrong information.

"A Proposal of a Probabilistic Framework for Web- Based Applications Quality" - G. Malak, H.A. Sahraoui, L. Badri and M. Badri

In this work, the authors try to introduce into the web-based applications quality some key issues inherent to this field such as causality, uncertainty and subjectivity. They propose a framework for assessing Web-based applications quality by using a probabilistic approach. The approach uses a model including most factors related to the evaluation of Web-based applications quality. A methodology regrouping these factors, integrating and extending various existing works in this field is proposed. A tool supporting the assessment methodology is developed. Some preliminary results are reported to demonstrate the effectiveness of the proposed model. During the discussion the authors explained that they use the uncertainty (that is different to weighting) because the result is not affected even if some errors appear into the probabilities. The authors were asked about some criteria of the proposal that are not automated and the problems derived from this fact. Authors think that there are some aspects on the web that are very difficult to automate. However, the important is not to automate but the time needed to do the calculation. In any case, they assume that if we want to measure a big amount of web sites, the subjective measures must be avoided.

"Investigating Refactoring Impact Through a Wider View of Software" - M. Lopez, N. Habra

On this work, the authors work about refactoring and the fact that the activity of refactoring is practiced by many software developers and when it is applied well, refactoring should improve the maintainability of software. To investigate this assumption, they propose a wider view of the software, which includes the different wellknown artifacts (requirements, design, source code, tests) and their relationships. This wider view helps analyzing the impact of a given refactoring on software quality. In this study, authors analyze the impact of the refactoring Replace Conditional with Polymorphsm by using this wider view of software. And, at the light of this global view of software, it is more difficult to accept that the analyzed refactoring Replace Conditional with Polymorphsm improves well the maintainability of software. Unfortunately the authors were not able to come to the session and there was no discussion.

"Relative Thresholds: Case Study to Incorporate Metrics in the Detection of Bad Smells" - Y. Crespo, C. López, and R. Marticorena

In order to detect flaws, bad smells, etc, quantitative methods: metrics or measures are usually used. It is common in practice to use thresholds setting the correctness of the measures. Most of the current tools use absolute values. Nevertheless, there is a certain concern about threshold applications on obtained values. Current work tries to accomplish case studies about thresholds on several products and different versions. By other side, product domain and size could also affect the results. The authors tackle if it is correct to use absolute vs. relative thresholds, seeing that effects could have in metric collection and bad smell detection. In the questions time the danger of using threshold values as a first step an after made them relative was discussed. The fact that if you use a threshold value wrong for a system, then the relative threshold will be worst, was remarked. So, some suggestion on the use of the use of data for calculating the threshold accompanied by some techniques as fuzzy logic, probability models, etc were suggested although the authors thought that their approach is also correct.

2.4   Session 4: Discussion

In this session five (5) open questions were selected and discussed. This section summarizes the discussions question by question.

1. Is it interesting to conduct empirical studies to prove obvious hypotheses about software quality? The majority of the participants agreed on the following aspects:
   - It is always worth to replicate previous studies that proved a particular hypothesis although replication studies are still not well considered in our community.
   - Studying obvious hypotheses can be a good mean to train students.
   - An obvious hypothesis can be transformed into a less obvious hypothesis if we target a particular context. For example, it seems obvious that design patterns improve the quality of object-oriented programs. However, is it really obvious that they improve a specific quality characteristic like performance?
   - The evaluation of an obvious hypothesis can be interesting is the results of the study are not a simple Yes/No answer. Detailed discussions of the results, treats to validity, etc. can be very valuable.
   - There is a gap between taught skills and required/performed skills in industry. What can seem obvious in academia may be not trivial in an industrial context.
   - In conclusion, proving obvious hypotheses can be interesting if well motivated, discussed and documented.
2. How to deal with threshold values in general and for anomaly detection in particular? The majority of the participants agreed on the following aspects:
   - Threshold values have a relative impact if the goal is not to decide automatically what is good and what is bad but just what is suspicious. Indeed, they can help to order suspected elements to prioritise the workload (for example testing activities).
   - We need to have explicit thresholds to explain analysis results to developers in industrial context, i.e., to have clear criteria. In particular, anti-pattern detection is hard to explain without clearly defined threshold values.

- To determine threshold values, two approaches are used. The first deals with expert knowledge or consensuses (practical approach). The second abstracts threshold values starting from a representative set of data. We need to define representative samples with respect to given sets of particular data, using an adequate sampling technique, when possible.
- In any case, we need to take into account the used technologies, company-wide standards, etc.

3. Generic model and uniform metrics, is it enough/possible? The majority of the participants agreed on the following aspects:
   - It is important to define metrics independently prom the programming language.
   - Achieving independence from programming languages means that any intermediate representation must take into account the operation semantic of each targeted language. In other words, Durant the mapping of a program to the intermediate representation, we must interpret syntactic constructs such as inheritance according to the used lookup algorithm.
   - An additional direction that seems promising is the consideration of domain ontologies to derive metric definitions automatically.
   - Finally, traceability can be also an avenue as it bridges the gap between models and source code.

4. Visualisation: what could be the paradigms to visualise data together? The majority of the participants agreed on the following aspects
   - It is important to go beyond tables andor aggregation of metrics (averages, summations, etc.) to visualize and exploit metrics. Visualization technique must allow displaying metric values for a large set of elements.
   - It is important to find tradeoffs between visualizing little information on large systems and visualizing lot of information on small systems. To this respect, cognitive science and scientific data visualisation are two domains were we can find inspiration.
   - We must find a balance between contextual information that is supposed to be present all the time and elements related to a specific problem that must be in first plan.
   - We have to find the balance also between offering customization capabilities and overriding the users with too many options.
   - Using metaphors is a promising direction for data visualization and navigation.

5. Beyond evaluation, how to provide feedback to improve programs? The majority of the participants agreed on the following aspects:
   - It is important to relate design/code anomalies (e.g., suspicious classes) and opportunities of corrections (e.g., refactorings). This can be done using metric definitions or general software engineering principles.
   - It is also important to consider metric-based quality evaluation as a day-to-day tool rather then a one-shot tool in an evaluation phase. After such an evaluation phase, it is generally too late. The cost of corrections is too high.

3   QAOOSE 2006 Participants

Organizers

Name	Affiliation
Fernando Brito e Abreu	Univ. of Lisbon, Portugal
Coral Calero	Univ. of Castilla, Spain
Yann-Gaël Guéhéneuc	Univ. of Montreal, Canada
Houari Sahraoui	Univ. of Montreal, Canada

Other Participants

Name	Affiliation
Regis Fleurquin	Univ. de Bretagne Sud, France
Carlos Lopez	Univ. Nova de Lisboa, Portugal
Guillaume Langelier	Univ. de Montréal, Canada
Rüdiger Lincke	Växjö Univ., Sweden
Macario Polo	Univ. Castilla-La Mancha, Spain
Haider Bilal	London South Bank Univ., UK
Javier Perez	Univ. de Valladolid, Spain
Gabriela Arevalo	LIRMM - Univ. de Montpellier, France
Thomas Fritz	Univ. of British Columbia, Canada
Jaqueline McQuillan	NUI Maynooth, Ireland
Norbert Pataki	Eötuös Lorand Univ. Budapest, Hungary
Christian Lange	TU Eindhoven, The Netherlands
Raul Marticorena	Univ. of Burgos, Spain
Yann Prieto	Ecole Centrale de Nantes, France
Cédric Bardet	SNCF, France
Naouel Moha	Univ. of Montreal, Canada
Christine Havart	SNCF, France
Olivier Beaurepaire	SNCF, France
Susanne Jucknath	TU Berlin, Germany

Architecture-Centric Evolution: New Issues and Trends

Report on the Workshop ACE at ECOOP'06

Paris Avgeriou[1], Uwe Zdun[2], and Isabelle Borne[3]

[1] Department of Mathematics and Computing Science,
University of Groningen, the Netherlands
paris@cs.rug.nl
[2] Distributed Systems Group,
Vienna University of Technology, Austria
zdun@acm.org
[3] VALORIA Laboratory,
University of South-Brittany, France
Isabelle.Borne@univ-ubs.fr

Abstract. Software evolution has largely been focused on low-level implementation artefacts through refactoring techniques rather than the architectural level. However code-centric evolution techniques have not managed to effectively solve the problems that software evolution entails. Instead a paradigm shift is emerging, where the evolution approaches put software architecture on the spotlight. This shift focuses on effectively documenting and modifying the architectural design decisions during system evolution, while synchronizing them with both the requirements and the implementation. The second workshop on the theme of Architecture-Centric Evolution attempted to explore the issues that such evolution approaches are dealing with, as well as the trends that emerge in this area. The workshop delved into this field, by presenting the latest research advances and by facilitating discussions between experts.

1 Introduction

Industry and academia have reached consensus that investing into the architecture of a system during the early phases of the system's lifecycle is of paramount importance to object-oriented software development. Moreover, there is an undoubted tendency to create an engineering discipline on the field of software architecture if we consider the published textbooks, the international conferences devoted to it, and recognition of architecting software systems as a professional practice. Evidently, there have been advances in the field, especially concerning design and evaluation methods, as well as reusable architectural artefacts such as architectural patterns and frameworks. And there is growing consensus nowadays about certain aspects of the task of software architecture description, such as the satisfaction of stakeholders' concerns through multiple views, and the use of UML for modelling architectures. Software architecture has become a key issue in the object-oriented community, as architecture is praised for facilitating effective communication between the stakeholders of the system, early analysis of the system, support of qualities and successful evolution of the system.

M. Südholt and C. Consel (Eds.): ECOOP 2006, LNCS 4379, pp. 97–105, 2007.

Unfortunately, in practice, the evolution of software systems largely takes place at the code level. For example, a substantial part of industrial practice of software evolution concerns storing code artefacts in configuration management systems and applying refactoring techniques on them. This hinders the development team from having an overview of the "big picture" and grasping the significant design decisions that appear only at a higher level of abstraction [4]. As a result, the new design decisions that are taken during evolution may compromise or even contradict fundamental principles or constraints of the system's architecture. Moreover, the most substantial properties of the system are its non-functional requirements, the so-called "quality attributes", and the evolution of such properties can only be tackled at the level of architecture. In essence, software architecture is good means for facilitating the synchronization of the system requirements, their evolution, and their implementation during evolution cycles of the system [2].

The theme of architecture-centric evolution is complex and multi-faceted, both in its core and in its relevance to other advances of software engineering. Essentially, it involves at least the following topics:

- Modeling architectures to support evolution of software systems
- Using ADLs or UML to model evolution
- Quality attributes and architectural evaluation in evolution
- Meta-modeling of architectural refactoring
- Architecture model transformations
- Evolution through software architecture patterns
- Architectural design decisions and architectural knowledge in evolution
- Evolution of legacy software through its architecture
- Architecture-centric evolution in the context of service-oriented architectures (SOA) or model-driven engineering (MDE)
- Software engineering processes and methods for architecture-centric evolution
- Theoretical aspects of architecture-centric evolution, e.g. causes of architectural changes
- Synchronizing requirements, architecture and code during evolution
- Evolution in product lines and system families
- Case studies of architecture-centric evolution
- Tools that foster architecture-centric evolution

This paper reports on the second workshop in the series of Architecture-Centric Evolution. The first workshop [5] had focused on the following topics: the metaphor of evolution, evolving components and product lines, languages to support evolution, and consistency of artifacts. The second workshop was of a more interactive nature and the discussion was directed towards the practical means to support evolution. The workshop consisted of four sessions, each lasting 1.5 hours. The first session included the presentation of three papers on formal methods, tools and frameworks to support architecture-centric evolution. The second session revolved around quality attributes in the evolution context, as well as the impact of aspects in the architectural design. The third session revolved around the industrial approach to architecture-centric evolution: tools and methods for architecture-centric evolution that are used in a large company were presented. The remaining time of the workshop was used to discuss the various issues and challenges that came out of the presentations and identify trends and challenges.

The rest of this workshop report is organized as follows: Section 2 outlines the contents of the papers that were presented in the workshop, as well as some of the discussion they raised. Section 3 describes the findings of the dialogue triggered by the previous sessions and the conclusions reached by the participants. Finally Section 4 concludes with a brief synopsis of the state-of-the-art and future trends.

2   Issues in Architecture-Centric Evolution

The essence of each paper as well as the key points of the raised discussions are summarized in the sub-sections below. The heading of each sub-section is the title of the corresponding paper. The papers presented during the workshop are available on-line at: *http://www.cs.rug.nl/ paris/ACE2006/*.

2.1   Modelling Software Evolution Using Algebraic Graph Rewriting

Selim Ciraci and Pim van den Broek have worked on an approach to formalize evolution requests with the help of algebraic graph rewriting. They considered UML class and interaction diagrams (especially classes, methods and parameters) as the main source of architectural information and proposed the transformation of these diagrams into colored graphs. Changes in these diagrams represent changes during system evolution, which can then be formalized by algebraic graph rewrite rules.

Ciraci and van den Broek claimed that their approach is language-independent and thus extensible for other kinds of UML diagrams or other Architecture Description Language (ADL) representations. As a natural follow-up question, the speaker was asked whether tool support was possible, given the independence of modeling languages. The answer was positive and the speaker asserted that tool support can be automated at two levels: first by converting models made in the specific modeling language to marked or colored graphs; second by subsequent transformation of the graphs when evolution requests occur (through the push-out mechanism). There is no automated tool support but the authors plan to implement appropriate tooling, firstly for the Unified Modeling Language. At the level of code, refactoring issues can also be tackled by this approach, as long as there is a possible reverse engineering of the code into the appropriate ADL.

2.2   Meta-architecture Tools: The Working Engines of the Company's Architectural Evolution

Ethan Hadar presented an industrial approach on the subject of architectural evolution, based on the paper he co-authored with Irit Hadar. Their perspective comes from a large multinational enterprise, that works with multiple different methodologies, products, product lines, technologies, tools, communities etc. In this context, architecture-centric evolution becomes a rather complex and risky issue. The speaker presented the Meta-Architecture tools constructed within their company and the corresponding method of operations, as well as its challenges and solutions. They focus on Software Architecture

Analysis and mainly work with three types of diagrams: business services, component interfaces and deployment. They pay particular attention to the traceability of the different artifacts produced. The presenter professed a rather radical view of their approach: the project management model follows the waterfall lifecycle model, while their development is rather agile. Furthermore the models produced are mainly aimed for use by managers, while the developers work with the source code.

According to the speaker, an architecture-centric evolution approach is not only a matter of implementing the appropriate methods and tools. Most importantly it is a matter of aligning the practices and goals of the organization with the corresponding line of thought. Another important remark is that in the pragmatic constraints of big corporate software development, research approaches, hypes and fashions are temporary and thus not so important. Their approach is to combine the best of all worlds. For instance they try to combine different concepts taken from the fields of Model Driven Architecture, Aspect-Oriented Programming, Software Architecture, etc., with the ultimate goal to make them work in practice and when needed.

2.3   Architectural Stability and Middleware: An Architecture-Centric Evolution Perspective

Rami Bahsoon presented a paper, co-authored by Wolfgang Emmerich, that focuses on architecture stability: how far a software system can endure changes in requirements, while leaving the architecture of the software system intact. They argue that architectural stability is more threatened by changes in non-functional rather than in functional requirements. They studied in particular architectures that are strongly based on middleware, and put specific emphasis on the non-functional requirements that are important in this area, such as scalability, fault tolerance, etc. The goal is to facilitate their evolution over time. Bahsoon and Emmerich have shown through a case study, how a software architecture, when induced by distinct middleware, differs in coping with changes in these non-functional requirements.

Bahsoon was asked about the relation of their approach to architectural patterns and styles, since they, just as middlewares, determine a great part of the system architecture. The presenter responded that architectural patterns have a large impact on architectural stability and therefore the system evolution. However, which architectural patterns are more stable in face of change, is still an open research question. It would thus be fruitful to conduct impact studies of architectural patterns to the system evolution and perhaps classify the patterns in this respect.

The discussion then revolved around the applicability of their approach with respect to the architectural documentation of middleware. In specific the question was raised whether, there exist documented reference architectures for middleware that can be reused in designing and evaluating the overall software system architecture. According to the speaker's experience, middleware architectures were rarely publicly documented, and the non-functional requirements (quality attributes) are difficult to assess. The only viable way is to study and use the middleware extensively.

The evolution of the middleware itself is not tackled in this approach, even though it apparently has a large impact on the overall system evolution. In principle, one can either treat it as a black box, waiting for the community to evolve it, or continue the development of the middleware with own resources.

2.4 Change Impact Analysis of Crosscutting in Software Architectural Design

Klaas van den Berg presented an approach for impact analysis of crosscutting dependencies in architectural design. According to the presenter, the analysis of the impact of changes in requirements can be based on the traceability of architectural design elements. Especially the crosscutting dependencies between the design elements may have a strong influence on the modifiability of software architectures. The proposed impact analysis is supported by a matrix representation of dependencies.

The presenter argued that crosscutting concerns must be represented at two levels: source and target. Source elements crosscut with respect to their mapping to the target elements. The type of dependencies between source and target are very important in this respect and one must explicitly define them or one must justify why one did not define them. Eventually there are numerous inter-level and intra-level dependencies that can be traced, but not all of them should be traced. Van de Berg stressed the importance to define the goal of traceability: why artifacts need to be traced (e.g. for testing or analysis purposes).

2.5 Using ATAM to Evaluate a Game-Based Architecture

Ahmed BinSubaih presented the next paper co-authored by Steve Maddock. Their research work examines the suitability of employing an off-the-shelf software architecture evaluation method, ATAM, in order to assess systems in the gaming domain. They conducted a case study of a specific game-based architecture, evaluating it for its key drivers. Their findings were encouraging, as the method can clearly reveal the strengths and weaknesses of the architecture, which can then be guarded and addressed respectively before evolving the architecture further. In addition they proposed a small extension to the method: a view that consolidates disparate outputs generated by ATAM.

The discussion that followed concerned the issue of traceability, and in particular that of the architectural decisions. The application of ATAM produced backwards traceability of the decisions to the requirements. However, the presenter agreed with the participants that architectural decisions should also be traced forward to the architectural models, to facilitate successful evolution.

2.6 Safe Integration of New Concerns in a Software Architecture: Overview of the Implementation

Olivier Barais presented a paper co-authored by Hanh-Missi Tran, Anne-Francoise Le Meur, and Laurence Duchien. This research concerned a framework for integrating new concerns into a software architecture, by factorizing the implementation of concerns into separate units, called 'patterns'. Their approach describes a rule language, that prevents erroneous concern integrations from being expressed, detects others by static verifications and identifies compatible join points between a 'pattern' and a basis architecture.

The presenter claimed that reusing components depends on a number of factors: making explicit all the dependencies of a component; separating the concerns in the software architecture; modularizing concerns in the form of aspects; applying an iterative integration process. The workshop participants discussed the notion of architectural mismatches caused by the assumptions made when integrating new components. The presenter argued that this approach provides a solution by making the assumptions explicit through both a static and a behavioral model, plus the necessary transformation rules. The presenter noted that the shortcoming of the approach is the focus on static analysis, since the mismatches cannot be explicitly documented and then tested at run-time.

The participants argued that the proposed approach has a shortcoming in the industrial context: one cannot really stop the development and freeze the code before a new component or aspect can be integrated. First, because there are many changes coming from different places that need to be accommodated simultaneously. Second, because not all 'patterns' and not all changes can be found and automatically accommodated; there needs to be some extent of manual intervention. The industrial point of view in such cases is to avoid automating everything; instead to allow for as much flexibility as possible.

This approach raises the process issues of architecture-centric evolution. The technical solutions need to be aligned to the pragmatic constraints, as they occur for instance in the industry. The importance of making the architectural knowledge explicit and sharing it with the stakeholders comes out as a necessity.

2.7   A Generic Framework for Integrating New Functionalities into Software Architectures

Guillaume Waignier presented a paper co-authored by Anne-Francoise Le Meur and Laurence Duchien, that was closely related to the previous presentation. The presentation concerned the evolution of software through a generic framework for automatically integrating new functionalities into an architecture description. In contrast to the previous presentation that was bound to a specific Architecture Description Language (ADL), this approach is ADL-independent. The research group conducted a domain analysis on ADLs and came up with a generic ADL model to manipulate and reason about architectural elements involved in integration. Their approach is complemented by high-level abstractions to describe different kinds of integration, as well as a generic integration engine.

The presenter stressed the added value of this approach: the focus on integration issues, when defining the common metamodel of Architecture Description Languages. The workshop participants noticed the lack of explicit Quality Attributes in the metamodel. The presenter explained that quality attributes can be dealt with in the traditional way: by combining their approach with an architecture evaluation method, such as ATAM. The proposed approach can however provide hints about a specific quality attribute: consistency of the architecture. Consistency can be automatically checked and furthermore it be associated to architectural tactics and patterns.

Finally, the participants discussed the issue of runtime reconfiguration with specific focus on integrating the components of the 'pattern' during runtime. This issue could also be dealt with in this approach, as long as the sequence of modifications is strictly kept.

3   Discussion and Outcomes

The last part of the workshop was a discussion session, in which we summarized the participants' insights into architecture-centric evolution gained from the presentations and discussions, and elaborated on the different concerns that arose.

First the workshop members agreed on the importance of tools on architecture-centric evolution. In fact, the different approaches seemed to have commonalities in the tools that support them. We can extract some useful conclusions by examining closer what exactly the different tools support and what kind of target users they are aimed at.

A recurring topic during the workshop was the gap between the industry and academia. It is a rather typical software engineering phenomenon: the distance between the researchers who propose novel methods and tools and the potential adopters in the industry is substantial. The academic approach on architecture-centric evolution is mostly theoretical and considers the processes and the models that need to be formalized to result in automatic or semi-automatic tools to help the developers. In the industry, economical and timing issues are crucial and consequently the area of software architecture and evolution is viewed from a pragmatic perspective.

Another significant parameter that was discussed is that of human behavior, e.g. communication issues between different stakeholders, the way architects take decisions etc. Just like any field of software engineering, the human aspect must be taken under consideration when dealing with architecture-centric evolution.

The workshop focused mostly on technological issues and approaches, but also there are important process issues and organization issues. It is quite common that these two worlds, technology and organization, are studied separately. To overcome this problem, the idea was discussed to apply something analogous to the architecture-business cycle [1] in order to bridge the gap between technology and process/organization. The result would be a paradigm that makes explicit the influence of one to another and vice versa in an iterative cycle.

During the workshop, some approaches were presented on automating the evolutionary mechanisms, e.g. the integration of aspects on an entire software architecture all at once. Integration concerns various kinds of elements, mainly components and objects, according to different techniques (e.g. marked graphs, separation of concerns). The participants agreed that we should not over-automate but rather allow for some flexibility in order to incorporate more human intervention and manual work into the processes. Architects and designers should be able to take decisions when appropriate. We should strike a balance between automation and manual work.

Another issue that is considered a 'hot' research topic, dynamic evolution, and particularly dynamic reconfiguration, is necessary and urgent for modern software development. However the workshop members were skeptical about how to implement such a mechanism due to unsolved problems, e.g. monitoring the run-time system, quality of service evaluation, etc. This is a crucial topic in cases where the system needs to evolve without being shut down, but indeed, its implementation is still problematic.

The workshop participants pondered over the meaning of architecture-centric evolution and how to achieve it. A simplistic but perhaps naive opinion that has been proposed in the past, is merely to synchronize architectural documentation when the software product is evolved. This can be achieved either by documenting the decisions taken by the developers, or after the fact, through reverse-engineering. However, this leads to code-centric rather than architecture-centric evolution. Updating the architecture document in this case is a side-effect of changing the code. Architecture is not in the center but is a by-product, a documentation outcome. A paradigm shift is necessary in order to move away from this code-centric approach and strive towards a real architecture-centric one. In architecture-centric evolution, the role of architecture is central to facilitating evolution. It is the starting point of incorporating changes and all other artifacts should follow. There are two trends towards this goal, that were identified during the presentations but also during the plenary discussion: the importance of traceability, and the emergence of the aspect-oriented paradigm.

First, the lack of effective traceability, was a recurring problem identified that currently hinders architecture-centric evolution. Traceability can be defined as "the degree to which a relationship can be established between two or more products of the development process, especially products having a predecessor-successor or master-subordinate relationship to one another" [3]. In the case of architecture-centric evolution, traceability is key in synchronizing the requirements specification, the architecture description, and the code. These three types of artifacts need to be traced backward and forward in order to keep them synchronized when one of them changes. This issue was also largely discussed in the first ACE workshop [5], where the consistency of artifacts between evolution was deemed of paramount importance. It is common place that traceability methods still need to be developed before they can successfully support Architecture-Centric Evolution.

Second, the role of *aspects* as a means to better manage evolution was largely discussed during the workshop. The rationale is that when we try to incorporate new requirements or concerns, these may be crosscutting in the architecture and need to be implemented horizontally. On the one hand, we must integrate them into the architecture by the means of a weaver. On the other hand, architectural artifacts must be connected (i.e. traceable) to other levels (e.g. to requirements and to the implementation), as well as to evolution versions and we can define crosscutting dependencies between the architectural artifacts. It is, however, not necessary that roundtrip traceability is supported.

4   Epilogue

The second workshop on the theme of Architecture-Centric Evolution (ACE 2006) hosted interesting presentations and discussions. The authors of the papers mainly focused on specific techniques and approaches from a technical point of view. We can claim that there are good practical and research solutions for particular technical problems. However, architecture-centric evolution is still quite preliminary and there are numerous open research issues that must be addressed. Specific issues that recurrently came up during the presentations and discussions were: how to connect architectural evolution and quality attributes; how to bridge the gap between research and practice; what is the role of aspects in architectural evolution; how to include organizational aspects and keep consensus between all stakeholders of a system. Even though architecture-centric evolution is still a young approach, there was consent among the participants that the approach is gaining importance both in research and practice. This is also apparent by the number of research projects, scientific papers, technical reports and tools that appear in this multi-faceted area.

References

1. L. Bass, P. Clements, and R. Kazman. *Software Architecture in Practice 2nd Edition*. Addison Wesley, Reading, MA, USA, 2003.
2. P. Clements, F. Bachmann, L. Bass, D. Garlan, J. Ivers, R. Little, R. Nord, and J. Stafford. *Documenting Software Architectures: Views and Beyond*. Addison-Wesley, 2002.
3. Institute of Electrical and Electronics Engineers. *A Compilation of IEEE standard Computer Glossaries*. IEEE, New York, NY, USA, 1990.
4. A. G. J. Jansen, J. van der Ven, P. Avgeriou, and D. K. Hammer. Tool support for architectural decisions. In *6th IEEE/IFIP Working Conference on Software Architecture (WICSA)*, Mumbai, India, January 2007.
5. U. Zdun and P. Avgeriou. Architecture-centric evolution. In *ECOOP 2005 Workshop Reader*, LNCS. Springer, 2006.

Appendix: Acknowledgement

We extend our thanks to all those who have participated in the organization of this workshop, particularly to the program committee, which is comprised of:

- Goedicke Michael, University of Essen, Germany
- Yann-Gael Gueheneuc, University of Montreal, Canada
- Guelfi Nicolas, University of Luxembourg, Luxembourg
- Dieter Hammer, University of Groningen, the Netherlands
- Heckel Reiko, University of Leicester, UK
- Laemmel Ralf, Microsoft Corporation, USA
- Oberleitner Joe, Technical University of Vienna, Austria
- Nicolas Revault, University of Cergy Pontoise, France
- Wermelinger Michel, Open University, UK

Component-Oriented Programming
Report on the WS WCOP at ECOOP'06

Wolfgang Weck[1], Ralf Reussner[2], and Clemens Szyperski[3]

[1] Independent Software Architect, Zürich, Switzerland
http://www.wolfgang-weck.ch
[2] University of Karlsruhe, Am Fasanengarten 5, D-76128 Karlsruhe, Germany
http://sdq.ipd.uka.de
[3] Microsoft, USA
http://research.microsoft.com/~cszypers

Abstract. This report covers the eleventh Workshop on Component-Oriented Programming (WCOP). WCOP has been affiliated with ECOOP since its inception in 1996. The report summarizes the contributions made by authors of accepted position papers as well as those made by all attendees of the workshop sessions.

1 Introduction

WCOP 2006, held in conjunction with ECOOP 2006 in Nantes, France, was the eleventh workshop in the successful series of workshops on component-oriented programming. The previous workshops were held in conjunction with earlier ECOOP conferences in Linz, Austria; Jyväskylä, Finland; Brussels, Belgium; Lisbon, Portugal; Sophia Antipolis, France; Budapest, Hungary; Málaga, Spain; Darmstadt, Germany, and Oslo Norway, and Glasgow, Scotland.

The first workshop, in 1996, focused on the principal idea of software components and worked towards definitions of terms. In particular, a high-level definition of what a software component is was formulated. WCOP97 concentrated on compositional aspects, architecture and gluing, substitutability, interface evolution and non-functional requirements. In 1998, the workshop addressed industrial practice and developed a major focus on the issues of adaptation. The next year, the workshop moved on to address issues of structured software architecture and component frameworks, especially in the context of large systems. WCOP 2000 focused on component composition, validation and refinement and the use of component technology in the software industry. The year after, containers, dynamic reconfiguration, conformance and quality attributes were the main focus. WCOP 2002 had an explicit focus on dynamic reconfiguration of component systems, that is, the overlap between COP and dynamic architectures. 2003, the workshop addressed predictable assembly, model-driven architecture and separation of concerns. The 2004 instance of the workshop focused on various technical issues and also on issues of industrialization of component-orientation. WCOP 2005 revolved around different aspects of trustworthiness with component-oriented programming. Considered were analyzing, asserting,

M. Südholt and C. Consel (Eds.): ECOOP 2006, LNCS 4379, pp. 106–116, 2007.

and verifying functional and non-functional properties of individual components as well as of assembled systems.

A central theme of WCOP 2006 was the composition and deployment of components, including component selection and adaption. A minor focus was the relation between components and aspects, that is between COP and AOP.

WCOP 2006 had been announced as follows:

> WCOP 2006 seeks position papers on the important field of component-oriented programming (COP). WCOP 2006 is the eleventh event in a series of highly successful workshops, which took place in conjunction with every ECOOP since 1996.

> COP has been described as the natural extension of object-oriented programming to the realm of independently extensible systems. Several important approaches have emerged over the recent years, including component technology standards, such as CORBA/CCM, COM/COM+, J2EE/EJB, and most recently .NET, but also the increasing appreciation of software architecture for component-based systems, and the consequent effects on organizational processes and structures as well as the software development business as a whole.

> COP aims at producing software components for a component market and for late composition. Composers are third parties, possibly the end users, who are not able or willing to change components. This requires standards to allow independently created components to interoperate, and specifications that put the composer into the position to decide what can be composed under which conditions. On these grounds, WCOP'96 led to the following definition:

>> A component is a unit of composition with contractually specified interfaces and explicit context dependencies only. Components can be deployed independently and are subject to composition by third parties.

> After WCOP'96 focused on the fundamental terminology of COP, the subsequent workshops expanded into the many related facets of component software.

> WCOP 2006 will emphasize reasons for using components beyond re-use. While consider software components a technical means to increase software re-use, other reasons for investing into component technology tend to be overseen. For example, components play an important role in framework and product-lines to enable configurability (even if no component is re-used).

> Another role of components beyond re-use is to use components to increase the predictability of the properties of a system. The use of components as contractually specified building blocks of software restricts the degrees of freedom during software development compared to classic line-by-line programming. However, this restriction is beneficial for the predictability of system properties. For an engineering approach to

software design, it is important to understand the implications of design decisions on the system's properties. Therefore, approaches to evaluate and predict properties of systems by analyzing its components and its architecture are of high interest.

To strengthen the relation between architectural descriptions of systems and components, a comprehensible mapping to component-oriented middleware platforms is important. Model-driven development, with its use of generators, can provide a suitable link between architectural views and technical component execution platforms.

Finally, in addition to submissions addressing the themes, we explicitly solicit papers reporting on experience with component-oriented software systems in practice, where the emphasis is on interesting lessons learned, whether the actual project was a success or a failure.

Submitted papers circled around composition mechanisms and infrastructure, reaching from AOP to scripting to adaptation and quality assurance.

Thirteen papers by authors were accepted for presentation at the workshop and publication in the workshop proceedings. Twenty participants from around the world participated in the workshop. The workshop was organized into three morning sessions with presentations, one afternoon breakout session with three focus groups, and one final afternoon session gathering reports from the breakout session and discussing future directions.

2   Presentations

This section summarizes briefly the contributions of the thirteen presenters, as grouped into three sessions, i.e. aspects and COP, component adaptation, and component composition and deployment. The full papers of all presentations mentioned below are collected on the workshops web-page[1] and in the WCOP proceedings (Technical Report No 2006-11 of the Faculty of Informatics of the University of Karlsruhe[2]).

2.1   Aspects and COP

This first session was concerned with the relation between component-oriented programming and aspect-oriented programming. Maarten Bynens presented in his talk "On the Benefits of using Aspect Technology in Component-Oriented Architectures" an approach, co-authored by Wouter Joosen, to include aspects into components, and as an alternative to include aspects into connectors. The pros and cons of both approaches were further discussed, while the relation to existing concepts like configurable containers have to be further explored.

The approach of Nicolas Pessemier, Lionel Seinturier, Laurence Duchien and Thierry Coupaye presented in the talk "A Safe Aspect-oriented Programming Support for Component-Oriented Programming" uses aspects to control the

---

[1] http://research.microsoft.com/~cszypers/events/WCOP2006

[2] http://www.ubka.uni-karlsruhe.de/cgi-bin/psview?document=ira/2006/11

openness of components. During the discussion the close relationship to controller/facet interfaces of the Fractal component model was realised. In addition, the unfinished concept of internal join points was discussed, as well as the question when to deploy aspects. It was stated, that aspects have to play the role of a additional component to be deployed with(in) the component being configured.

The talk of Romain Rouvoy on "Leveraging Component-Oriented Programming with Attribute-Oriented Programming" motivated the work of him and his co-workers by the overhead of component-oriented technology, such as requiring several different files for configuring and deploying the component. In the proposed approach, attributes for specifying deployment parameters are included as annotations in the component's code. During the discussion, the approach was seen closer to model-driven approaches than to aspect-orientation. Whether the flexibility of adding arbitrary attributes is actually needed remained open. However, a dependency on the used generator is created and has to be taken into account when re-using components in different contexts.

2.2   Component Adaptation

In this session different approaches to component adaptation were presented.

Jürgen Wolff von Gudenberg presented in his talk "Automated Component Bridge Generator" joint work with Dominik Glaser and Gregor Fischer on a generator to create adapters for COM components. These adapters are used to call COM components from Java. The generator is included in an Eclipse environment. Preliminary tests may indicate that the performance of the bridges generated by model-driven techniques is faster than some currently available commercial solutions of this problem. The automated adapter generation works, as the adapters focus on a very specific class of technical interoperability problems and all information to generate the adapter is contained in the signature given by the interface of the COM component.

The approach of Inès Mouakher, Arnaud Lanoix and Jeanine Souquières, presented by the first author in her talk "Component Adaptation: Specification and Verification" took a different way to component adaptation. In the approach of her and her co-authors, component interfaces are specified in B and the adapter generator also needs a specification on the adapter as input in addition to the interfaces. The benefit is that adapters can also bridge semantic interoperability problems, although a precise characterisation of the bridgeable interoperability problems remains open.

The talk "Profitability-oriented Component Specialisation" by Ping Zhu presented joined work with Siau Cheng Khoo on a specific form of adaptation, namely the specialisation of components depending on their usage context. This specialisation is meant to resolve the antagonism between a component's genericity and efficiency, given a cost-function to optimise for. In the discussion the relation to partial evaluation was raised, as well as the use of component profiling information for specialisation.

2.3   Component Composition and Deployment

The third session was opened by Steffen Becker presenting joint work with Jens Happe and Heiko Koziolek. Their proposal was to explicitly model the relevant context to enable QoS prediction. It was observed that the QoS of a deployed component depends next to its actual implementation on three context parameters: the environment (hardware, distribution, etc.), the QoS of connected services that are used, and the usage profile. To allow such context parameters to become part of QoS analysis, with the component one needs to provide a description that can be parameterized accordingly - an extension of parametric contracts. From the parameter attributes, which must be specified for each actual context, other attributes can be computed. The paper provides a list of some attributes of each kind. The authors were asked, whether they use a specific language to specify the attributes. Currently, a a DSL is used to describe the component model at higher level. Model characteristics are then incrementally refined, as prediction experiments show misprediction patterns.

Next, Francisco Domínguez-Mateos presented joint work with Raquel Hijón-Neira about using architecture to solve heterogeneous interoperation problems with middleware, such as CORBA, DCOM, WebServices, Java, .Net. At the solution's core is a bidirectional mapping to a common type system (bus) based on a common abstract machine model, which is extended towards the individual middleware standards. Using wrappers, objects and services from each platform are represented in others as if they would exist there. Each such connection needs exactly two indirections in form of proxies - one mapping from the source environment to the own abstract machine and one mapping from there to the target environment. The respective proxy code is generated either from reflection or from IDL. From the audience, questions arose, whether a new platform is needed, beyond .Net CLR or CORBA. The answer was, that the new platform also allows to connect non-CLR platforms and that it has a focus on full reflection incl. runtime modification.

The talk "Automated Deployment of Component Architectures with Versioned Components" by Leonel Gayard was on a generator-based approach to generate code to instantiate and deploy components taking their versioning into account. Instead of hardwiring component instantiation in component code or deployment scripts, the proposed tool "CosmosLoader" loads components from a repository, instantiates and connects them at run-time. The stronger integration with component repositories is considered as future work. After the talk, the relation to OSGi was discussed which also contains support for connectivity, versioning and instantiation, but not for architectural views.

The work of Sérgio Lopes, Adriano Tavares, João Monteiro and Carlos Silva was presented by the first author. In his talk on "Describing the static structure of frameworks" a approach of promoting interfaces with UML annotations was introduced. This word is motivated by observed difficulties of framework reuse due to the complexity caused by the usuall yrequired flexibility of frameworks and the reverse of control-flow. The approach introduces so-called black-box variation points and call-points. Therefore a novel UML profile "UML-FD" is introduced. During the discussion the general applicability of the approach was elaborated. In principle, it could be used by any framework provider, who is willing to extend the documentation of variation point in terms of the new profile.

The presentation of Sean McDirmid was canceled due to certain technical problems with the projector and the author's relaxedness on that. Anyhow, his paper describes SuperGlue, a promising language and visual tool to compose components. SuperGlue is declarative and contains signals and rules which can abstract over time and space. The approach looks promising while its relation to coordination languages (e.g., work by Nierstrasz) remains open. The benefit compared to scripting languages is SuperGlue's declerative nature. The limitations imposed by the Java interface model on the "richness" of connectors remain open.

Markus Reitz used a poster to demonstrate his work on "Active Documents". These are meant to support end users to perform component composition. The motivation is to use component technology to create user-configurable and personalisable software. One specific feature of Active Documents is the ability to express structural and semantic constraints on the entities to be composed. By that, it goes beyond visual programming environments or OLE-technology. During the discussion, the role of domain specific composition operators for constraining component composition were elaborated.

Emmanual Renaux presented "A component-based method for enterprise application design". This joined work with Eric Lefebvre is motivated by a lack of consistency between different partitions in classical engineering. The traceability between various models (for analysis, design or deployment) is rarely defined or maintained. A global view on links between such models often lacks, as different stakeholders contribute to different models and often communicate outside the channels defined by a normative workflow. The proposed model-driven approach includes a meta-model with OCL rules and asks for the identification of components in early stages of development, although reuse of existing components may be hindered by this.

3   Break-Out Sessions

In the afternoon the workshop participants were organized in break-out sessions addressing three specific topics, aspects and components, component adaptation and component deployment.

Each group had a nominated scribe who, as named in the subsection titles below, took notes which were used by the authors to write the session summaries.

3.1   Aspects and Components (Wolff von Gudenberg)

This break out group is motivated by the papers in the first morning session and is concerned about the relation between aspects and components. First, aspects were described as cross-cutting concerns which strongly relate to non-functional properties. Technically they are realised by pointcuts and advices, i.e., as a modification of behaviour. By this, aspect orientated programming (AOP) is closely related to the areas of meta-programming, code-injection and rule-based dispatch. Therefore, the specific contribution of AOP is to be discussed. For certain challenges, aspect orientation is thought to be the right approach, such as logging, authentification and the creation of product families.

Now, looking to aspects from a component-perspective, asks for the definition of specific terms, such as "aspect connector", "aspect context" and "aspect functionality". Regarding the use of aspects for a component oriented system, aspects can connect components and aspects can, of course, modify components. It was seen, that aspects lead to a tighter coupling of components. However, aspects are only one possible realisation of a connector. Other options include interfaces and procedure calls or rule-based dispatching. It was concluded by th members of this break out group, that the addition of aspects as a way to realise connectors is beneficial for the component community.

The following discussion of these results from the break out groups within all participants of the workshop was concerned with two topics:

The open problems of AOP: Despite the efforts of the AOP community for the past ten years, crucial problems remain open. In particular, the claim that software maintenance gets simpler by the factorisation of code into several aspects has not been validated. In fact, the concurrent maintenance of several aspects requires that the software developer is able to foresee the consequences of an aspect-local change to the overall system behaviours. Given the difficulty of this task, the hypothesis (opposite to the original claim) that AOP hinders maintenance of large software systems seems also quite natural. Besides, it remains unclear, whether the flexibility of AOP is really needed. It should be investigated whether a limited and fixed set of aspects and pointcuts is sufficient for a domain.

The current use of AOP in component systems: In enterprise systems, some aspects have been clearly identified, including transactionality, authentification, logging, persistency. In Enterprise Java Beans (EJB), containers exist as an execution environment for components. These containers can be configured with the above mentioned aspects. Some EJB applictaion servers, such as JBoss even allow user defined aspects to configure the container. It remains open, whether the current research on the relation between aspects and components really goes beyond these existing possibilities and whether a higher flexibility (i.e., arbitrary pointcuts) is really useful in practice.

3.2   Context Agility (Steffen Becker)

This breakout group was concerned with a component's context and its dynamic change. First of all, it was suggested to distinguish between design-time contexts and run-time contexts of a component. Design time contexts specify all influencing factors of a component which are defined at design-time. This includes the connection of components to other components, the deployment to resources, and the usage profile. Run-time contexts includes exactly the above, but in it can change now during run-time, as in dynamic architectures or agent systems. Therefore, a strong relation to context aware computing exists and the context includes now location and user awareness. Context changes are caused by run-time triggers (or activators) which also have to be defined within the context.

A result from the sequel discussion is that the context model always depends on the results of compositional reasoning. However, current commonly accepted context models for software components are lacking. One was wondering whether this absence of common context models is due to a strong platform dependency. It was concluded, that the various differing component concepts mainly hinder a shared context model, as the context model naturally strongly depends on the component model itself. It was agreed that for reasoning, component models must be parameterised on context properties and that parametric contracts are an example of this parametric component models.

3.3 Software Architectures and Connectors (Leonel Gayard, Jens Happe)

The definition of connectors strongly depends on the application domain. Especially the embedded system and business application domains seem to have different views on connectors. In embedded systems, connectors are often regarded as first class entities as they have to be mapped to physical entities, such as hardware buses. For business applications that use a middleware platform, like J2EE or .Net, connectors rarely provide their own functionality. Usually, the application server handles things like distributed service calls and security issues. Therefore, it is unclear whether connectors necessarily must be considered as first class entities in this domain.

The information that is required to specify the complete functionality of a connector depends on the type level at which the system is modeled. Cheesman and Daniels (UML Components) distinguish four levels at which a component can exist: Component specification - At this level only a description of the component exists that specifies its provided functionality and its requirements. For example, the description of the functionality to create slides (like OpenOffice Impress or Power Point) can be regarded as a component specification. Component implementation - At this level a component is implemented according to a given specification, e.g. Power Point 2003 and OpenOffice can be regarded as implementations of the same specification. Deployed component - That is a component which has been installed and configured for a actual machine. For example your installation of Power Point is a deployed component. Executing component - A component that is executed on an actual machine. For example, if you start Power Point you get an executing component. Note that the relation between two levels is always one to many. For one specification there can be many implementations, for one implementation there can be many deployed components and so on.

Only on the lowest level (deployed component), it is possible to know the complete functionality of a connector. The information about the component allocation is required to decide whether a connector needs to support remote procedure calls, security, or anything else to handle distribution. This strong dependency on the component allocation does imply that connectors cannot be considered as first class entities.

However, in embedded systems hardware and software co-design is a common practice. So, each component-based system has exactly one execution environment and deployment. Connectors that enable component communication need to be implemented in hardware. In this case, connectors can be regarded as first class entities, because they exist independently as hardware. However, this hardware can likewise also be regarded as component.

This confusing results of the break out group on the role of connectors lead to a small role play on the arguments for and against connectors as a first class entites. (Where Clemens argued against connectors as a first class entity, while Ralf – of course only pretending – argued for connectors as a first class entity.

Connectors are first class entities, because	– they are not, because

- connectors can be complex
- support of "rich reasoning"
  (e.g., data flow analysis for QoS)
- components compute,
  connectors mediate,
  hence they are different
- of clearity
	- what connects the connector
	  and the component?
	- interaction is fixed by
	  component anyway.
	- if interaction is an entity by
	  its own mean (composable, reusable)
	  it should be modelled as a component

4   Final Words

We, the organizers, look back on a more than ten years' series of very successful workshops on component-oriented programming. It is good to see, how over the years the range of topics constantly evolves, while the increasing importance of the aspects trust, quality attributes, architecture, and industrial engineering is well recognized. The field of component orientation is now well connected to many other research areas, such as prediction of extra-functional properties, software architecture modeling and even aspect orientation. We have traveled a long way from the first WCOP in 1996 in Linz and look forward to the continuing journey.

With respect to WCOP 2006, we would like to thank all participants and contributors. In particular, we would like to thank the scribes of the break-out groups.

5 Accepted Papers

The full papers of all presentations are collected on the workshops web-page[3] and in the WCOP proceedings (Technical Report No 2006-11 of the Faculty of Informatics of the University of Karlsruhe[4]).

The following list of accepted and presented papers is sorted by the order of the presentation.

1. Maarten Bynens, Wouter Joosen (KU Leuven, Belgium). *On the Benefits of using Aspect Technology in Component-Oriented Architectures*

2. Nicolas Pessemier, Lionel Seinturier, Laurence Duchien (INRIA/LIFL), Thierry Coupaye (France Telecom R&D, France) *A Safe Aspect-Oriented Programming Support for Component-Oriented Programming*

3. Romain Rouvoy (Jacquard Project - INRIA Futurs LIFL, France) *Leveraging Component-Oriented Programming with Attribute-Oriented Programming*

4. Dominik Glaser, Gregor Fischer, Jürgen Wolff von Gudenberg (University of Würzburg, Germany) *Automated Component Bridge Generator*

5. Inès Mouakher, Arnaud Lanoix, Jeanine Souquières (LORIA - CNRS - Université Nancy 2, France) *Component Adaptation: Specification and Verification*

6. Ping Zhu, Siau Cheng Khoo (National University of Singapore, Singapore) *Profitability-oriented Component Specialization*

7. Steffen Becker (University of Karlsruhe, Germany), Jens Happe, Heiko Koziolek (University of Oldenburg, Germany) *Putting Components into Context – Supporting QoS-Predictions with an explicit Context Model*

8. Francisco Domínguez-Mateos, Raquel Hijón-Neira (University Rey Juan Carlos, Spain) *An Architectural Component-Based model to solve the Heterogeneous Interoperability of Component-Oriented Middleware Platforms*

9. Leonel Aguilar Gayard, Paulo Astério de Castro Guerra, Ana Elisa de Campos Lobo, Cecília Mary Fischer Rubira (UNICAMP, Brazil) *Automated Deployment of Component Architectures with Versioned Components*

10. Sérgio Lopes, Adriano Tavares, João Monteiro and Carlos Silva (University of Minho, Portugal) *Describing Framework Static Structure: promoting interfaces with UML annotations*

11. Sean McDirmid (EPFL, Switzerland) *Interactive Component Assembly with SuperGlue*

12. Markus Reitz (University of Kaiserslautern, Germany) *Active Documents – Taking advantage of component-orientation beyond pure reuse*

13. Emmanuel Renaux (University of Lille, France) Eric Lefebvre (École de Technologie Supérieure Montréal, Canada) *Component based method for enterprise application design*

---

[3] http://research.microsoft.com/~cszypers/events/WCOP2006
[4] http://www.ubka.uni-karlsruhe.de/cgi-bin/psview?document=ira/2006/11

List of Participants

Name	Affiliation, Country
Steffen Becker	Universität Karlsruhe (TH), Germany
Maarten Bynens	K.U. Leuven, Belgium
Francisco Domínguez-Mateos	Universidad Rey Juan Carlos, Spain
Leonel Gayard	JC Unicamp, Brazil
Jürgen Wolff von Gudenberg	Universität Würzburg, Germany
Jens Happe	Universität Oldenburg, Germany
Heiko Koziolek	Universität Oldenburg, Germany
Sérgio Lopes	University of Minho, Portugal
Sean McDirmid	EPFL, Switzerland
Lior Meister	RAFAEL, Israel
Inès Mouakher	LORIA / Université Nancy 2, France
Nicolas Pessemier	INRIA / LIFL, France
Markus Reitz	Universität Kaiserslautern, Germany
Emmanuel Renaux	University of Lille, France
Ralf Reussner	Universität Karlsruhe (TH), Germany
Romain Rouvoy	INRIA Futurs LIFL, France
Dietmar Schreiner	TU Wien, Austria
Clemens Szyperski	Microsoft, USA
Wolfgang Weck	Indep. Software Architect, Zurich, Switzerland
Ping Zhu	National University of Singapore, Singapore

Fractal Component-Based Software Engineering
Report on the WS Fractal at ECOOP'06

Thierry Coupaye[1] and Jean-Bernard Stefani[2]

[1] France Telecom R&D
thierry.coupaye@orange-ftgroup.com
[2] INRIA
Jean-Bernard.Stefani@inrialpes.fr

Abstract. This article is a report on the 5th international workshop devoted to the Fractal component model that took place the 4th of July 2006 in Nantes, France, as an ECOOP workshop. Prior to that, the article provides some background on the Fractal project and previous Fractal workshops for readers who are not familiar with Fractal.

1 Introduction

We are witnessing a tremendous expansion in the use of software in scientific research, industry, administration and more and more in every day life. With the advent of the Internet and more globally the convergence between telecommunications and computing, software has become omnipresent, critical, complex. Time-to-market of services, which rely on system engineering (operating systems, distributed systems, middleware), is becoming a strategic factor in a competitive market in which operation (deployment, administration) costs are much higher than development costs.

In this context, component-based software architectures have naturally emerged as a central focus and reached momentum in different fields of computing because Component-Based Software Engineering (CBSE) is generally recognized as one of the best way to develop, deploy and administrate increasingly complex software with good properties in terms of flexibility, reliability, scalability[1] - not to mention lower development cost and faster time-to-market through software reuse and programmers productivity improvements.

Fractal is an advanced component model and associated on-growing programming and management support devised initially by France Telecom and INRIA since 2001. Most developments are framed by the Fractal project inside the ObjectWeb open source middleware consortium. The Fractal project targets the development of a reflective component technology for the construction of highly adaptable and reconfigurable distributed systems.

---

[1] As stated in the conclusions of the 7th International Symposium on CBSE (Edinburgh, Scotland, 2004): "Components are a way to impose design constraints that as structural invariants yields some useful properties".

M. Südholt and C. Consel (Eds.): ECOOP 2006, LNCS 4379, pp. 117–129, 2007.
© Springer-Verlag Berlin Heidelberg 2007

2   The Fractal Ecosystem

2.1   Component Model

The Fractal component model relies on some classical concepts in CBSE: *components* are runtime entities that conforms to the model, *interfaces* are the only interaction points between components that express dependencies between components in terms of *required/client* and *provided/server* interfaces, *bindings* are communication channels between component interfaces that can be primitive, i.e. local to an address space or composite, i.e. made of components and bindings for distribution or security purposes.

Fractal also exhibits more original concepts. A component is the composition of a *membrane* and a *content*. The membrane exercices an *arbitrary reflexive control* over its content (including interception of messages, modification of message parameters, etc.). A membrane is composed of a set of *controllers* that may or may not export control interfaces accessible from outside the considered component. The model is *recursive (hierarchical) with sharing* at arbitrary levels. The recursion stops with base components that have an empty content. Base components encapsulate entities in an underlying programming language. A component can be shared by multiple enclosing components. Finally, the model is programming *language independent* and *open*: everything is optional and extensible[2] in the model, which only defines some "standard" API for controlling bindings between components, the hierarchical structure of a component system or the components life-cycle (creation, start, stop, etc).

The Fractal component model enforces a limited number of very structuring architectural principles. Components are runtime entities conformant to a model and do have to exist at runtime per se for management purposes. There is a clear separation between interfaces and implementations which allow for transparent modifications of implementations without changing the structure of the system. Bindings are programmatically controllable: bindings/dependencies are not "hidden in code" but systematically externalized so as to be manipulated by (external) programs. Fractal systems exhibits a recursive structure with composite components that can overlap, which naturally enforces encapsulation and easily models resource sharing. Components exercise arbitrary reflexive control over their content: each component is a management domain of its own. Altogether, these principles make Fractal systems self-similar (hence the name of the model): architecture is expressed homogeneously at arbitrary level of abstraction in terms of bindings an reflexive containment relationships.

2.2   Implementations

There exist currently 8 implementations (platforms)[3] providing support for Fractal components programming in 8 programming languages:

---

[2] This openness leads to the need for conformance levels and conformance test suites so as to compare distinct implementations of the model.

[3] Julia, AOKell, ProActive and THINK are available in the ObjectWeb code base. FracNet, FractTalk and Flone are available as open source on specific web sites.

– *Julia* was historically (2002) the first Fractal implementation[4], provided by France Telecom. Since its second version, Julia makes use of AOP-like techniques based on interceptors and controllers built as a composition of mixins. It comes with a library of mixins and interceptors mixed at loadtime (Julia relies very much on loadtime bytecode transformation as the main underlying technique thanks to the ASM Java bytecode Manipulation Framework). The design of Julia cared very much for performance: the goal was to prove that component-based systems were not doomed to be inefficient compared to plain Java. Julia allows for intra-components and inter-components optimizations which altogether exhibit very acceptable performance.

– *THINK* is a C implementation of Fractal, provided by France Telecom and INRIA Sardes, with a growing participation of STMicroelectronics and CEA, geared at operating and especially embedded systems development. Using THINK, OS architects can build OS kernels conforming to any kernel architecture: exo-kernel, micro-kernel... Minimal kernels can be built on bare hardware and basic functions such as scheduler and memory policies can be easily redefined or even not included. This helps achieve speed-ups and low memory footprints over standard general-purpose operating systems. THINK is also suggested for prototyping when using a complete OS would be a too heavy solution. It can also be used when implementing application-specific kernels, especially when targeting small platforms embedding microcontrollers. THINK comes along with KORTEX, a library of already existing system components, implementing various functions (memory management, schedulers, file systems, etc.) on various targets (e.g. ARM, PPC, x86).

– *ProActive* is a distributed and asynchronous implementation of Fractal targetting grid computing, developed by INRIA Oasis with a participation of France Telecom. It is a grid middleware for parallel, distributed, and concurrent computing, also featuring mobility and security in a uniform framework. It mixes the active object paradigm for concurrent programming (objects executing their own asynchronous activity in a thread) and the component paradigm for deployment and management.

– *AOKell* is a Java implementation by INRIA Jacquard and France Telecom similar to Julia, but based on standard AOP technologies (static weaving with AspectJ in AOKell v1 and loadtime weaving with Spoon in AOKell v2) instead of mixins. Also AOKell v2 is the first Fractal implementation that supports component-based membranes: Fractal component controllers can themselves be implemented as Fractal components. AOKell offers similar performance to Julia.

– *FractNet* is a .Net implementation of the Fractal component model developed by the LSR laboratory. It is essentially a port of AOKell on .Net, in which AspectDNG is used as an alternative aspect weaver to AspectJ or Spoon. FractNet provides for Fractal component programming in J#, C#, VB.Net and Cobol.Net languages.

---

[4] And sometimes considered for this reason as "the reference implementation" in Java.

- *Flone* is a Java implementation of the Fractal component model developed by INRIA Sardes for teaching purposes. Flone is not a full-fledge implementation of Fractal: it offers simplified APIs that globally reduce the openness and use of reflection of the general Fractal model so as to make teaching of component-based programming easier for students.
- *FracTalk* is an experimental SmallTalk implementation of the Fractal component model developed at Ecole des Mines de Douai. FracTalk focuses very much on dynamicity in component-based programming thanks the intrinsic dynamic nature of the SmallTalk language.
- *Plasma* is a C++ experimental implementation of Fractal developed at INRIA Sardes (with a participation of Microsoft Research) dedicated to the construction of self-adaptable multimedia applications.

2.3 Languages and Tools

A large number of R&D activities are being conducted inside the Fractal community around languages and tools, with the overall ambition to provide a complete environment covering the complete component-based software life cycle covering modelling, design, development, deployment and (self-)management. A representative but not exhaustive list of such activities is the following:

- development of formal foundations for the Fractal model, typically by means of calculi, essentially by INRIA Sardes,
- development of basic and higher levels (e.g. transactional) mechanisms for trusted dynamic reconfigurations, by France Telecom, INRIA Sardes and Ecole des Mines de Nantes (EMN),
- support for configuration, development of ADL support and associated tool chain, by INRIA Sardes, Jacquard, France Telecom, ST Micoelectronics,
- support for packaging and deployment, by INRIA Jacquard, Sardes Oasis, IMAG LSR laboratory, ENST Bretagne,
- development of navigation and management tools, by INRIA Jacquard and France Telecom,
- development of architectures that mix components and aspects (AOP), at the component (applicative) level and at the membrane (technical) level, by INRIA, France Telecom, ICS/Charles University Prague,
- development of specification models, languages and associated tools for static and dynamic checking of component behaviour, involving ICS/Charles University Prague, I3S/U. Nice, France Telecom, Valoria/U. Bretagne Sud,
- development of security architectures (access control, authentication, isolation), by France Telecom,
- development of QoS management architectures and mechanisms, for instance in THINK-based embedded systems, by France Telecom, or multimedia services with Plasma, by INRIA Sardes,
- development of semi-formal modelling and design methodologies (UML, MDA), models and tools, by CEA, Charles University Prague and others,
- ...

The most mature among these works are typically incorporated as new modules into the Fractal code base. Examples of such modules are the following:

- Fractal RMI is a set of Fractal components that provide a binding factory to create synchronous distributed bindings between Fractal components (la Java RMI). These components are based on a re-engineering process of the Jonathan framework.
- Fractal ADL (Architecture Description Languages) is a language for defining Fractal configurations (components assemblies) and an associated retargetable parsing tool with different back-ends for instantiating these configurations on different implementations (Julia, AOKell, THINK, etc.). Fractal ADL is a modular (XML modules defined by DTDs) and extensible language to describe components, interfaces, bindings, containment relationships, attributes and types - which is classical for an ADL - but also to describe implementations and especially membrane constructions that are specific to each Fractal implementation, deployment information, behaviour and QoS contracts or any other architectural concern. Fractal ADL can be considered as the favourite entry point to Fractal components programming (its offers a much higher level of abstraction than the bare Fractal APIs) that embeds concepts of the Fractal component model[5].
- FractalGUI is a graphical editor for Fractal component configurations which allows for component design with boxes and arrows. Fractal GUI can import/export Fractal configurations from/to Fractal ADL files.
- FScript is a scripting language used to describe architectural reconfigurations of Fractal components. FScript includes a special notation called FPath (loosely inspired by XPath) to query, i.e. navigate and select elements from Fractal architectures (components, interfaces...) according to some properties (e.g. which components are connected to this particular component? how many components are bound to this particular component?). FPath is used inside FScript to select the elements to reconfigure, but can be used by itself as a query language for Fractal.
- Fractal Explorer is a "graphical" (in fact a multi-textual windows system) management console that allows for navigation, introspection and reconfiguration of running Fractal systems in Java.
- Fractal JMX is a set of Fractal components that allows for automatic, declarative and non-intrusive exposition of Fractal components into JMX servers with filtering and renaming capabilities. Fractal JMX allows administrators to see a Fractal system as if it was a plain Java system instrumented "by hand" for JMX management: Fractal components are mapped to MBeans that are accessible by program or with a JMX console through a JMX server.

---

[5] It is worth noticing that Fractal ADL is not (yet) a complete component-oriented language (in the Turing sense), hence the need for execution support in host programming languages a.k.a. "implementations".

2.4   Component Library and Real Life Usage

Fractal has essentially been used so far to build middleware and operating system components. The current library of components engineered with Fractal that are currently available inside ObjectWeb include:

- DREAM, a framework (i.e. a set of components) for building different types (group communications, message passing, event-reaction, publish-subscribe) of asynchronous communication systems (management of messages, queues, channels, protocols, multiplexers, routers, etc.)
- GOTM, a framework for building transaction management systems (management of transactions demarcation, distributed commit, concurrency, recovery, resources/contexts, etc.)
- Perseus, a framework for building persistence management systems (management of persistency, caching, concurrency, logging, pools, etc.),
- Speedo, an implementation of the JDO (Java Data Object) standard for persistence of Java objects. Speedo embeds Perseus,
- CLIF, a framework for performance testing, load injection and monitoring (management of blades, probes, injectors, data aggregators, etc.)
- JOnAS, a J2EE compliant application server. JOnAS embeds Speedo (hence Perseus, Fractal, Julia, ASM),
- Petals, an implementation of Java Business Integration (JBI) platform, i.e. an Enterprise Software Bus.

Some of these components that embed Fractal technology are used operationally, for instance JOnAS, Speedo and CLIF by France Telecom: JOnAS is widely used by France Telecom[6] for its service platforms, information systems and networks by more than 100 applications including vocal services including VoIP, enterprise web portals, phone directories, clients management, billing management, salesman management, lines and incidents management.

3   Organization of the Workshop

3.1   History of Fractal Workshops

The Fractal CBSE workshop at ECOOP 2006 was the 5th in the series[7].

The first workshop was held in January 2003 as an associated event of an ObjectWeb architecture meeting. The attendance was of about 35 people. 15 talks were given, organized in 5 sessions. The first session was a feedback session about the use of Fractal in Jonathan (a flexible ORB), JORAM (a JMS-compliant MOM) and ProActive (a distributed computing environment based on active objects). The second session was dedicated to Fractal implementation,s

---

[6] See http://jonas.objectweb.org/success.html for a more comprehensive list of operational usage of JOnAS.

[7] All programs and talks from Fractal CBSE workshops are available on the Fractal project web site at http://fractal.objectweb.org

namely Julia and THINK. The third sessions was devoted to configuration tools, namely Kilim and Fractal GUI. The fourth session was dedicated to management and deployment, especially JMX management with Fractal JMX and connection with J2EE management and OSGi. The last session presented a conceptual comparison of Fractal and other component models.

The second workshop was held in March 2004 as an associated event of an ObjectWeb architecture meeting and ITEA Osmose project meeting. The attendance was of about 30 people. 10 talks were given, organized in 3 sessions. The first session was dedicated to tutorials on the Fractal model and Java tools (Fractal ADL, Fractal GUI, Fractal Explorer). The second session was dedicated to feedback from practical usage of Fractal in the Dream communication framework, the CLIF framework for load injection and performance evaluation and the GoTM open transaction monitor. The third session was dedicated to work in progress: components for grid computing with Fractal and ProActive, components and aspects, convergence of the Fractal and SOFA component models.

The third workshop was held in June 2005, again as an associated event of an ObjectWeb architecture meeting. The attendance was of about 20 people. It was mostly dedicated to discussions about components and aspects around AOKell (aspect-oriented programming of Fractal component membranes), FAC (Fractal Aspect Components: reification of aspects as components), and "micro-controllers". Another talk was given about the development of a formal and dynamic ADL.

The fourth workshop was held in November 2005 as a satellite of the ACM /IFIP/USENIX Middleware conference. The attendance was of more than 50 people. 8 talks about work in progress were given, framed by an introduction to Fractal and the Fractal project, and a final discussion about the evolution of the Fractal project. The technical talks described the recent developments concerning the Fractal ADL tool chain, the Fractal RMI ORB, the AOKell and ProActive implementations, reliability of Fractal components thanks to contracts (ConFract), behaviour protocols and model checking, with an original talk from the Nokia research center about dynamic and automatic configuration of components.

3.2   Call for Proposals

The call for proposals, that was publicized on several mailing-lists (ObjectWeb, DBWorld, seworld, ACM SIGOPS France...), contained:

- – a description and rationale for component-based architecture and its interest for the ECOOP conference;
- – the expected audience: the Fractal community inside the ObjectWeb community hopefully enlarged thanks to ECOOP;
- – the definition of scope of expected proposals: implementation and conformance test suites, model extensions, languages and tools, practical usage and feedback;
- – and finally a description of the submission and selection process.

The submission and selection processes were rather light. Submissions were asked to contain 2 to 4 pages describing the work to be presented during the workshop. No full-length articles were asked for submission[8].

3.3   Selection and Call for Participation

More than 20 propositions were received, evaluated and discussed by the workshop organisers. Among them, 11 were selected for regular talks during the workshop. The selection was based on several individual criteria (technical maturity, originality, novelty) and also globally so as to cover a wide spectrum of activities around the Fractal component model and to make an interesting program with potential vivid discussions among participants. Most other proposals were very relevant but unfortunately could not fit in a one-day workshop, and were proposed to give place to poster presentations during breaks and lunch.

The final call for participation repeated the general items of the call for proposals and gave the detailed program with the list of regular talks and posters.

4   Tenue of the Workshop

The workshop took place the 3rd of July 2006. It was organized around 11 talks (typically 20 mn talk + 10 mn discussion) grouped in 5 sessions: Implementation and Basic Tools, Higher Languages and Tools, UML and MDA Design, Verification and Predictable Assembly, and Applications. 3 poster sessions also took place during coffee breaks and lunch. A final free discussion involving the around 30 participants closed the workshop.

4.1   Presentations and Discussions

The first morning session was devoted to implementations and basic tools for Fractal component programming.

L. Seinturier presented a joint work between INRIA Jacquard (L. Seinturier, N. Pessemier) and IMAG LSR laboratory (D. Donsez, C. Escoffier) towards a reference model for implementing the Fractal specifications in Java and the .Net platform. This preparatory work, fuelled by the development of the AOKell Fractal implementation and its port on the .Net platform, and a comparative analysis of the Julia implementation, advocates for a greater interoperability between Fractal implementations. The purpose of a Fractal implementation is to support the Fractal APIs and to offer mechanisms to compose control aspects inside membranes. Of course, all Fractal implementations support the Fractal API (with possible different conformance levels however) but offer generally different and incompatible mechanisms for building membranes. The aim of this line of work is to define some "Service Provider Interfaces" (SPI) that would

---

[8] A post-workshop editing and publishing activity to produce post-workshops proceedings was planned however.

embody programming conventions; implementations should follow these conventions so as to build assembly of, for instance, Julia and OAKell components and hopefully mix controllers/interceptors from different implementations. This line of work was acknowledged by the audience as very useful and important, and probably strongly connected to necessary efforts towards the definition of compliance test suites and benchmarks for Fractal implementations.

E. Özcan presented a status of the work in progress around THINK by STMicrolectronics (E. Özcan, M. Leclerc), France Telecom (J. Polakovic) and INRIA Sardes (J.-B. Stefani). The talk focused on recent developments of the ADL tool-chain for THINK (Fractal ADL Factory) so as to make it more modular (finer-grained), extensible and retargetable, i.e. able to consider different back-ends corresponding to different hardware platforms. The talk concluded by listing other recent R&D activities and additions to the Kortex component library such as support for multi-processor platforms and support for customizable multimedia applications. The following discussion was not so much technical but concerned the collaborative management of the THINK code base. The THINK code base was historically managed by a few individuals from France Telecom and INRIA, with a quite clear direction and minimal collaborative decision making. Now, the growing implication of STMicrolectronics and others raises the question of how to choose between alternative propositions, e.g. concerning the design of the ADL tool chain for THINK, who is authorized to commit in the code base, who is authorized to create branches, etc.

The second session was devoted to higher languages and tools.

P.-C. David presented the work he did on FScript with T. Ledoux at Ecole des Mines de Nantes and France Telecom. FScript is a scripting language that allows for expressing reconfigurations of Fractal systems much more concisely, thanks to a higher level of abstraction than the bare Fractal APIs. FScript also includes FPath, a sublanguage/subsystem for navigation/query in Fractal architectures. It only comes with a Java backend for the time being but works are ongoing, e.g. at France Telecom, to use FScript to express reconfigurations in the THINK platform. One focus of the talk was the ACID-like transactional properties of FScript that would allow for *safe* reconfigurations. The vivid discussion following the talk revealed that this important but complex matter would/should require more developments.

R. Rouvoy presented the work on attribute-oriented programming around Fraclet with N. Pessemier, R. Pawlack and P. Merle at INRIA Jacquard. Fraclet is an annotation framework for Fractal components in Java. The motivation for this work is that component programming can be considered as verbose - and hence time consuming - by developers because the components code has to respect some conventions and provide meta-information as required by the Fractal model. Fraclet is composed of a library of annotations and plugins to generate[9] automatically various artifacts required by the Fractal component model (a.k.a. callbacks). Annotations provide a way to describe the component

---

[9] Fraclet and attribute-oriented programming in general takes its roots in generative programming and aspect-oriented programming.

meta-information directly in the source code of the content Java class. Fraclet plugins generate either Fractal component glue (use of Fractal APIs) or FractalADL definitions. Two implementations of the Fraclet annotation framework exist: Fraclet XDoc and Fraclet Annotation. Fraclet XDoc uses the XDoclet generation engine to produce the various artifacts required by the Fractal component model. Fraclet Annotation uses the Spoon transformation tool to enhance the handwritten program code with the non-functional properties of the component model. The talk emphasised two benefits of the approach. First, a reduction in development time and in the size of the components code produced "by hand". Second, a better support for software deployment and evolution: the presence in components code of architecture/deployment concerns facilitates the co-evolution of business and architecture/deployment code. This second benefit appeared as arguable from an industrial point of view: mixing, within the same file, business and deployment concerns might not appear as such a pleasant idea for software administrators. Also, a massive use of annotations is quite questionable with respect to code analysis and dependability in general. Most participants to the workshops were rather programmers than industrials and appeared quite enthusiastic about annotations and Fraclet anyway!

The third session was devoted to component modelling and more specifically to UML and MDA design.

V. Mencl presented a study with M. Polak at Charles University, Prague. They used their comparative analysis of UML 2.0 components and Fractal components to discuss possible mappings of Fractal concepts in UML. They actually proposed one specific mapping and instrumented it as a plug-in for the Enterprise Architect platform which is able to generate the Fractal ADL component descriptions, Java interfaces and a *skeleton* of the actual Java code of components. In the after-talk discussion, some possible future extensions were mentioned such as to *reverse engineer* UML models from Fractal ADL descriptions or runtime capture and representation in UML of a running Fractal system.

F. Loiret presented a study with D. Servat at CEA/LIST and L. Seinturier at INRIA Jacquard about modelling real-time Fractal components. This early work includes the definition of a EMF (Eclipse Modelling Framework) meta-model of Fractal IDL and ADL description, as well as the development of an Eclipse plug-in for actual generation of Fractal components targetting the THINK platform. The perspectives that were discussed include an extension of the meta-model to describe components behaviour and a reverse engineering tool chain to extract behaviour from the code of components.

The general discussion at the end of this modelling session acknowledged that there is probably not a unique direct mapping between UML and Fractal, especially because of specificities of Fractal such as component sharing and reflection (components controllers and membranes). However, thanks to UML/MDA (meta)modelling capabilities, different UML (meta)models could be defined to tackle Fractal specificities. People/teams interested by this line of work inside the Fractal community were encouraged to discuss further and hopefully to converge towards a common meta model (or at least to assess if one such a common model would make sense).

In the afternoon, the fourth session was devoted to verification tools and predictable assembly.

J. Kofron presented the work on behaviour protocols by J. Adamek, T. Bures, P. Jesek, V. Mencl, P. Parizek and F. Plasil at Charles University, Prague. Behaviour protocols are basically a formalism that allows for the specification of the expected behaviour of components in terms of legal sequences of operation invocations on components interfaces. A static behaviour protocol checker has been developed in the context of the SOFA component models for several years by Charles University. Recently, behaviour protocols have been ported on the Fractal platform through a partnership between Charles University and France Telecom. The result is a static checker and a dynamic checker that include Java code analysis of primitive components with the JavaPathFinder (JPF) model checker.

E. Madelaine presented a case-study of verification of distributed components behaviour with L. Henrio and A. Cansado at INRIA Oasis/I3S/U. Nice. The case study application itself has been defined in a partnership between Charles University and France Telecom to experiment behaviour protocols (cf. previous paragraph). E. Madelaine and al. used this application to experiment with their own verification formalism, *parameterized networks* with their supporting verification platform Vercors. This formal approach allows for model-checking of components behaviour (typically deadlock and reachability checking). The work also mentioned the proposition of a new Fractal ADL module (defined in collaboration with Charles University) for attaching behaviour specification and associated verification tools in architecture descriptions.

D. Deveaux presented a work with P. Collet, respectively at Valoria/U. Bretagne Sud and I3S/U. Nice, on contract-based built-in testing. The approach leverages previous works on built-in testing of Java classes by Valoria and ConFract, a contracting system for Fractal by I3S and France Telecom. It proposes to instrument each component under test (CUT) with, for instance, ConFract contracts which embody the particular testing information of this component and a test controller that would generate a test bed component encapsulating (containing) each CUT. A prototype is currently under development. Some questions arose from the audience concerning the adherence to ConFract and if the approach was only applicable during the design phase or whether it would be used in a deployed system. D. deveaux explained that the system would exhibit low dependancy to the contracting system (alternative contract systems may be used instead of ConFract) and would not be limited to unit testing, but could also handle admission, integration and regression test thanks to the dynamic configuration management capabilities in Fractal.

The fifth and last session was devoted to applications in real life of the Fractal technology.

N. Rivierre presented the work around JMXPrism with T. Coupaye at France Telecom. JMXPrism is a mediation layer that stands between the systems to be managed through JMX and management consoles or applications. JMXPrism provides a unique access point (embedding a JMX server) for managers that allows for the definition and management of *logical views* on the managed systems. JMXPrism prevents managers to access directly the managed systems and allows for filtering, renaming, etc. JMXPrims is implemented in Fractal which makes it very dynamic, allowing views and other components of a JMXPrims server to be changed very easily. JMXPrism embeds Fractal JMX, which was released some time ago as open source in the Fractal code base, and which allows for a declarative and non-intrusive exposition of Fractal components in JMX. JMXPrism has been used inside France Telecom to build a toy autonomic prototype controlling the creation of threads correlated to memory consumption. It has also been used more operationally in a grid information system project in partnership with Fujitsu to provide an homogenous view of resources in cluster on which resource sharing control was exercised to arbitrate two concurrently running applications: a visio-conference application exhibiting real-time QoS constraints and a batch-oriented scientific computing application.

G. Huang presented the last work with L. Lan, J. Yang and H. Mei at Peking University, Beijing, China on next generation J2EE servers. The work advocates for a combined use of reflective (applicative) components as embodied in Fractal or the ABC tool chain from Peking University and reflective middleware (especially EJB container) in future J2EE servers. Experiments are been conducted in PKUAS, an J2EE-compliant J2EE application server developed at Peking University. The talk raises up the engaged collaboration between ObjectWeb and OrientWare[10], a Chinese open source middleware consortium, as a suitable context for this line of work.

4.2 Final Discussion

The open discussion session was launched by a short talk by D. Caromel from INRIA Oasis, who reported on the Grid Component Model (GCM). GCM is an component model dedicated to grid systems that is being defined by the IST CoreGrid[11] network of excellence (NoE) along with the IST STREP project GridCOMP which is in charge of implementing, tooling and experimenting GCM. Fractal is considered as the basis for GCM and also as the main candidate to emerge as the standard component model for grid computing, at least in Europe. The talk recalled for some changes in the Fractal APIs that would be suitable for grid environments and that were discussed in previous Fractal workshop (e.g. multicast interfaces) but, more importantly, advocates for a close synergy between ObjectWeb/Fractal and CoreGrid/GridCOMP, i.e. a support of Fractal in CoreGrid and symmetrically a commitment from the Fractal community. This point was largely acknowledged as an important matter for the visibility and future of Fractal.

The discussion on the expected synergy between ObjectWeb/Fractal and CoreGrid/GridCOMP raised up a more general discussion about the evolution of

---

[10] http://www.orientware.org

[11] http://www.coregrid.net/

the Fractal project. Some time ago was announced an evolution towards "Fractal v3". Some points were discussed during the previous Fractal workshop (November 2005), namely: i) evolution of the Fractal model specification (e.g. removal of some semantic ambiguities, changes and additions required for grid computing), including evolution in the organisation of the work on the specification with editors, editing committee and contributors, ii) evolution in the management of the Fractal code bases (e.g. cartography/matrix of (in)compatibilities between implementations and tools, conformance test suites) and iii) evolution of the Fractal web site (e.g. bibliography, success stories) and more generally of the management of the Fractal community (e.g. more structured workshops with CFP, program committee, proceedings; working groups inside the Fractal project). Since then, some elements contributed to "Fractal v3" in a quite informal way e.g. reflections on interoperability between Fractal implementations (cf. work by Seinturier and al. in the previous section), organisation of the two last workshops as satellite events of Middleware and ECOOP conferences (including CFP, PC and hopefully post-proceeding for Fractal Workshop at ECOOP), additions to the Fractal code base(s) (e.g. AOKell, FScript) and web site. The discussion at ECOOP, as well as previous informal discussions in particular on the Fractal mailing-list, revealed that some people were perhaps expecting a quicker evolution. Again, after a lively discussion, the workshop organisers pointed out that there might have been a misunderstanding and that what was intended by "Fractal v3" does not boild down to just a evolution of the specification of the model itself but refers to a collective effort with implication of many individuals that are part of the Fractal community so as to tackle the different issues at stake (implementations engineering and interoperability, conformance test suites, tools, common code base for uses cases and demonstrators, management of commit in code bases, web site, etc.).

From the evolution of Fractal, the discussion then jumped to the standardisation of Fractal. Several participants advocated for a more volunteer approach of the Fractal community towards standardization organisms. A vivid discussion took place to assess which standard committees/organizations would be most appropriate (ISO, IUT, Sun JCP, OMG...). Some others pointed out that standardization in the middleware area is a huge effort and the return on this investment not always remunerating. Most participants agreed that the group or institution they represent would not have much resources for such activities anyway. The question of standardization activities around Fractal remains largely open.

Acknowledgments. We would like to thank the ECOOP conference and workshop organizers for their assistance in the preparation of this workshop. We would like to thank the Fractal community for its vitality, for having proposed so many talks at this workshop even though this was the 3rd Fractal workshop in less than a year. Thanks to A. Lefebvre for his careful reading and comments.

Object Technology for Ambient Intelligence and Pervasive Computing: Language Constructs and Infrastructures

Holger Mügge[1], Pascal Cherrier[2], Wolfgang De Meuter[3], and Éric Tanter[4]

[1] University of Bonn, Germany
[2] France Telecom, France
[3] Vrije Universiteit Brussels, Belgium
[4] University of Chile, Chile

Abstract. This report summarizes the main activities held during the second workshop on object-technology for Ambient Intelligence and Pervasive Computing held at ECOOP 2006. The workshop covered topics varying from low-level considerations such as garbage collection and object migration, via programming language infrastructure such as reflection and context-oriented programming, to engineering applications using maturing techniques such as aspects.

1 Introduction

In the near future, a new level of dynamicity will be required in order to construct software that is highly context-dependent due to the mobility of both the software itself and its users. This peculiar setting has been given different names like Ambient Intelligence (AmI), Pervasive Computing or Ubiquitous Computing with slightly different meanings. We use the term Ambient Intelligence but address equally all kinds of mobile, distributed software from the software engineering point of view. The idea of Ambient Intelligence is that everybody will be surrounded by a dynamically-defined processor cloud, of which the applications are expected to cooperate smoothly.

Currently, Ambient Intelligence seems to incorporate aspects from previously unrelated fields such as ubiquitous computing, mobility, intelligent user interaction, context dependency, domotics, etc. Early experiments in these fields, as conducted for example by Philips and MIT, already indicate that a full realization of their potential will need a new generation of concepts. These concepts need to support software which is able to operate in extremely dynamic hardware and software configurations. Ambient Intelligence is put forward as one of the major strategic research themes by the EUs IST Advisory Group for the financing structure of the 6th Framework of the EU. "The focus of IST in FP6 is on the future generation of technologies in which computers and networks will be integrated into the everyday environment [...]. This vision of 'ambient intelligence' places the user, the individual, at the centre of future developments for an inclusive knowledge-based society for all." (from the overall vision of the working programme of IST in FP6).

M. Südholt and C. Consel (Eds.): ECOOP 2006 Ws, LNCS 4379, pp. 130–140, 2007.

2   Scope of the Workshop

2.1   Goals

Important goals of the workshop were to identify and discuss the impact of
Ambient Intelligence on object-oriented technologies and vice versa, and to outline some fruitful paths for future research concerning the connection between
Ambient Intelligence and object-oriented programming languages and systems.
In this context, we understand the term object technology to cover the whole
range of topics that have evolved around the notion of object-orientation in the
past decades, starting from programming language design and implementation,
ranging over software architectures, frameworks and components, up to design
approaches and software development processes.

We expect a special emphasis on the (seemingly?) conflicting forces of high
dynamicity as offered, for example, by delegation- and reflection-based object-
oriented systems that provide a high level of adaptability on the one hand, and
peoples needs for security, safety and stability on the other hand. How can these
forces be resolved, and does the notion of Ambient Intelligence with its concept
of high availability of services even lead to new opportunities in this regard?

2.2   Topics

In the call for participation, the following non-exhaustive list of potential topics
was included:

- Programming languages: Concepts for coping with new levels of dynamicity
  and security.
- Reflection: Why could it still be interesting to imagine a better reflective
  virtual machine and what about security and reflection: Can a reflective
  (structural / behavioural) object-oriented virtual machine be secured?
- Software evolution: Mobile software must continually adapt itself to potentially unanticipated environments. How can this be tackled?
- Context Modelling: What are the most promising ways to model context and
  integrate it into the software architecture?
- Adaptivity: What are the requirements for adaptive software? What do current methods and tools provide for building adaptive systems and what is
  missing?
- Quality of Service: What software engineering techniques support depend-
  able, reliable and safe systems? How to bridge the gap between (too) low-level
  and (too) high-level rules? How to take structural constraints into account?
- Software development processes: Are the current approaches to analysis,
  modelling and development able to cope with the specific demands of mobile
  software?
- Human-device interactions: What is new in comparison to the good old
  model view controller? What are good new ways for GUI design and implementation? What about extending to 3D graphics and sounds? What
  about multimodalities?

- Device-device interaction: What are the requirements for embedded virtual machines? How do the existing models (Java, Smalltalk, Scheme, Python) differ from each other in handling events and communicating with people and other devices? Do they enable the software to exploit spontaneous collaborations between multiple devices and people?
- Constrained resources: Specificities of small mobile equipments, impact on the software in terms of object oriented concepts.

This topic list led to the submission of seven papers with topics varying from low level considerations such as garbage collection and object migration, via programming language infrastructure such as reflection and context-oriented programming, to engineering applications using maturing techniques such as aspects.

3   Workshop Organization

The workshop organisation was centred around two invited talks that were scheduled in the morning and in the afternoon. Apart from the invited talks, authors have presented their position papers according to the following schedule. In the schedule, the actual presenter is indicated in a boldfaced fashion.

Time	Content
9:00	Start: Welcome and Introduction
9:30	Invited Talk by **Jacques Malenfant** "Programming for Adaptability in Ambient Computing: Towards a Systemic Approach"
10:30	"Using Mixin Layers for Context-Aware and Self-Adaptable Systems" (**B. Desmet**, J.V. Vargas, S. Mostinckx and P. Costanza)
11:00	"Prototypes with Multimethods for Context-Awareness" (**S. Gonzáles**, K. Mens and S. Mostinckx)
11:30	"Semi-Automatic Garbage Collection for Mobile Networks" (**E.G. Boix**, T. Van Cutsem and S. Mostinckx)
12:00	"Design of a Multi-level Reflective Architecture for Ambient Actors" (D. Standaert, **É. Tanter** and T. Van Cutsem)
14:00	Invited talk by **Bill Griswold**: "Software Architectures for Context-Aware Computing - Experience and Emerging Challenges"
15:00	"Towards an Integration Platform for AmI: A Case Study" **A. Fortier**, J. Munoz, V. Pelechano, G. Rossi and S. Gordillo
15:30	"Towards Context-Sensitive Service Aspects" **T. Rho** and M. Schmatz
16:00	"Context-Aware Adaptive Object Migration" R. Kapitza, **H. Schmidt**, F.J. Hauck
16:30	Summary and roundup discussions
17:00	End

4   Summary of Contributions

This section summarizes the main points of the submitted position papers. These papers can be downloaded from the workshop's home page at

   http://sam.iai.uni-bonn.de/ot4ami/Wiki.jsp?page=Program

Using Mixin Layers for Context-Aware and Self-Adaptable Systems by B. Desmet. This talk was about technology that allows an application to dynamically adapt its behaviour according to changes in the context in which the application operates. Current-day technology typically consists of a series of programming patterns to achieve such dynamic behaviour adaptation. As a consequence, combining different contexts in such systems has proven to be far from trivial. The talk proposed the use of mixin layers to modularize the context-dependent adaptations separate from the application core logic, together with a composition mechanism that deals with runtime context interactions. Since the classes in mixin layers have no fixed superclasses, they can be combined easily to reflect different combinations of context. The relationships between the different mixin-layers was proposed to be programmed in a declarative way. This enables a dynamic composition mechanism to construct and apply valid compositions of mixin layers according to context changes. The combination of using mixin layers and a declarative language to describe relationships between mixin layers was argued to be a powerful mechanism to deal with the continuously varying behaviour of context-aware systems.

Prototypes with Multimethods for Context-Awareness by S. Gonzales. The talk argued that the incorporation of context information into running mobile applications is currently often achieved using ad hoc mechanisms. To allow for an application to behave differently in a given context, this context-specific behaviour is typically hard-wired in the application under the form of if -statements scattered in method bodies or by using design patterns (e.g. Visitor, State, Strategy) and best-practice patterns (e.g. Double Dispatch). Therefore, the talk explores the Prototypes with Multiple Dispatch (PMD) object model in the light of context-aware mobile applications. The proposal provides a structured mechanism to deal with contextual information in a flexible and fine-grained manner. Context-aware mobile applications rely on a context architecture that aggregates the input from sensors (and possibly other applications) in a way that is accessible to the application. Using multiple dispatch the aggregated context directly influences the dispatch of methods, thereby avoiding hard-wiring context-related behaviour in the application. In other words, the programming model directly supports Context-Oriented Programming as recently proposed by P. Costanza.

Semi-Automatic Garbage Collection for Mobile Networks by E.G. Boix. In recent years remarkable progress has been made in the fields of mobile hardware and wireless network technologies. Devices communicate by means of such wireless infrastructure with other devices in their environment in ad hoc way spontaneously creating networks. However, developing applications for such devices is very complex due to the lack of support in current programming languages to deal with the specific properties that distinguish mobile networks from the traditional distributed systems. The research presented in this talk focusses on providing programming language support to alleviate the complexity encountered when developing such applications. The talk identified the following phenomena intrinsic to mobile networks: connection volatility, ambient resources, autonomy.

The Ambient-Oriented Programming paradigm was postulated as a new computing paradigm which incorporates these hardware phenomena at the heart of its programming model in order to ease the development of applications for mobile networks. The talk gave an overview of this paradigm and then focussed on the issues of distributed garbage collection for mobile networks. Subsequently a new family of distributed garbage collection mechanisms to cope with them was introduced. It requires annotations from programmers to steer the garbage collection mechanism and is therefore called semi-automatic garbage collection.

Design of a Multi-level Reflective Architecture for Ambient Actors by É. Tanter. This work describes a multi-level reflective architecture for a language that automatically supports open network topologies where devices may join and leave at any point in time, where reliance on central servers is usually impractical and where the connection between two communicating devices is often volatile due to the limited wireless communication range. Rather than requiring the developer to manually deal with the difficult issues engendered by the ambient hardware at the base level, where this code would be severely tangled with and scattered throughout the functional code, the research proposes to offer the programmer a means to express a solution for the issues in a generic manner, at the metalevel. This metalevel is structured according to different levels of abstraction, which gives rise to what is known as a multi-model reflection framework. This structure is simply derived from the fact that not all distribution-related issues are expressible at the same level of abstraction.

The talk proposed a multi-level reflective architecture for ambient actors and its instantiation in the AmOP language AmbientTalk. The architecture combines (a) the engineering benefits of multi-model reflection by structuring metalevel facilities according to different levels of abstraction (passive objects, active objects, virtual machine), (b) the extreme encapsulation properties of mirror methods by ensuring that objects that are reflected upon can themselves restrict access to their meta-level facilities depending on the client, and this at all levels, and (c) the power offered by an extensible virtual machine in which facilities are made accessible to actors so that they can customize their execution environment, as well as adapting their own behavior according to it. The resulting MOP respects the extreme encapsulation principle thanks to its systematic use of mirror methods.

Towards an Integration Platform for AmI: A Case Study by A. Fortier. Creating intelligent environments requires knowledge from different disciplines such as HCI, artificial intelligence, software engineering and sensing hardware to be combined to produce an application. Therefore, the integration of independently components developed will be necessary. This talk argues that what is needed to support this is an integration framework (comprising formalisms, tools and a software platform), which allows different components to seamlessly interact, to provide pervasive services and ambient intelligence. In such framework one should be able to specify, in an abstract way, the contextual information that a certain software module needs to perform his task, so that the integration platform can dynamically discover which providers can fit the module needs.

As a contribution towards the development of an integration platform, the talk presents a concrete example of systems cooperation. This example involves two different projects developed at different universities. Both projects address the problem of building ubiquitous software, but they do so using somewhat different approaches. The Software Engineering And Pervasive Systems (SEAPS) project, being developed in the OO-Method research group from the UPV, focuses on the development of a model driven method for the automatic generation of pervasive systems from abstract specifications. The systems that are generated by this method are used to provide services in a particular environment, generally smart homes. To implement the systems, the OSGi middleware, which is based on Java, was used. On the other hand, the Context-Aware (CA) project being developed at LIFIA, in the UNLP, focuses on the user as a service consumer. In this view of a pervasive system, the user carries a mobile device most of the time, which is used to present services according to his context, which can vary dynamically. This framework is implemented in Smalltalk.

By integrating both systems the authors expect to improve the SEAPS project with dynamically-varying context information, to extend the CA project so that it can remotely manipulate SEAPS services, and to build a context model based on the information sensed by the SEAPS. They also expect to gain knowledge about more generic integration needs, to be able to effectively build the integration platform mentioned before. As a result of the work carried out, the talk presents as its contributions: the presentation of a concrete case of independent systems integration, the identification of a set of problems encountered during the integration process and the presentation of the lessons learned for others.

Towards Context-Sensitive Service Aspects by T. Rho. The talk argued that context-aware behavior is usually hard-coded into the application itself using the deployed libraries on the device. Since these have to be known at development time context-processing is limited to the known libraries on the corresponding target device. Besides that, not all context-sensitivity can be anticipated. Being bound to one device neither composition nor sharing of context information is possible. To build flexible applications that adapt themselves to the current situation, the underlying architecture must provide the means to dynamically reconfigure the application based on context information.

Service-oriented architectures (SOA) help to support the dynamic reconfiguration of applications. They modularize applications by decomposing them into distributed components, so called services. Ap- plications are build by composing these services and configuring them at runtime. Therefore the architecture is based on service-orientation.

Aspects help to improve the software design by encapsulating the unstable composition concern. AOP frameworks like have been proposed which realize this concept. Ambient intelligence introduces an even more unstable element —the varying context—, which influences the runtime adaptation of the service composition. Using AOP to encapsulate the service composition the services stay compact and stable because they are independent of adaptation strategies and context information. However, common aspect languages only consider the event flow of programs. The AOP terminology for program flow events is join point. Typical join points are method calls, field accesses or thrown exceptions. In an ambient intelligence setting these join points are not sufficient. The properties of the environment must also be taken into account. To combine contexts and join points a powerful pointcut language is needed.

One cannot apply AOP techniques in full extend on the SOA level, because the concrete implementation of services is, at most times, not accessible to a local system. And even if the service implementation is available there may still be different views onto the same service from the local or a remote system which are in a different contexts. The authors therefore restrict the join point model to calls on the service level. This paper introduces the Ditrios architecture and the service aspect language CSLogicAJ, which provide context-sensitive services aspects for the service-oriented architecture OSGi.

Context-Aware Adaptive Object Migration by H. Schmidt. There is an ongoing trend to integrate and link the physical world to the virtual world of computing resources and applications. Techniques like RFID (radio frequency identifications), sensors (e.g. BTNodes 1) and mobile devices, but also positioning systems like GPS (global positioning system) and wireless communication of all kinds, push this trend. Accompanied with this evolution and the rising diversity of systems, new concepts and techniques to provide adaptable and context-aware applications are required. Often, these applications will migrate between different platforms during their lifetime. As a typical example, a follow me application (e.g. personal information manager application) can have a different interface and state on a laptop, a cellular phone or a publicly accessible web-terminal. In other words, we expect that a mobile application has to adapt its state, the provided functionality and the implementation basis to its execution context, the target system and application-dependent restrictions.

Most recent object-based middleware and agent platforms restrict migration support to a certain programming language and environment. In this talk, the concept of adaptable mobile objects was proposed. These objects are capable of adapting their state, functionality and underlying code basis during migration to the requirements of the target platform and the needs of the object itself. We focus on weak migration. This means that only the state of an object is migrated but no execution-dependent state like, e.g., values on the stack. The proposed research builds on our recent platform- and ORB-independent implementation of the CORBA Life-Cycle Service that is based on CORBA value types, a standard CORBA mechanism for passing objects by value. This service combined with a logical separation of the mobile objects state, functionality and code enables support for adaptive ob ject migration in heterogeneous environments. In fact, our current prototype of a dynamic adaptation service for mobile objects, the adaptive ob ject migration (AOM) service, supports the migration of ob jects between Java and C++. Supporting other CORBA-supported languages requires only moderate implementation effort. To assist the developer during the implementation process, the AOM tool was presented. Additionally, mobile objects acting as mobile agents (an object having an own thread that executes autonomously on behalf of a user) is supported.

5   Summary of Invited Talks

We were happy to welcome two invited talks:

- "Programming for adaptability in ambient computing: towards a systemic approach" by Jacques Malenfant, Universit Pierre et Marie Curie, Paris, France (http://www-poleia.lip6.fr/~malenfant/)
- "Software Architectures for Context-Aware Computing - Experience and Emerging Challenges" by Bill Griswold, University of California, San Diego, USA (http://www.cs.ucsd.edu/~wgg/)

This section briefly summarizes these talks. The slides shown by the presenters during the talks can be downloaded from the workshop's website:
http://sam.iai.uni-bonn.de/ot4ami/Wiki.jsp?page=Program.

Programming for adaptability in Ambient Computing: Towards a systemic approach by Jacques Malenfant. The talk starts by motivating the point of view that ambient systems are systems that have to survive in a constantly evolving context or environment and that disconnection is no longer a fault but a feature of ambient systems. This challenges all aspects of software deployment. It has repercussions on such things as dynamic installations, quality of service and software reconfigurations. The answer to this problem is "dynamic adaptability": the application should react to changes in the execution context. A very fundamental problem here is that — during the application adaptation — time goes by. This means that the environment is changing *while* the application is adapting itself. This is a very well-known problem since the advent of radar-controlled antiaircraft guns in world war two: the fact that the target moves after having shot has to be taken into account when aiming.

Looking at the architectural considerations of ambient systems, it is probably worthwhile taking into account IBM's vision on the Automatic Computing Blueprint. The main idea is to allow computers to configure themselves and manage their own adaptations. Keywords are self-gouvernance, self-configuration, self-optimization, self-healing, self-protection and self-maintenance. This requires biologically inspired computing which we will call "systemic programming". Systemics is the science that studies systems that are too complex to be tackled through the traditional reductionist approach. It has applications in domains as diverse as biology, sociology and economy. The main idea of systemic programming is to have a large distributed self-control with a higher goal (i.e. evolve over time by learning from interactions with the environment). Challenges of systemic programming include modelling techniques (how do adequate local and globally emerging control models look like) and decision techniques (e.g., control theory, markovian decision processes, AI-heuristics). Furthermore, we need languages, methodologies and tools to program such systems.

The talk then continues by presenting the presenter's view on how to arrive at systemic programming. Two models are required: a reflection model and a decision model. The reflection model is the answer to the need for obtaining a static and dynamic model of the managed elements. It is used to reify representation of the managed elements. The presenter's view is that classical computational reflection is insufficient to tackle systemic needs. Current models for reflective computation usually take some metacircular form where the meta level implements the base level in a causally connected way. The major drawbacks of these models is that they are based on a strong and strict single threaded coupling between the base level and the meta level. Furthermore, they cannot tackle distribution because no global representation of the system can effectively be built. Finally, they cannot take into account he environment of a computing device because this is not necessarily causally connected.

The presenter moves on to present a new form of computational reflection, to wit asynchronous reflection. In this form of reflection, the meta level is no longer the language processor but takes the form of a general processor that controls the base level, in a concurrent way. It has many drawbacks over the current "synchronous" model of reflection: the base level and meta level keep each other informed about their evolution in terms of notifications and therefore, the meta level can sense events in the environment.

The second requirement for systemic programming is the presence of a decision model that decided on when the system should adapt itself. In classical computational reflection it is the task of the base level to decide when to "escape" to the meta level. In the model presented here adaptation is triggered based on occurrences of events in the environment. The presenter subsequently moves on to present a number of potential decision policies. They all reflect a sequence of decisions to take given a certain state of the system.

Software Architectures for Context-Aware Computing: Experience and Emerging Challenges by William Griswold. The presenter begins the talk by listing a number of facts. He states that there are many real needs and opportunities, yet very little progress. It appears as if the evolution is to have ever more nomadic systems that are increasingly *unaware* of their environment surrounding them: "I still can't find the printer when I need one". Furthermore, we are connected with a reasonable sensor platform (85 percent of Europe carries a mobile phone). Last, he states that mobile phones, as a commodity technology, must be part of the solution.

Next, a big experiment — called ActiveCampus — was presented. It is an ambient system on a university campus that gives students and professors an integrated access to all kinds of material such as librarie, courseware and administration. Furthermore, it offers a few innovative services such as place-its which can be considered as context-aware post-its: they pop up on your mobile phone whenever you arrive in a certain context. E.g., in a supermarket that has a good selection of wines, a "buy wine" place-it might pop up. The main goal of ActiveCampus is to increase social awareness of its users.

The presenter presents his major claims which boil down to the following:

- First, context-aware computing is governed by "the three laws of context-aware computing", namely the Ubiquity Law, the Commodity Law and the Systems Law. These are further explained in detail (see below).
- A number of complex phenomena arise from these laws. One of them is that failure becomes a normal mode of operation.
- The presenter acknowledges that most academic work acknowledges the same issues. These issues are not to be dealt with as an afterthought: they actually shape systems.

The three laws of context-aware computing in detail:

1. **The Ubiquity Law:** *A context-aware system is useful to the degree that a person can use it everywhere and that everyone can use it.* An example of this law are the omnipresence of the ability to place the place-its described above. All they need is a phone that is location-aware.
2. **The Commoditization Law:** *The cost pressures of ubiquity lead to commoditization, thereby increasing heterogeneity, interoperability, and fragility.* Again the place-its example is taken to explain the law.
3. **The Systems Law:** *Successfully designing a component of a context-aware system requires understanding key aspects of the whole.* As an example used to explain this, ActiveClass was used. This is a web-enabled "backchannel" to enable students to anonymously ask questions in class at any time. The presenter uses the example to show that adding a small feature (or component) can destroy the entire idea behind a system.

These three laws engender a number of key consequences and the presenter has spent a lot of time describing how his projects as UCB have tried to cope with them. The consequences are:

- Commoditization makes failure a normal mode of operation. The question then becomes how to design for this and how to make progress given this fact. Failures cannot be abstracted away. They are manifested in objects and interfaces. Furthermore, applications should remain useful and profoundly rich instead of confusing or hobbled.
- The commoditization and the systems law can be tackled somewhat using object technologies. However, the systems law implies the presence of system-wide interactions that complicate a design. Issues such as failure interweave and crosscut other components. Much of failure has to be designed into the application metaphor. This needs a holistic design. The presenter explains the usefulness of architecture-governed design patterns, AOP, reflection, publish/subscribe architectures and remote objects with rollback/replay facilities in this light.

The presenter finishes by stating that Ubiquity + Failure means that it "is better to operate 20% of the time in 100% of the world rather than 100% of the time in 20% of the world."

6   Discussions and Upcoming Issues

Although the workshop schedule was tight, there were vivid discussions among the 26 participants. We list some of the most prominent open questions here and hope that they will be addressed in later workshops or joint work.

- *Adaptivity and Autonomy:* The invited talk by Jacques Malenfant raised the question whether techniques of autonomous and self-organized systems should be taken into account. In particular when thinking of unanticipated situations, emergent behavior becomes an issue. The relation between programming techniques for adaptivity on the one side and for autonomous systems on the other might be fruitful area for further research.
- *Dynamically vs. statically typed languages and reflection vs. aspects:* On the language level two competing approaches are status quo: dynamically typed languages with reflection on the one hand and statically typed languages enhanced with aspects on the other. The question under which circumstances which of these alternatives is more adequate is still not fully answered.
- *Frameworks, component systems, and programming languages:* Another question involves the language level as well as the component level: Do we need AmI-specific languages, or can we cope the requirements on the component or service level? How do they depend on each other or are open to be combined?
- *Systematic comparison of different techniques:* A basis for a systematic comparison between different programming instruments is missing. A start in this direction could be to create a concise catalogue of technical requirements. An example are typical security and privacy issues and how they can be achieved using reflection or aspects.
- *Context Representation:* How should context be represented? In which should we model is as data and in which as an activity?
- *Limits of Ontology-based approaches:* In order to allow context-driven adaptations to be performed without full anticipation, ontologies will play an important role (e.g. for detecting adequate services in a given application situation). It has to be expected that ontology-based work for service selection will face basically the same problems that were encountered in artificial intelligence (i.e. you cannot compare mathematic functions).

Parallel/High-Performance Object-Oriented Scientific Computing Today
Report on the WS POOSC at ECOOP'06

Kei Davis[1] and Jörg Striegnitz[2]

[1] Modeling, Algorithms, and Informatics, CCS-3, MS B256
Los Alamos National Laboratory
Los Alamos, NM 87545, U.S.A.
Kei.Davis@lanl.gov
http://www.c3.lanl.gov/~kei
[2] University of Applied Sciences Regensburg
93053 Regensburg, Germany
Tel.: +49 94 19 43 13 14; Fax: +49 94 19 43 14 26
joerg.striegnitz@informtik.fh-regensburg.de

Following is the report on the workshop on Parallel/Object-Oriented Scientific Computing 2006 (POOSC'06) held at the European Conference on Object-Oriented Programming, 20th edition, July 3–7, Nantes, France.

1 Motivation, History, and Abstract

In this section we attempt to motivate the appropriateness of an ongoing workshop series on parallel/high-performance object-oriented scientific computing, give a brief history of the workshop series, and state our current working purview via the current abstract.

1.1 Motivation

Scientific programming has reached an unprecedented degree of complexity. Sopisticated algorithms, a wide range of hardware environments, and an increasing demand for system integration, portability, and fault tolerance have shown that language-level abstraction must increase; at the same time performance must not be compromised.

Work presented at previous POOSC workshops has shown that the OO approach provides an effective means for the design of highly complex scientific systems, and that it is possible to design abstractions and applications that fulfill strict performance constraints.

However, OO still isn't embraced in high performance computing and there is still demand for and active interest in research and discussion. Previous POOSC workshops have proven that a workshop is an ideal venue for this, that new approaches and techniques are being developed, and that researchers and developers are keen to share these in a live, interactive setting.

M. Südholt and C. Consel (Eds.): ECOOP 2006 Ws, LNCS 4379, pp. 141–145, 2007.

1.2 History

The current organizers, with various changes in personnel over the years, have organized successful POOSC workshops several times, once at OOPSLA'01 and the others at previous ECOOP conferences. Response to the CFP has always been sufficiently good that a formal reviewing process had to be imposed. The workshops themselves have been lively forums for debate and discussion and have resulted in a number of new collaborations.

1.3 Abstract

While object-oriented programming has been embraced in industry, particularly in the form of C++, Java, and Python, its acceptance by the parallel scientific programming community is for various reasons incomplete. Nonetheless, various factors practically dictate the use of language features that provide higher level abstractions than FORTRAN or C, including increasingly complex numerical algorithms, application requirements, and hardware (e.g. deep memory hierarchies, rapidly increasing numbers of processors, multi-core processors, communication, and I/O, and the need for user-level fault tolerance).

This workshop series seeks to bring together practitioners and researchers in this growing field to 'compare notes' on their work. The emphasis is on identifying specific problems impeding greater acceptance and widespread use of object-oriented programming in scientific computing; proposed and implemented solutions to these problems; and new or novel frameworks, approaches, techniques, or idioms for object-oriented scientific and/or parallel computing. Presentations of work in progress are welcome.

2 Summary of Call for Participation

While object-oriented programming is being embraced in industry, particularly in the form of C++ and to an increasing extent Java and Python, its acceptance by the parallel scientific programming community is still tentative. In this latter domain performance is invariably of paramount importance, where even the transition from FORTRAN 77 to C is incomplete, primarily because of real or perceived loss of performance. On the other hand, various factors practically dictate the use of language features that provide better paradigms for abstraction: increasingly complex numerical algorithms, application requirements, and hardware (e.g. deep memory hierarchies, numbers of processors, multi-core processors, communication and I/O); and the need for user-level fault tolerance.

This workshop seeks to bring together practitioners and researchers in this growing field to 'compare notes' on their work. The emphasis is on identifying specific problems impeding greater acceptance and widespread use of object-oriented programming in scientific computing; proposed and implemented solutions to these problems; and new or novel approaches, techniques or idioms for scientific and/or parallel computing. Presentations of work in progress are welcome.

Specific areas of interest include, but are not limited to:

- tried or proposed programming language alternatives to C++;
- performance issues and their realized or proposed resolution;
- issues specific to handling or abstracting parallelism;
- specific points of concern for progress and acceptance of object-oriented scientific computing;
- existing, developing, or proposed software;
- frameworks and tools for scientific object-oriented computing;
- schemes for user-level fault tolerance;
- grand visions (of relevance).

The workshop will consist of a sequences of presentations each followed by a discussion session. The workshop will conclude with an overall discussion. We expect the majority of the participants to give presentations.

3   Summary of Contributions

This section briefly describes each of the contributions, and attempts to put each in a larger context motivating the problems to be solved.

In the paper *The dimension-independent programming paradigm and its application in the deal.II finite element library*, Wolfgang Bangerth revisited a long-standing problem in scientific C++ programming: how to codify a programming style, metaprogramming using the C++ template mechanism, that yields both a dimension-independent interface *and* no significant loss in efficiency.

Fortran 95 was designed to support object-oriented programming, though its facilities are not nearly as powerful or expressive as those of C++. In the paper *Object-oriented programming in Fortran95: Patterns and process*, Henry Gardner developed this theme to demonstrate how design patterns may be expressed in Fortran 95, and how their use can benefit the software engineering development and maintenance cycle in this context.

Rene Heinzl, P. Schwaha, M. Spevak, and T. Grasser, in the paper *Performance aspects of a DSEL for Scientific Computing with C++*, addressed a number of topics in scientific OO programming: the embedding of a domain-specific language in C++, multi-paradigm programming in C++—functional programming in their case, and the mitigation of resulting performance issues.

Effective decomposition (or partitioning) and distribution of data structures for parallel computing is problematic when the data structures are 'inhomogeneous,' for example for sparse structures. The problem of obtaining good parallel speed-up is worsened when allowing a heterogeneous computing platform, including computational grids. In the paper *Parallel Object Programming in Pop-C++: a case study for sparse matrix-vector multiplication*, Clovis Dongmo Jiogo, Kevin Cristiano, Pierre Kuonen, Pierre Manneback, and Tuan Anh Nguyen directly addressed these problems, with a detailed case study, in POP-C++ ("Parallel Object Programming with C++"), a framework for providing service abtraction for Grid middleware.

Toon Knapen and Karl Meerbergen addressed a long-standing tension in scientific computing: providing generic interfaces without loss of performance. In the presentation entitled *Generic interface to linear algebra operations that allows maximal performance as well as convenience* they describe a framework *glas* (generic linear algebra software) that seeks to provide a truly generic interface to various existing, highly optimized, numerical backends via a modular architecture.

In the paper *Typesafe and Size-Deducing Fast Expression Templates for Small Arrays*, Andrea Lani and Herman Deconinck explicated a number of techniques for improving C++ expression template performance for regular array operations. One significant issue addressed was preventing reinstantiation of their FET (fast expression template) objects by dynamically loaded libraries. Another was compile-time detection of fixed-size (as opposed to dynamically allocated) arrays to allow complete loop unrolling.

Tiago Quintino and Herman Deconinck proposed a solution to the management of large numbers of data types and associated algorithms typically found in coupled multi-physics simulations, with automatic enforcement of type safety. In *A context architecture for managing data collections in multi-method parallel environments*, they described an approach based on a *context architecture*, where methods expose typed data sockets as part of their interfaces to allow compile-time guarantees of type correctness.

A known problem in C++ template metaprogramming is that multiple formulations of an algorithm must be explicity coded by the programmer to achieve performance commensurate with possible parameter properties (roughly, whether they are static or dynamic). Andreas Priesnitz and Sibylle Schupp, in *From Generic Invocations to Generic Implementations*, described a technique that allows an algorithm to be implemented generically by a single definition, wherein the choice of argument representation determines how the algorithm is evaluated, and so implicitly what versions of the code are generated.

Viktória Zsók, Zoltán Hernyák, and Zoltán Horvath, in *Distributed Computation on Cluster D-Clean and D-Box*, described a multi-paradigm environment for distributed computation. Their approach used a two-level abstraction: a higher-level coordination language for abstracting the distributed computation of purely functional subtasks, and lower-level 'computatonal boxes' and embodied the subtasks. While these subtasks were expressed in a purely functional language, they pointed out that it is only necessary that the semantics be purely functional, that these subtasks could be implemented in a number of supported OO languages including C++, Java, and Python.

4   The Great Debate

The final discussion session of the workshop was devoted to open commentary: the value of this workshop, the appropriateness of a POOSC workshop in general, and the most fitting venues for the workshop. To the first two considerations there was unanimity that the workshop was worthwhile and the series should be continued.

A spirited debate arose, however, about choice of venue or venues for the workshop. To date they have been held at ECOOP with two exceptions: in 2001 a POOSC workshop was held at OOPSLA (Object-Oriented Programming, Systems, Languages, and Applications), and in 2002 at OOPSLA where it was coalesced with JavaGrande.

The debate regarding venue was initiated during the last discussion session of the day, and continued by email after the conference, with most participants tendering opinions.

The essence of the argument was whether the workshop is more appropriate to a computer science/languages conference, or a computational science/software frameworks conference. Some computational scientists present deemed the workshop interesting and worthwhile, but found the ECOOP conference as a whole too far out of field to be of interest. The computer scientists, in contrast, revel in both the content and atmosphere of ECOOP.

One prospective participant has since organized a software frameworks workshop at an applied mathematics conference, and this branching is not unwelcome: it provides a venue for those not interested in the *programming language* aspects of parallel object-oriented scientific computing. We elect to retain the qualification of scientific computing because we wish to remain focused on true parallel computing and not consider the much broader field of distributed computing.

5   Conclusion

The POOSC workshop remains an attractive venue for both computer scientists, and to a lesser extent computational scientists, to showcase and discuss their current research, as evidenced by the level of contribution and participation. The field is active, with significant progress being made on numerous problematic fronts, and specifically on many of those enumerated in the call for papers.

Tenth Workshop on Pedagogies and Tools for the Teaching and Learning of Object Oriented Concepts
Report on the WS TLOOC at ECOOP'06

Jürgen Börstler

Umeå University, Sweden
jubo@cs.umu.se

Abstract. This report summarizes the results of the tenth workshop on pedagogies and tools for the teaching and learning of object-oriented concepts. The focus of this year's workshop was on examples, modelling and abstraction. Participants agreed that carefully developed scaffolded examples are a key element for learning to program. For the teaching of modelling and abstraction this area, however, seems badly neglected. The workshop gathered 12 participants, all from academia, from 10 different countries.

1 Introduction

It is generally accepted that transitioning to object-oriented development implies a paradigm shift. Compared to procedural development it requires different ways of thinking and different ways of approaching problems. Very likely, it therefore also requires a different way of teaching. Although the object-oriented paradigm has become mainstream long ago, approaches for teaching introductory programming courses are still heavily discussed [7].

Traditionally, programming concepts have been systematically introduced one after one, each building nicely on the concepts already learned. Abstract and advanced concepts, like for example modules and abstract data types, could be handled in later courses. In the object-oriented paradigm, on the other hand, the basic concepts are tightly interrelated and cannot easily be taught and learned in isolation. Furthermore, the basic object-oriented concepts are on a higher level of abstraction. Together this results in a higher threshold for the learner.

The complexity of common languages, libraries and tools add to this problem [1]. It is therefore important to share experiences and explore ideas that can help us to improve the teaching and learning of object technology.

This was the tenth in a series of workshops on issues related to the teaching and learning of object technology. Reports from previous workshops and links to the accepted contributions of most workshops can be found at the workshop series home page[1].

---

[1] http://www.cs.umu.se/research/education/ooEduWS.html

M. Südholt and C. Consel (Eds.): ECOOP 2006, LNCS 4379, pp. 146–156, 2007.

The workshop format makes it possible to present and discuss actual results as well as early ideas for approaches and tools to support the teaching and learning of object-oriented concepts. For 2006, we particularly invited submissions on the following topics:

- successfully used exercises, examples and metaphors;
- approaches and tools for teaching object-oriented concepts;
- approaches and tools for teaching analysis and design;
- ordering of topics, in particular when to teach analysis and design;
- teaching outside the CS curriculum;
- experiences with innovative CS1 curricula and didactic concepts;
- learning theories and pedagogical approaches / methods;
- misconceptions related to object technology; and
- learners' views on object technology education.

2 Workshop Organization

Participation at the workshop was by invitation only. The number of participants was limited to encourage lively discussions. Potential attendees were required to submit either a full research paper or experience report, or a position paper or vision statement.

Out of the 11 contributions that were submitted, 3 papers were selected for formal presentation at the workshop (30 minutes each). An additional 5 papers were selected for short presentations (15 minutes each). All accepted contributions were made available on the workshop's home page some weeks before the workshop, to give attendees the opportunity to prepare for the discussions.

All formal presentation activities were scheduled for the morning sessions to get enough time for discussions around particular questions. The full workshop program can be found in table 1.

The workshop gathered 12 participants from 10 different countries, all of them from academia. A complete list of participants together with their affiliations and e-mail addresses can be found in table 3.

3 Summary of Presentations

This section summarizes the main points of the presented papers and the main issues raised during the morning discussions. Copies of the presented papers can be obtained from the workshop's home page[2].

3.1 Short Papers

Irit Hadar (University of Haifa, Israel) claimed that abstraction is one of the most important skills for successfully applying object technology. Abstraction is also commonly identified as one of the fundamental concepts of object technology [3].

---

[2] http://www.cs.umu.se/~jubo/Meetings/ECOOP06

Table 1. Workshop program

9:00   **Welcome and introduction**
9:15   **SHORT PAPERS**
– **Iterative Cycle for Teaching Object Oriented Concepts: From Abstract Thinking to Specific Language Implementation,** *Irit Hadar and Ethan Hadar, Israel*
– **Visualize and Open Up,** *Michela Pedroni and Till G. Bay, Switzerland*
– **Teaching Multiparadigm Programming Based on Object-Oriented Experiences,** *Zoltán Porkoláb and Viktória Zsók, Hungary*
– **Learning by Doing: Using an Extendible Language to Teach OO Concepts,** *Dehla Sokenou and Stephan Herrmann, Germany*
– **A Design for Trustability Approach to Teach Object-Oriented Program Development,** *Daniel Deveaux, France*
10:30   **Coffee break**
11:00   **FULL PAPERS**
– **Appreciation of Software Design Concerns via OpenSource,** *Christopher P. Fuhrman, Canada*
– **Computer Aided Modelling Exercises,** *Monique Snoeck, Ralf Haesen and Manu De Backer, Belgium*
– **Teaching/Learning a First Object-Oriented Programming Course Outside the CS Curriculum,** *Jorge Villalobos and Rubby Casallas, Colombia*
12:30   **Lunch break**
13:30   **Working group discussions**
15:00   **Coffee break**
15:30   **Working group discussions contd.**
16:30   **Summary and wrap-up**
17:00   **Closing**

Developing abstract thinking skills takes a long time. Novices are known to have difficulties in practising abstract thinking. When solving problems they tend to think at low abstraction levels and therefore often cannot see the forest for the trees. However, Irit's research shows that even experienced developers think at lower levels of abstraction than appropriate [12].

So, how can we support the learning of abstract thinking from the very beginning? Teaching design or modelling early seems a good idea [5,14]. However, understanding abstract concepts requires a good understanding of the concrete concepts they are based on [2]. Abstract knowledge constructed without a good understanding of the underlying concrete concepts is therefore fragile.

To overcome these problems, Irit proposed an iterative teaching approach switching constantly between abstraction levels. A visual modelling language (UML) is used as a tool to support abstract thinking. Concepts are always

Table 2. Categorization of contributions

	Group	Problem	Solution	Validation
Hadar, Hadar	Novices	Abstraction	Iterate between abstract models (in UML) and concrete code	Initial experience
Pedroni, Bay	Novices	Motivation	Open project assignments using advanced multimedia libraries	Course evaluations (2005-2006)
Porkoláb, Zsók	2nd year	Multiple paradigms	Teach many paradigms; show many examples	By experience (since 1995)
Sokenou, Herrmann	3rd year	Teaching OO concepts	Let students implement an "object system" using a simple interpreter language	By experience (since 1999)
Deveaux	Varies	Software quality	Semi-formal V&V; "a software project is a documentation project, not a coding project"	By experience (since 2000)
Fuhrman	Advanced	Design evaluation	Reverse engineer and analyse software from open-source projects	Initial experience
Snoeck, Haesen, De Backer	Non-CS	OOA	Usage of the didactical tool **Mermaid** for basic model checking and feedback	Course and tool evaluations (2004-2005)
Villalobos, Casallas	Novices	Motivation	Active learning based on fully worked examples; proceed in very small steps	Course evaluation (2006); detailed evaluation in progress

presented and explained in abstract/concrete pairs; UML models and the concrete corresponding code. During the course, models and code are always kept consistent. This helps students to internalize the abstract/concrete correspondencies.

The visual models constitute "abstraction barriers" and force students to focus attention at certain levels of abstraction. In a class diagram for example, attention cannot be shifted to details of method code, since it cannot be expressed at this level of abstraction.

According to Irit, initial experience with this approach is quite positive.

Michela Pedroni (ETH Zürich, Switzerland) presented experience from a redesigned introductory programming course at ETH Zürich using the inverted curriculum approach [13] and open project assignments. In this approach the students start from a consumer perspective. They learn to use existing objects and (library) components as "black boxes" before learning about implementation details. For the open project assignment, students extend or employ existing libraries or applications. Some of them have been specifically been developed for this purpose,

Table 3. List of workshop participants

Name	Affiliation	E-mail Address
Meriem Belguidoum	*ENST Bretagne, France*	meriem.belguidoum@enst-bretagne.fr
Jürgen Börstler	*Umeå University, Sweden*	jubo@cs.umu.se
Rubby Casallas	*University of Los Andes, Colombia*	rcasalla@uniandes.edu.co
Daniel Deveaux	*Université de Bretagne-Sud, France*	daniel.deveaux@univ-ubs.fr
Christopher Fuhrman	*École de Technologie Superieure, Canada*	christopher.fuhrman@etsmtl.ca
Irit Hadar	*University of Haifa, Israel*	hadari@mis.haifa.ac.il
Stephan Herrmann	*Technische Universität Berlin, Germany*	stephan@cs.tu-berlin.de
Michela Pedroni	*ETH Zürich, Switzerland*	pedronim@inf.ethz.ch
Zoltán Porkoláb	*Eötvös Loránd University Budapest, Hungary*	gsd@elte.hu
Monique Snoeck	*Katholieke Universiteit Leuven, Belgium*	monique.snoeck@econ.kuleuven.be
Darren Willis	*Victoria University of Wellington, New Zealand*	darren@mcs.vuw.ac.nz
Viktória Zsók	*Eötvös Loránd University Budapest, Hungary*	zsv@inf.elte.hu

like for example a traffic simulation framework, built on `EiffelMedia`, a multimedia library for the programming language Eiffel[3].

Using these tools, students can develop quite advanced applications at the end of their introductory programming course, which increases their motivation and enthusiasm for the field. Open project assignments make it possible for the students to define projects after their own interests, typically computer games in the case of young men and "meaningful" applications in other areas than computer science for young women.

Course evaluations show that the open project component has increased student's satisfaction with the course significantly.

Zoltán Porkoláb (Eötvös Loránd University Budapest, Hungary) described his experience from teaching multiple paradigms to second year students. He too believes that abstraction is a central skill for computer scientists. The development of abstractions is highly influenced by the paradigm used for problem understanding and decomposition.

He argued that most real problems are so complex and multi-faceted that they cannot be solved in a good way using a single paradigm. It is therefore necessary to teach multiple paradigms (functional, object-oriented, aspect-oriented, metaprogramming, etc.), so students can choose the tools best suited for the

---

[3] See `http://se.ethz.ch/download/index.html` for more information on the tools.

problem at hand. In his presentation Zoltán gave several examples where switching paradigms can be an advantage, for example to improve run-time efficiency.

Although the audience supported most of Zoltán's ideas, there were several questions with respect to the teaching of such an approach. Since there are no explicit criteria for the selection of a paradigm, teaching is mainly example-based. How then can a student know whether a particular problem can be more easily or better solved using another paradigm? Solutions could be found in multiparadigm-oriented analysis and design as proposed by Coplien [8] or multiparadigm software metrics [15].

Stephan Herrmann (Technische Universität Berlin) talked about his experience teaching object-oriented concepts independently of a particular object-oriented language. The basic idea is to let students implement their own object system using the simple interpreted language Lua[4]. Lua is an imperative language with a Pascal-like syntax, one rich datatype, automatic garbage collection and extensible semantics.

Different programming languages can give quite different meanings to object-oriented concepts. Inheritance for example is realized quite different in C++, Smalltalk or CLOS. In this course students are introduced to many object-oriented languages and use Lua to implement different flavours of object-oriented concepts. An implementation of dynamic binding, for example, takes only about 15 lines of Lua code.

Stephan's experience shows that students learn to differentiate between general object-oriented concepts and their realization in a particular programming language. This leads to a better understanding of these concepts.

Lua is very easy to learn and use for students with an imperative or object-oriented background. That is a big advantage over for example Scheme, which could also be used for the same purpose. This approach has been successfully used to teach a variety of programming language concepts.

Daniel Deveaux (Université de Bretagne-Sud, France) talked about "Design for Trustability" (DfT). The main idea behind DfT is to make software quality and customer satisfaction central to development. Verification and Validation (V&V) are important activities in industrial software development, but they are often neglected in educational programs.

Daniel and his colleagues have developed a complete development process supporting DfT, which is taught (with variations) in several courses at Université de Bretagne-Sud. In DfT documentation is central. The documentation constitutes a description of the knowledge of the development group. It is the basis for exchanging information and building up trust in customers. He therefore claims that "a software project is a documentation project, not a coding project".

The documentation is also the basis for V&V activities, by means of semi-formal contracts. Experiences from using DfT in many courses are very positive. The DfT framework can be easily adapted to a particular goal of a course.

---

[4] http://www.lua.org

Emphasis can be put on modelling, traceability of models, derivation of tests, actual testing or coding (according to given contracts).

The biggest problem in using this approach is the lack of integrated tools. This makes it difficult and time-consuming for students to keep all documentation (models, contracts, test cases, etc.) consistent and up-to-date.

3.2 Full Papers

Christopher P. Fuhrman (École de Technologie Superieure, Canada) shared his experience of using open-source software as a resource in a professional masters course on software design.

In textbooks one rarely can find convincing examples conveying the real importance of topics like notation, architecture, documentation of design decisions or assessment of design qualities. Christopher proposes to use open-source software to overcome this motivational problem.

Students analyse real code from real (open-source) projects with the goal of identifying problems and proposing solutions to mitigate these problems. First, students have to select an open-source project with at least 25 classes. Then they reverse engineer the software to produce a documentation (mainly UML diagrams) that can be understood by their classmates. This step is supported by Omondo[5], an Eclipse plug-in for reverse/round-trip engineering for Java/UML. This first exercise helps students appreciate design notations.

As a second exercise, students have to assess the quality of the software of a reverse engineered project. They choose a quality factor they aim to assess, like for example maintainability. Then they have to identify and discuss measurable characteristics (metrics) that can be used in this assessment. The linkage between the metrics used and the design qualities has to be supported by at least two sources (books, articles, etc.). This step is supported by Eclipse plug-in for metrics[6] and static code analysis (PMD[7]).

In their third exercise students propose improvements to the software analysed before. Usually this involves the application of design patterns.

According to Christopher, students like course and the tools, and appreciate the limitations of metrics.

Monique Snoeck (Katholieke Universiteit Leuven, Belgium) talked about her experience using the didactical CASE-tool Mermaid[8] for teaching object-oriented domain and business modelling to a diverse group of non-CS students.

Mermaid supports two kinds of models; data models (UML class diagrams) and behavioural models (finite state machines). The tool has several pedagogical features for validation/feedback. The data model can be converted to plain text, which is particularly useful for students totally unfamiliar with domain and

---

[5] http://www.omondo.com
[6] http://sourceforge.net/projects/metrics
[7] http://sourceforge.net/projects/pmd
[8] http://sourceforge.net/projects/merode

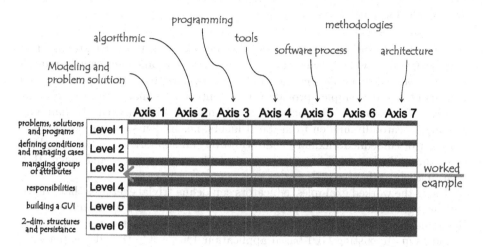

Fig. 1. The role of worked examples in relation to thematic axes and levels (©Rubby Casallas, used with permission)

business modelling. For the state machines the tool provides basic model checking for completeness and consistency.

The tool can also generate prototypes from the models using AndroMDA[9]. This helps students in validating their models against the original user requirements and building mental models of both the data and the behavioural views.

Evaluations show that students find the tool useful. The tool has also been shown to improve the students' modelling skills.

Rubby Casallas (University of Los Andes, Colombia) presented first experiences from a new approach to introductory programming. The approach builds on seven thematic axes of fundamental knowledge and skills for software development. Course topics are structured along these axes and introduced step by step by means of fully worked examples. Each example is a working GUI-based Java application with a complete set of documentation (detailed specification, design, various kinds of diagrams, test cases, code and manuals) [18].

The course topics, and hence the thematic axes, are furthermore organized into six levels; from "Problems, solutions and programs" to "Two dimensional structures and persistence". Each level gradually introduces new concepts and reinforces topics from lower levels, see figure 1. At level six the students eventually develop a simple application from scratch.

The approach has been developed as a collaborative project between several colombian universities. It has been successfully tested in an introductory programming course with 900 students, mostly engineers. Initial course evaluations show promising results. The student satisfaction rate increased from from 70-74% to 87% and the failure rate dropped from 26-30% to 16%.

---

[9] http://andromda.org/

4 Discussions

During the afternoon sessions, several aspects of the approach presented by Rubby Casallas were discussed in more detail. The audience considered the levelled worked examples as one of the main strengths of the approach. One one hand, these examples provide a rich context that makes it easy to define "meaningful" exercises. On the other hand, most of this context (GUI handling, testing) is carefully hidden from the students, i.e. students are not scared away by a lot of embedded auxiliary code. However, all supporting material is there, if required. Such a scaffolding reduces students' cognitive load and makes their learning more effective [17].

Using the worked examples, educators can define trivial exercises that still result in significant changes in program behaviour. On level 1 for example, which lasts the first three weeks, students only change and test a few very small code snippets in an existing GUI-based application. On level 6, they develop a small but complete application (including GUI and JUnit tests) given a set of functional requirements.

Currently, about 60 worked examples exist. In addition there are also some training tools to exercise certain topics.[10]

The project consumed huge effort and would not have been possible without collaborating with other universities. According to Rubby, about 20 people worked half-time on this project over 3.5 years! The project is supported by a "learning community" for sharing materials for courses based on this approach. Currently, about 35 educators are actively participating in this community.

Despite these efforts, the approach did not succeed in attracting students from various engineering disciplines to computer science. This was one of the original goals for the project. However, at least the drop-outs from computer science programs could be stopped.

Another aspect discussed in the afternoon was modelling and abstraction. How can we help students understand and appreciate models? How can we prevent them from jumping into details too early and/or too often? Even for the educators this is very difficult. Like in the case of programming examples, we likely need better examples to establish models (usually UML diagrams) as "thinking tools". As long as models are treated as add-ons that take a lot of extra time to develop, their teaching will be difficult.

The approaches proposed by Irit Hadar, Christopher P. Fuhrman and Monique Snoeck actually use models as tools. Doing so can provide educators with convincing arguments in favour of modelling. When the code is too complex to understand or can be generated (derived) from a model that is easier to develop than the raw code, modelling makes a lot of sense.

The often claimed "naturalness" of object-orientation was identified as another factor contributing to student problems with modelling and abstraction. This naturalness is often equated with "simple" and may lead students to premature

---

[10] Many worked examples and "training wheels" can be downloaded from http:// cupi2.uniandes.edu.co

solutions. They can for example miss that the behaviour of model objects can be quite different from their real-life counterparts. A die in a model for example will likely know its face value and take care of rolling (changing its face value). Furthermore, model objects are always honest. A borrower object could for example be responsible for the book-keeping of its own fines and will always answer correctly (if not implemented otherwise). The often cited closeness between objects/classes in the problem domain and the solution domain only exists at a very high abstraction level. Taking the correspondence too far will lead to deficient or even erroneous models.

These lessons can only be learned when educators offer good role models. If students never encounter interesting modelling problems and discussions, they will never learn to appreciate modelling and abstraction as useful thinking tools. We must therefore provide rationale for our own models, before jumping to a particular solution. We must make clear the process (the How) and the reasoning (the Why) that lead us to a particular solution (the What). Students must also be rewarded for their modelling rationale, instead of possibly premature solutions alone.

This raises two important issues; examples and assessment. Where do we find suitable examples? Textbooks rarely, if ever, provide How and Why. Furthermore, how do we determine the quality of a model? As for code, syntactical correctness and consistency are important, but insufficient to assess the quality of a model.

There is a large body of literature on design qualities, principles, heuristics and patterns (e.g., [4,9,10,11,16]). However, only the latter topic has made it into the educational literature, although on the What-level only. The rest is largely ignored.

Investigating this body of literature would help in identifying a set of core guidelines for educational purposes. Likewise, it seems useful to investigate recurring problems in the (premature) models developed by students. This could help to extend the guidelines by anti-patterns [6] or code smells [10] which would be very useful for quality control.

5   Summary and Conclusions

This was the tenth workshop in a series of workshops on pedagogies and tools for the teaching and learning of object-oriented concepts. It gathered 12 participants, who shared experiences from a wide range of teaching contexts.

The presentations revealed that, in certain contexts, a good idea can be sufficient to solve a particular teaching/learning problem. On the other hand, huge efforts can be necessary to solve more basic problems in more general ways.

Our discussions focused mainly on the importance of examples for learning and teaching programming as well as modelling. The conclusions can be summarized as follows.

- *Use worked examples.* They lower the threshold for learning to program. They also make it easier for educators to define meaningful examples.
- *Modelling and abstraction are important.* They are at the core of the object-oriented paradigm. Students should learn to appreciate modelling and abstraction as useful "thinking tools".

- *Integrate models/abstraction in your teaching.* This can be done explicitly, like in the models-early approach presented by Irit Hadar (see sec. 3.1) or implicitly, like in the inverted curriculum approach as presented by Michela Pedroni (see sec. 3.1).
- *Provide rationale.* Educators should provide the reasoning that leads to a particular solution. For the students, the How and Why are as valuable as the actual result.
- *Don't ignore research.* There is a large body of literature on design. This should be exploited for courseware development.

References

1. ACM Java Task Force: Java Task Force materials, Version 1.0 (2006) `http://jtf.acm.org/index.html`, accessed 2006-10-05
2. Aharoni, D., Leron, U.: Abstraction is Hard in Computer-Science too. Proceedings of the 21st Conference of the International Group for the Psychology of Mathematics Education, Vol. 3 (1997) 2-9–2-16
3. Armstrong, D. J.: The Quarks of Object-Oriented Development. Communications of the ACM **49** (2) (2006) 123–128
4. Basili, V. R., Briand, L. C., Melo, W. L.: A validation of Object-Oriented Design Metrics as Quality Indicators. IEEE Transactions on Software Engineering **22** (10) (2004) 751–761
5. Bennedsen, J., Caspersen, M. C.: Programming in Context—A Model-First Approach to CS1. Proceedings of the 35th SIGCSE Technical Symposium on Computer Science Education (2004) 477–481
6. Brown, W. J., Malveau, R. C., Mowbray, T. J.: AntiPatterns: Refactoring Software, Architectures, and Projects in Crisis Wiley (1998)
7. Bruce, K.: Controversy on How to Teach CS 1: A Discussion on the SIGCSE-members Mailing List. SIGCSE Bulletin – Inroads **36** (4) (2004) 29–35
8. Coplien, J.O.: Multi-Paradigm Design for C++. Addison-Wesley (1998)
9. Eichelberger, H.: Nice Class Diagrams Admit Good Design? Proceedings Software Visualization (2003) 159–167, 216
10. Fowler, M.: Refactoring: Improving the Design of Existing Code. Addison-Wesley (1999)
11. Gamma, E., Helm, R., Johnson, R., Vlissides, J.: Design Patterns: Elements of Reusable Object-Oriented Software. Addison-Wesley (1995)
12. Hadar, I.: The Study of Concept Understanding via Abstract Representation: The Case of Object Oriented Design. PhD thesis. Technion – Israel Institute of Technology (2004)
13. Meyer, B.: Towards an Object-Oriented Curriculum. Journal of Object-Oriented Programming **6** (2) (1993) 76–81
14. Moritz, S. H., Blank, G. D.: A Design-First Curriculum for Teaching Java in a CS1 Course. SIGCSE Bulletin **37** (2) (2005) 89–93
15. Porkoláb, Z., Sillye, Á.: Towards a Multiparadigm Complexity Measure. ECOOP – QAOOSE Workshop (2005) 134–142
16. Riel, A.: Object-Oriented Design Heuristics. Addison-Wesley (1996)
17. Sweller, J., van Merriënboer, J., Paas, F.: Cognitive Architecture and Instructional Design. Educational Psychology Review **10** (3) (1998) 251–296
18. Villalobos, J. G., Casallas, R.: Fundamentos de Programación: Aprendizaje Activo Basado en Problemas. In Spanish. Prentice-Hall (2006)

Author Index

Lecture Notes in Computer Science

For information about Vols. 1–4347

please contact your bookseller or Springer

Vol. 4398: S. Marchand-Maillet, E. Bruno, A. Nürnberger, M. Detyniecki (Eds.), Adaptive Multimedia Retrieval: User, Context, and Feedback. XI, 269 pages. 2007.

Vol. 4397: C. Stephanidis, M. Pieper (Eds.), Universal Access in Ambient Intelligence Environments. XV, 467 pages. 2007.

Vol. 4396: J. García-Vidal, L. Cerdà-Alabern (Eds.), Wireless Systems and Mobility in Next Generation Internet. IX, 271 pages. 2007.

Vol. 4395: M. Daydé, J.M.L.M. Palma, Á.L.G.A. Coutinho, E. Pacitti, J.C. Lopes (Eds.), High Performance Computing for Computational Science - VEC-PAR 2006. XXIV, 721 pages. 2007.

Vol. 4394: A. Gelbukh (Ed.), Computational Linguistics and Intelligent Text Processing. XVI, 648 pages. 2007.

Vol. 4393: W. Thomas, P. Weil (Eds.), STACS 2007. XVIII, 708 pages. 2007.

Vol. 4392: S.P. Vadhan (Ed.), Theory of Cryptography. XI, 595 pages. 2007.

Vol. 4391: Y. Stylianou, M. Faundez-Zanuy, A. Esposito (Eds.), Progress in Nonlinear Speech Processing. XII, 269 pages. 2007.

Vol. 4390: S.O. Kuznetsov, S. Schmidt (Eds.), Formal Concept Analysis. X, 329 pages. 2007. (Sublibrary LNAI).

Vol. 4389: D. Weyns, H.V.D. Parunak, F. Michel (Eds.), Environments for Multi-Agent Systems III. X, 273 pages. 2007. (Sublibrary LNAI).

Vol. 4385: K. Coninx, K. Luyten, K.A. Schneider (Eds.), Task Models and Diagrams for Users Interface Design. XI, 355 pages. 2007.

Vol. 4384: T. Washio, K. Satoh, H. Takeda, A. Inokuchi (Eds.), New Frontiers in Artificial Intelligence. IX, 401 pages. 2007. (Sublibrary LNAI).

Vol. 4383: E. Bin, A. Ziv, S. Ur (Eds.), Hardware and Software, Verification and Testing. XII, 235 pages. 2007.

Vol. 4381: J. Akiyama, W.Y.C. Chen, M. Kano, X. Li, Q. Yu (Eds.), Discrete Geometry, Combinatorics and Graph Theory. XI, 289 pages. 2007.

Vol. 4380: S. Spaccapietra, P. Atzeni, F. Fages, M.-S. Hacid, M. Kifer, J. Mylopoulos, B. Pernici, P. Shvaiko, J. Trujillo, I. Zaihrayeu (Eds.), Journal on Data Semantics VIII. XV, 219 pages. 2007.

Vol. 4379: M. Südholt, C. Consel (Eds.), Object-Oriented Technology. VIII, 157 pages. 2007.

Vol. 4378: I. Virbitskaite, A. Voronkov (Eds.), Perspectives of Systems Informatics. XIV, 496 pages. 2007.

Vol. 4377: M. Abe (Ed.), Topics in Cryptology – CT-RSA 2007. XI, 403 pages. 2006.

Vol. 4376: E. Frachtenberg, U. Schwiegelshohn (Eds.), Job Scheduling Strategies for Parallel Processing. VII, 257 pages. 2007.

Vol. 4374: J.F. Peters, A. Skowron, I. Düntsch, J. Grzymała-Busse, E. Orłowska, L. Polkowski (Eds.), Transactions on Rough Sets VI, Part I. XII, 499 pages. 2007.

Vol. 4373: K. Langendoen, T. Voigt (Eds.), Wireless Sensor Networks. XIII, 358 pages. 2007.

Vol. 4372: M. Kaufmann, D. Wagner (Eds.), Graph Drawing. XIV, 454 pages. 2007.

Vol. 4371: K. Inoue, K. Satoh, F. Toni (Eds.), Computational Logic in Multi-Agent Systems. X, 315 pages. 2007. (Sublibrary LNAI).

Vol. 4370: P.P Lévy, B. Le Grand, F. Poulet, M. Soto, L. Darago, L. Toubiana, J.-F. Vibert (Eds.), Pixelization Paradigm. XV, 279 pages. 2007.

Vol. 4369: M. Umeda, A. Wolf, O. Bartenstein, U. Geske, D. Seipel, O. Takata (Eds.), Declarative Programming for Knowledge Management. X, 229 pages. 2006. (Sublibrary LNAI).

Vol. 4368: T. Erlebach, C. Kaklamanis (Eds.), Approximation and Online Algorithms. X, 345 pages. 2007.

Vol. 4367: K. De Bosschere, D. Kaeli, P. Stenström, D. Whalley, T. Ungerer (Eds.), High Performance Embedded Architectures and Compilers. XI, 307 pages. 2007.

Vol. 4366: K. Tuyls, R. Westra, Y. Saeys, A. Nowé (Eds.), Knowledge Discovery and Emergent Complexity in Bioinformatics. IX, 183 pages. 2007. (Sublibrary LNBI).

Vol. 4364: T. Kühne (Ed.), Models in Software Engineering. XI, 332 pages. 2007.

Vol. 4362: J. van Leeuwen, G.F. Italiano, W. van der Hoek, C. Meinel, H. Sack, F. Plášil (Eds.), SOFSEM 2007: Theory and Practice of Computer Science. XXI, 937 pages. 2007.

Vol. 4361: H.J. Hoogeboom, G. Păun, G. Rozenberg, A. Salomaa (Eds.), Membrane Computing. IX, 555 pages. 2006.

Vol. 4360: W. Dubitzky, A. Schuster, P.M.A. Sloot, M. Schroeder, M. Romberg (Eds.), Distributed, High-Performance and Grid Computing in Computational Biology. X, 192 pages. 2007. (Sublibrary LNBI).

Vol. 4358: R. Vidal, A. Heyden, Y. Ma (Eds.), Dynamical Vision. IX, 329 pages. 2007.

Vol. 4357: L. Buttyán, V. Gligor, D. Westhoff (Eds.), Security and Privacy in Ad-Hoc and Sensor Networks. X, 193 pages. 2006.

Vol. 4355: J. Julliand, O. Kouchnarenko (Eds.), B 2007: Formal Specification and Development in B. XIII, 293 pages. 2006.

Vol. 4354: M. Hanus (Ed.), Practical Aspects of Declarative Languages. X, 335 pages. 2006.

Vol. 4353: T. Schwentick, D. Suciu (Eds.), Database Theory – ICDT 2007. XI, 419 pages. 2006.

Vol. 4352: T.-J. Cham, J. Cai, C. Dorai, D. Rajan, T.-S. Chua, L.-T. Chia (Eds.), Advances in Multimedia Modeling, Part II. XVIII, 743 pages. 2006.

Vol. 4351: T.-J. Cham, J. Cai, C. Dorai, D. Rajan, T.-S. Chua, L.-T. Chia (Eds.), Advances in Multimedia Modeling, Part I. XIX, 797 pages. 2006.

Vol. 4349: B. Cook, A. Podelski (Eds.), Verification, Model Checking, and Abstract Interpretation. XI, 395 pages. 2007.

Vol. 4348: S.T. Taft, R.A. Duff, R.L. Brukardt, E. Ploedereder, P. Leroy (Eds.), Ada 2005 Reference Manual. XXII, 765 pages. 2006.

Lecture Notes in Computer Science

Sublibrary 4: Security and Cryptology

For information about Vols. 1– 3935
please contact your bookseller or Springer

Vol. 4582: J. López, P. Samarati, J.L. Ferrer (Eds.), Public Key Infrastructure. XI, 375 pages. 2007.

Vol. 4579: B.M. Hämmerli, R. Sommer (Eds.), Detection of Intrusions and Malware, and Vulnerability Assessment. X, 251 pages. 2007.

Vol. 4575: T. Takagi, T. Okamoto, E. Okamoto, T. Okamoto (Eds.), Pairing-Based Cryptography – Pairing 2007. XI, 408 pages. 2007.

Vol. 4567: T. Furon, F. Cayre, G. Doërr, P. Bas (Eds.), Information Hiding. XI, 393 pages. 2008.

Vol. 4521: J. Katz, M. Yung (Eds.), Applied Cryptography and Network Security. XIII, 498 pages. 2007.

Vol. 4515: M. Naor (Ed.), Advances in Cryptology - EUROCRYPT 2007. XIII, 591 pages. 2007.

Vol. 4499: Y.Q. Shi (Ed.), Transactions on Data Hiding and Multimedia Security II. IX, 117 pages. 2007.

Vol. 4464: E. Dawson, D.S. Wong (Eds.), Information Security Practice and Experience. XIII, 361 pages. 2007.

Vol. 4462: D. Sauveron, K. Markantonakis, A. Bilas, J.-J. Quisquater (Eds.), Information Security Theory and Practices. XII, 255 pages. 2007.

Vol. 4450: T. Okamoto, X. Wang (Eds.), Public Key Cryptography – PKC 2007. XIII, 491 pages. 2007.

Vol. 4437: J.L. Camenisch, C.S. Collberg, N.F. Johnson, P. Sallee (Eds.), Information Hiding. VIII, 389 pages. 2007.

Vol. 4392: S.P. Vadhan (Ed.), Theory of Cryptography. XI, 595 pages. 2007.

Vol. 4377: M. Abe (Ed.), Topics in Cryptology – CT-RSA 2007. XI, 403 pages. 2006.

Vol. 4356: E. Biham, A.M. Youssef (Eds.), Selected Areas in Cryptography. XI, 395 pages. 2007.

Vol. 4341: P.Q. Nguyên (Ed.), Progress in Cryptology - VIETCRYPT 2006. XI, 385 pages. 2006.

Vol. 4332: A. Bagchi, V. Atluri (Eds.), Information Systems Security. XV, 382 pages. 2006.

Vol. 4329: R. Barua, T. Lange (Eds.), Progress in Cryptology - INDOCRYPT 2006. X, 454 pages. 2006.

Vol. 4318: H. Lipmaa, M. Yung, D. Lin (Eds.), Information Security and Cryptology. XI, 305 pages. 2006.

Vol. 4307: P. Ning, S. Qing, N. Li (Eds.), Information and Communications Security. XIV, 558 pages. 2006.

Vol. 4301: D. Pointcheval, Y. Mu, K. Chen (Eds.), Cryptology and Network Security. XIII, 381 pages. 2006.

Vol. 4300: Y.Q. Shi (Ed.), Transactions on Data Hiding and Multimedia Security I. IX, 139 pages. 2006.

Vol. 4298: J.K. Lee, O. Yi, M. Yung (Eds.), Information Security Applications. XIV, 406 pages. 2007.

Vol. 4296: M.S. Rhee, B. Lee (Eds.), Information Security and Cryptology – ICISC 2006. XIII, 358 pages. 2006.

Vol. 4284: X. Lai, K. Chen (Eds.), Advances in Cryptology – ASIACRYPT 2006. XIV, 468 pages. 2006.

Vol. 4283: Y.Q. Shi, B. Jeon (Eds.), Digital Watermarking. XII, 474 pages. 2006.

Vol. 4266: H. Yoshiura, K. Sakurai, K. Rannenberg, Y. Murayama, S.-i. Kawamura (Eds.), Advances in Information and Computer Security. XIII, 438 pages. 2006.

Vol. 4258: G. Danezis, P. Golle (Eds.), Privacy Enhancing Technologies. VIII, 431 pages. 2006.

Vol. 4249: L. Goubin, M. Matsui (Eds.), Cryptographic Hardware and Embedded Systems - CHES 2006. XII, 462 pages. 2006.

Vol. 4237: H. Leitold, E.P. Markatos (Eds.), Communications and Multimedia Security. XII, 253 pages. 2006.

Vol. 4236: L. Breveglieri, I. Koren, D. Naccache, J.-P. Seifert (Eds.), Fault Diagnosis and Tolerance in Cryptography. XIII, 253 pages. 2006.

Vol. 4219: D. Zamboni, C. Krügel (Eds.), Recent Advances in Intrusion Detection. XII, 331 pages. 2006.

Vol. 4189: D. Gollmann, J. Meier, A. Sabelfeld (Eds.), Computer Security – ESORICS 2006. XI, 548 pages. 2006.

Vol. 4176: S.K. Katsikas, J. López, M. Backes, S. Gritzalis, B. Preneel (Eds.), Information Security. XIV, 548 pages. 2006.

Vol. 4117: C. Dwork (Ed.), Advances in Cryptology - CRYPTO 2006. XIII, 621 pages. 2006.

Vol. 4116: R. De Prisco, M. Yung (Eds.), Security and Cryptography for Networks. XI, 366 pages. 2006.

Vol. 4107: G. Di Crescenzo, A. Rubin (Eds.), Financial Cryptography and Data Security. XI, 327 pages. 2006.

Vol. 4083: S. Fischer-Hübner, S. Furnell, C. Lambrinoudakis (Eds.), Trust and Privacy in Digital Business. XIII, 243 pages. 2006.

Vol. 4064: R. Büschkes, P. Laskov (Eds.), Detection of Intrusions and Malware & Vulnerability Assessment. X, 195 pages. 2006.

Vol. 4058: L.M. Batten, R. Safavi-Naini (Eds.), Information Security and Privacy. XII, 446 pages. 2006.

Vol. 4047: M. Robshaw (Ed.), Fast Software Encryption. XI, 434 pages. 2006.

Vol. 4043: A.S. Atzeni, A. Lioy (Eds.), Public Key Infrastructure. XI, 261 pages. 2006.

Vol. 4004: S. Vaudenay (Ed.), Advances in Cryptology - EUROCRYPT 2006. XIV, 613 pages. 2006.

Vol. 3995: G. Müller (Ed.), Emerging Trends in Information and Communication Security. XX, 524 pages. 2006.

Vol. 3989: J. Zhou, M. Yung, F. Bao (Eds.), Applied Cryptography and Network Security. XIV, 488 pages. 2006.

Vol. 3969: Ø. Ytrehus (Ed.), Coding and Cryptography. XI, 443 pages. 2006.

Vol. 3958: M. Yung, Y. Dodis, A. Kiayias, T. Malkin (Eds.), Public Key Cryptography - PKC 2006. XIV, 543 pages. 2006.

Vol. 3957: B. Christianson, B. Crispo, J.A. Malcolm, M. Roe (Eds.), Security Protocols. IX, 325 pages. 2006.

Vol. 3956: G. Barthe, B. Grégoire, M. Huisman, J.-L. Lanet (Eds.), Construction and Analysis of Safe, Secure, and Interoperable Smart Devices. IX, 175 pages. 2006.